The Critical Shaw

on

Politics

Edited by
L.W. Conolly

RosettaBooks®

The Critical Shaw: On Politics
Editorial material © 2016 by L.W. Conolly

All primary source material © the Estate of Bernard Shaw: *A Manifesto. Fabian Tracts, no. 2.* © 1884 *The Manifesto of the Fabian Parliamentary League* © 1887 Excerpt from "The Transition to Social Democracy" © 1888 Excerpt from "What Socialism Is," *Fabian Tract no. 13.* © 1890 Excerpt from "The Impossibilities of Anarchism" © 1891 Excerpt from the *Fabian Election Manifesto 1892* © 1892 Excerpt from "What Socialism Will be Like" © 1896 Excerpt from "The Illusions of Socialism" © 1896 Excerpt from "The Revolutionist's Handbook and Pocket Companion" © 1903 by the Estate of Bernard Shaw Excerpt from "Why All Women are Peculiarly Fitted to be Good Voters." © 1907 "The Crime of Poverty" © 1912 Excerpt from *Common Sense About the War* ©1914 Excerpt from "Cataclysm" © 1917 Excerpt from *How to Settle the Irish Question* © 1917 Monarchy v. Republicanism: An Unpublished Letter to *The Times*, 22 April 1917 © 1917 Excerpt from "Peace Conference Hints" © 1919 Excerpt from "The Dictatorship of the Proletariat" © 1921 Excerpt from *The Intelligent Woman's Guide to Socialism and Capitalism* © 1928 Excerpt from the Preface to *The Apple Cart* © 1930 "Fascism" © 1931 "The Only Hope of the World," © 1931 "Look, You Boob! A Little Talk on America" © 1931 Excerpt from *The Political Madhouse in America and Nearer Home* © 1933 "Halt, Hitler!" © 1933 Excerpt from the Preface to *On the Rocks* © 1933 Excerpt from the Preface to *The Millionairess* © 1935 Excerpt from "The Unavoidable Subject" © 1940 Excerpt from *Everybody's Political What's What?* © 1944 Excerpt from the Preface to *Geneva* © 1945 Excerpt from "Sixty Years of Fabianism" © 1947

All rights reserved. No part of this book may be used or reproduced in any form or by any electronic or mechanical means, including information storage and retrieval systems, without permission in writing from the publisher, except by a reviewer who may quote brief passages in a review.

Published 2016 by RosettaBooks
ISBN (paperback): 978-0-7953-4895-2
Cover design by David Ter-Avanesyan / Ter33Design
Cover illustration by Corina Lupp
ISBN (EPUB): 978-0-7953-4690-3
ISBN (Kindle): 978-0-7953-4766-5

www.RosettaBooks.com

RosettaBooks®

Contents

Acknowledgments 5
General Editor's Preface 7
Introduction....................................... 9
Bernard Shaw and His Times: A Chronology 23
A Note on the Text................................ 29
Part I: Fabian Socialist 31
   1. A Manifesto. Fabian Tracts, no. 2. 1884................ 32
   2. The Manifesto of the Fabian Parliamentary League, 1887 34
   3. From "The Transition to Social Democracy," 1888 ... 36
   4. From "What Socialism Is," 1890 52
   5. From "The Impossibilities of Anarchism," 1891 53
   6. From the Fabian Election Manifesto 1892............ 67
   7. From "What Socialism Will be Like," 1896 74
   8. From "The Illusions of Socialism," 1896 82
Part II: Resolute Socialist, Disillusioned Democrat...... 99
   1. From "The Revolutionist's Handbook and Pocket Companion," 1903 100
   2. From "Why All Women are Peculiarly Fitted to be Good Voters," 1907 112
   3. "The Crime of Poverty," 1912 120
Part III: War and Revolution......................... 125
   1. From Common Sense About the War, 1914............. 126
   2. From "Cataclysm," 1917 153
   3. From How to Settle the Irish Question, 1917 157
   4. Monarchy v. Republicanism, 1917.................. 163
   5. From "Peace Conference Hints," 1919 167
Part IV: Democracy, Communism, Fascism, Capitalism . 173
   1. From "The Dictatorship of the Proletariat," 1921 174

2. From *The Intelligent Woman's Guide to Socialism and Capitalism*, 1928 182
3. From the Preface to *The Apple Cart*, 1930 205
4. Fascism. *Daily Telegraph*, 25 February 1931. 215
5. "The Only Hope of the World," 1931. 215
Part V: America 223
   1. "Look, You Boob! A Little Talk on America," 1931. . 224
   2. From *The Political Madhouse in America and Nearer Home*, 1933 234
Part VI: The Dictators 251
   1. "Halt, Hitler!," 1933 252
   2. From the Preface to *On the Rocks*, 1933–34 255
   3. From the Preface to *The Millionairess*, 1935 265
   4. From "The Unavoidable Subject," 1940. 275
Part VII: Last Thoughts 279
   1. From *Everybody's Political What's What?* 1944 280
   2. From the Preface to *Geneva*, 1945 295
   3. From "Sixty Years of Fabianism," 1947 297
Sources and Further Reading 305

Acknowledgments

I am most grateful to RosettaBooks for their expert support during the preparation of this book, particularly Jonathan Ward, Hannah Bennett, and Jay McNair. My thanks also to fellow editors in this Critical Shaw series: Brigitte Bogar, Dorothy Hadfield, Christopher Innes, Michel Pharand, and Gustavo Rodriguez Martin. As always, my wife, Barbara Conolly, has been an invaluable advisor and sounding board.

General Editor's Preface

Bernard Shaw is not the household name he once was, but in the 1920s and 1930s he was certainly the world's most famous English-language playwright, and arguably one of the most famous people in the world. His plays were internationally performed and acclaimed, his views on matters great and small were relentlessly solicited by the media, he was pursued by paparazzi long before the word was even invented, the biggest names in politics, the arts, entertainment, even sports—Gandhi, Nehru, Churchill, Rodin, Twain, Wells, Lawrence of Arabia, Elgar, Einstein, Garbo, Chaplin, Stalin, Tunney and many more—welcomed his company, and his correspondents in the tens of thousands of letters he wrote during his long lifetime constitute a veritable who's who of world culture and politics. And Shaw remains the only person ever to have been awarded both a Nobel Prize and an Oscar.

Shaw's reputation rests securely not just on his plays, a dozen or so of which have come to be recognized as classics—*Man and Superman*, *Major Barbara*, *Pygmalion*, and *Saint Joan* perhaps now the most familiar of them—but also on his early work as a music, art, literary, and theater critic, and on his lifelong political activism. After he moved to London from his native Dublin in 1876, and after completing five novels, he established himself as one of London's most controversial, feared, and admired critics, and while he eventually retired from earning his living as a critic in order to focus on playwriting, he continued to lecture and write about cultural and other issues—religion, for example—with scorching intelligence. As for politics, his early commitment to Socialism, and his later expressed admiration for Communism and contempt for Capitalism, meant that while his views were relentlessly refuted by the establishment press they could rarely be ignored—hardly surprising given the logic and passion that underpinned them.

Winston Churchill once declared Shaw to be "the greatest living master of letters in the English-speaking world," and the selections from Shaw's reviews, essays, speeches, and correspondence contained in the five volumes of this Critical Shaw series provide abundant evidence to validate Churchill's high regard. Shaw wrote—and spoke—voluminously, and his complete works on the topics covered by this series—Literature, Music, Religion, Theater, and Politics—would fill many more than five volumes. The topics reflect Shaw's deepest interests and they inspired some of his most brilliant nondramatic writing. The selections in each volume give a comprehensive and representative survey of his thinking, and show him to be not just the great rhetorician that Churchill and others acknowledged, but also one of the great public intellectuals of the twentieth century.

Leonard Conolly
Robinson College, Cambridge
December 2015

Introduction

While Bernard Shaw is remembered today principally for his plays—*Mrs Warren's Profession, Caesar and Cleopatra, Man and Superman, Major Barbara, Pygmalion, Heartbreak House,* and *Saint Joan,* among many others—he also devoted a great deal of his time, energy, and intellectual effort to politics. It would be an exaggeration to rank Shaw as a political thinker alongside great British philosophers such as Thomas Hobbes (1588–1679), John Locke (1632–1704), David Hume (1711–76), or John Stuart Mill (1806–73), but his ability to engage intelligently, provocatively, and profusely with the many huge political issues that paralleled his long life (1856–1950) made him one of the most important public intellectuals in Great Britain from the heyday of high Victorianism to the creation of the welfare state by the Labour government elected at the close of the Second World War.

The subjects he addressed in his numerous political books, speeches, essays, and broadcasts continue to have a familiar ring: income inequality, corporate excess, unemployment, dysfunctional government, political ideologies, totalitarian regimes, poverty, gender discrimination, the role of the state, the inefficiency of democracy, war, nationalism, party politics. Shaw's unwavering commitment to Socialism and—in the deeply troubling social and economic turmoil of the 1930s—Communism, and his equally unwavering denunciation of Capitalism are not well received by all readers today; indeed, his language and his values frequently offend and shock. Many Americans do not take kindly to Shaw's description of the Statue of Liberty as "a monstrous idol," which ought to bear Dante's inscription on the Gate of Hell, "All hope abandon, ye who enter here" (page 239). And Americans are not alone in finding Shaw's embrace of Stalin and his horrendous crimes unfathomable and unforgivable. Yet for as many who are shocked and offended by Shaw's political stances, multitudes have been challenged and provoked into thinking and rethinking—and perhaps even reshaping—their deepest political beliefs by his contentiousness. Labour Prime Minister Ramsay MacDonald (1866–1937) went out on a very thin limb in lauding Shaw's *Intelligent Woman's Guide to Socialism and Capitalism* as "after the Bible… the most important book that humanity possesses" (Holroyd III:133), but no serious political discussion could occur in Great Britain between the two world wars without taking Shaw's views into account.

Bernard Shaw's political journey began in the slums of Dublin in the 1860s. Although he was born (in 1856) into relatively comfortable, though by no means wealthy, circumstances, he became familiar with those slums through visits with his nanny to her friends. He "loathed" their sights and smells, a loathing deepened by his experience of the slums of London after he moved there in 1876. Having received no formal education in Dublin beyond the age of 15, Shaw set about educating himself in the British Museum in London, which is where, in 1883, he read (in a French translation) Karl Marx's *Das Kapital*, another major influence on his political thinking. A year later, he joined the newly founded Fabian Society (www.fabians.org.uk), a left-wing organization dedicated to achieving fundamental economic and political reform in Great Britain through democratic, nonviolent means. Shaw quickly became one of the Fabian Society's most active and influential members, giving numerous speeches (all unpaid) at gatherings around the country on behalf of the Society, and writing many of its publications. He also gained practical political experience by successfully standing for election to the Vestry of the Parish of St Pancras (i.e., municipal government) in 1897, a position he held until 1903.

Shaw's early political values and objectives are reflected in the opening selections in this book, all related to what he calls the "sacredly imperative" goals of Socialism: the nationalization of industries and resources, restraints on commercial competition, elimination of poverty, the extension of the franchise (to women equally with men), devolution of political authority from central to local government, and the creation of a "genuine Working Class party" (page 70). It's an ambitious agenda, but one tempered by reality, including the "impossibility" of rapid reform, the need for hard work and pragmatism ("you cannot convert first and third class carriages into second class... by merely singing the Marseillaise" [page 40]), and the difficulty of marshalling the working class—many of whom, he had to concede, "care more for drinking and gambling than for freedom"—into an effective political force. In addition, there were deep divisions among his Socialist colleagues. Socialism, Shaw declared, "would spread fast enough if it were not for the Socialists" (page 55). Included among the Socialists who impeded progress were the anticompromise idealists—"whatever is not white [Socialism] is black [Capitalism]" (page 58)—and the far-left Anarchists, who believed that cooperation with established political structures gave undeserved legitimacy to what they wanted to destroy.

The impediments to social progress, created by friends as well as enemies, were formidable and sorely tested Shaw's commitment to the democratic process and perhaps even to an active involvement in the political process at all. After lecturing to Fabians in Glasgow in early October 1903, he returned to London bemoaning the "prodigious expenditure of nervous energy... merely to drive a little common sense into a crowd, like nails into a very tough board"; the effort, he said, "leaves one empty, exhausted, disgusted" (letter to Siegfried Trebitsch, 7 October 1903, *Collected Letters* II:375). What's more, he complained to Trebitsch, he had to "work like a dog" on political manifestos, speeches, and books, rather than "setting to at a new play." And then, in the following March, he was defeated in a bid to gain a seat on the London County Council, his last effort to win political office. In only a matter of a few weeks he entered a theatrical partnership with Harley Granville Barker and John Vedrenne at London's Royal Court Theatre, a partnership that over the next three years—with the production of 11 of his plays—cemented Shaw's reputation as the leading playwright in Great Britain.

Playwright or political activist? Which road would Shaw take? In a word—both. To some degree, Shaw had always managed to combine his creative work with his political views. The title and subject matter of his fifth (and final) novel, *An Unsocial Socialist,* written in 1883, are indicative of this, and his first play, *Widowers' Houses,* which he started writing in 1884, is a powerful indictment of exploitation of the poor by slum landlords. And it went on: *Mrs Warren's Profession, The Philanderer, The Devil's Disciple, Caesar and Cleopatra,* all of which have political elements, practical and theoretical. And then came *Man and Superman,* the most successful of the Royal Court plays (176 performances), and written as both his political enthusiasm and his political creed were undergoing significant reassessments.

The protagonist of *Man and Superman,* John Tanner, is the author of *The Revolutionist's Handbook and Pocket Companion,* the text of which Shaw included as an appendix in the published play (1903). Tanner is a character in the play, not Shaw himself, but Tanner's *Handbook* captures and expresses Shaw's growing doubts about working through established democratic structures to implement political reform. Universal suffrage is "a political panacea" that in practice "withers" because "Democracy cannot rise above the level of the human material of which its voters are made." Hence the need, says Tanner/Shaw, for "selective breeding" so that "we can have a Democracy of Supermen." The breeding will be administered by a "State Department of Evolution" on a "human stud farm."

How much of the selective breeding nonsense is Jack Tanner and how much Bernard Shaw is hard to say, though there can be no doubt about Shaw's enthusiasm for the Superman concept (from German philosopher Friedrich Nietzsche's Übermensch). Be that as it may, Shaw wasn't yet ready to abandon Democracy entirely. He continued to argue for universal suffrage for adult men and women, and to advocate core Socialist objectives such as the elimination of poverty ("an abominable disease and... a very horrible crime") and a legislated minimum income for all. Perhaps, he suggested in a 1912 speech on poverty (page 120), social reformers could learn something from the militant strategies of the suffragette movement.

And then everything changed for Shaw, and, indeed, the world. The assassination of Archduke Franz Ferdinand of Austria on 28 June 1914 led inexorably to world war, the German invasion of Belgium on 3 August 1914 precipitating Britain's declaration of war on Germany the following day. Four years later some 15 million military personnel and civilians had been killed.

Shaw was not a pacifist, but in his long essay *Common Sense About the War*, one of his most important, and certainly one of his most courageous political statements, he raged against the war, seeing it as essentially a class war ("war is always waged by working men who have no quarrel") and urging soldiers on both sides to "shoot their officers and go home to gather in their harvests in the villages and make a revolution in the towns." For this suggestion Shaw was universally reviled and ostracized.

It is sometimes forgotten, however, that Shaw ends *Common Sense* with a ringing declaration that while "Militarism is a rusty sword that breaks in the hand," "Democracy is invincible." But is it?

Common Sense was published on 14 November 1914. Three years into the war another event that shook the world took place, but in this instance it was an event that was enthusiastically welcomed by Shaw and also one that shaped his political thinking for the rest of his life.

In October 1917 Vladimir Ilyich Lenin and his supporters overthrew the Russian government and installed a Communist administration under Lenin's leadership. It was, Shaw approvingly wrote "the crash of an epoch" (page 153). "The mountainous dyke within which western Capitalism had been working for centuries cracked and left a gap the whole width of Europe from the Baltic to the Black Sea". The following July Czar Nicholas II and his family were executed, and, despite civil war (which ended in 1921), Communism would become secure in Russia for decades to come, ruthlessly implemented by both Lenin and Joseph Stalin.

Until he visited Russia in 1931 Shaw relied mainly on press reports (usually biased against Russia) to learn about the progress of Communism. In the meantime, he continued to maintain a high profile as a playwright and political speaker and essayist. There were, for instance, troubles in his native Ireland to comment on (page 157). He opposed an independent Ireland, urging instead—presciently—devolution of power to Irish, Scottish, Welsh, and English parliaments in a federal system. And as the First World War finally drew to a close he warned of the dangers—and events in the 1930s proved him absolutely right—of punitive treatment of Germany. He saw much greater hope for world peace in

Woodrow Wilson's proposal for a League of Nations, which, "within certain limits" (page 167), he supported.

Shaw's support for Democracy, on the other hand, was rapidly diminishing. Even if Democracy was "invincible," he no longer saw it as essential for the creation of a Socialist society. In a remarkable *volte-face*, he now declared (in a 1921 essay) that "adult suffrage will make all changes impossible" (page 175). Historically and currently (i.e., in Russia), he argued, fundamental political change is achieved by autocrats, not democrats. One of John Tanner's "Maxims for Revolutionists" in *Man and Superman* is that "Democracy substitutes election by the incompetent for appointment by the corrupt few," and Shaw himself came to view Democracy as an inefficient, time-wasting, obfuscatory barrier to social progress. More and more, Shaw found validity in the ruthless efficiency of dictatorship. Shaw's version of Socialism had no room for "parasitic idleness" (from rapacious landlords to striking miners); work would be compulsory, "with death as the final penalty" (page 177), he said. Was he serious? Probably not, but as economic conditions worsened through the 1920s, and as Shaw (and many others) got even more deeply disillusioned with the seeming inability of democratic structures to deal with widespread poverty and unemployment, Shaw's solutions (and rhetoric) grew exponentially.

But first he had some explaining to do. In 1924 his sister-in-law asked him to explain his views on Socialism. His response took four years (during which time he largely neglected his playwriting) and came in the form of a 470-page book, *The Intelligent Woman's Guide to Socialism and Capitalism*. The book is a measured and carefully reasoned discussion of political theory and practice, largely free of inflammatory rhetoric; Michael Holroyd (III:132) has described it as "Shaw's political autobiography in the form of a socialist Sermon on the Mount."

There are 84 chapters and an appendix in *The Intelligent Woman's Guide*, covering an astonishing range of subjects. On one subject—Communism—Shaw remained resolute: "Would you ever have supposed from reading the newspapers that Communism, instead of being the wicked invention of Russian revolutionaries and British and American desperadoes, is a highly respectable way of sharing our wealth... and an indispensable part of our own daily life and civilization?" Despite never becoming a member of the Communist Party, Shaw was convinced that Russia had got it right: "The more Communism, the more civilization," he believed.

Capitalism, on the other hand, he argued in a 1929 BBC Radio talk, meant "control by gigantic trusts wielding great power without responsibility, and having no object but to make as much money out of us as possible," while Democracy was a washout. Who, said Shaw, "can blame Signor Mussolini for describing it as a putrefying corpse" (page 213)?

In July 1931 Shaw finally visited Russia. He spent ten days in Moscow and Leningrad, met Maxim Gorky, had a two-hour private meeting with Stalin, took escorted tours of factories, barracks, and collective farms, and celebrated his 75th birthday with 2,000 guests in Moscow's Concert Hall for Nobles. He returned home full of praise for Russia's achievements ("here at last is a country which has established Socialism"), brushing aside criticism that he was shown only the positive aspects of Communism ("I don't want to go to Russia to see what remains of poverty and ignorance from the Capitalist system. I can see that within twenty minutes of my own door in London. I want to see the best that can be done"), and acknowledging, but not criticizing, Stalin's summary execution of political dissidents [page 216].

Shaw's fervent support of Communism was matched by his intense aversion to Capitalism, which naturally led him to be critical of the United States. Just as he had praised Russia before visiting there, so he criticized—taunted would be more accurate—the United States before seeing the country for himself. As the American Depression deepened following the 1929 Wall Street crash, with unemployment nearing 25 percent, he contrasted (in a shortwave radio broadcast in October 1931 [page 224]) the economic and political strength of Russia with the "business incompetence, political helplessness, and financial insolvency" of the United States. He challenged Americans to visit Russia, but warned them that they would be greeted "with a mixture of pity for you as a refugee from the horrors of American Capitalism, with a colossal intellectual contempt for your political imbecility in not having established Communism in your own unhappy country." The broadcast contained some of Shaw's most powerful rhetoric on Communism and Capitalism. There is still in Russia, he conceded, "a good deal of the poverty, ignorance, and dirt we know so well at home," but "there is hope everywhere in Russia because these evils are retreating there before the spread of Communism as steadily as they are advancing upon us before the last desperate struggle of our bankrupt Capitalism to stave off its inevitable doom...."

Provoking and insulting Americans from a microphone on the other side of the Atlantic was one thing. Doing it in person was another. But when the opportunity arose to do just that, Shaw, to his credit, did not shrink from it. His first visit to the United States took place in 1933, beginning in Honolulu on 16 March and ending in New York on 12 April. On the evening before his departure from New York, at the invitation of the American Academy of Political Science, Shaw spoke on "The Future of Political Science in America" to an audience of 3,500 in the Metropolitan Opera House, with live broadcast on the NBC radio network. Speaking for an hour and forty minutes, he delivered a pro-Russian and anti-American harangue (Shaw's word) that was a volatile mix of reason and vituperation. He attacked American sacred idols such as the Constitution ("a Charter of Anarchism");

mocked the "Hundredpercent American" as "ridiculous" and "futile"; and attacked financiers ("your country is run by them"), stockbrokers, politicians, newspaper proprietors, and other bulwarks of a Capitalist system that had "broken down" (The Political Madhouse in America and Nearer Home).

Despite this criticism, however, and his ongoing and unswerving support of Communism, Shaw had not given up entirely on America. If Capitalism was a discredited and broken system, it was America's "most pressing job to find a better one," he said, and maybe Communism wasn't the be-all and end-all: "possibly America may save human society yet by solving the great political problems which have baffled and destroyed all previous attempts at permanent civilization" (page 241).

In the meantime there were ominous developments in Europe. Stalin's farm collectivization program and his labor camps were killing millions of Russians. In Italy Benito Mussolini was consolidating power as dictator. And in January 1933 Adolf Hitler had become Chancellor of Germany. Fascism was on the rise.

Shaw was unmoved by the carnage in Russia. "A well-kept garden must be weeded" he told Americans in his 1931 broadcast, and he callously defended Stalin's brutality by arguing (in the preface to *On the Rocks*) that all governments are "obliged" to kill citizens "on a scale varying from the execution of a single murderer to the slaughter of millions of quite innocent persons." Shaw's claim that "capital punishment is abolished in Russia" (page 232) is staggering in its sophistry. What he said about Fascism was equally disquieting. In a 1931 interview he blamed the rise of Fascism on the failure of "liberal parliamentarism on the English model" to provide the kind of "positive and efficient State control" that Hitler was implementing in Germany (page 215). Shaw later said that the Nazi movement "is in many respects one which has my warm sympathy" (page 252). When the BBC invited him early in 1940 to talk about the war he declared that "Mr Hitler did not begin this war; we did" (page 275). tracing the origin of Hitler's rise to the punitive measures taken against Germany at the end of the First World War. The BBC, unsurprisingly, banned the talk (Conolly, 106–14).

Shaw's praise of Hitler, however, was strictly limited to his success in leading Germany to economic recovery, with massive industrial expansion and a rapid decline in unemployment—in marked contrast to Great Britain with its unemployment (up to 70 percent of the workforce in some parts of the country) and subsequent poverty and hunger marches.

Where Shaw parted company with Hitler was in what he called Hitler's Judophobia, which, he argued, "is not a part of Fascism but an incomprehensible excrescence on it" (page 253). While he never unequivocally condemned the unspeakable atrocities of the Nazi extermination camps, he fully supported the fight against Hitler. In the suppressed BBC talk he made it clear that despite his admiration of Hitler's economic achievements, it's not "his virtues" that matter now, it's his "persecutions and dominations" (page 278).

By the end of the Second World War Shaw was approaching his ninetieth birthday, yet he was far from a spent force. He continued to revise his 1938 play, *Geneva* (in which he mocks Hitler, Mussolini, and Franco—but not Stalin), to bring it into line with current events, and he wrote a new preface for the 1945 edition of the play. In that preface, harking back to comments he had made in the preface to *The Millionairess* about Mussolini's leadership, he continued to argue that Democracy was not an effective way of implementing change. In the 1930s in Great Britain, Parliament, Shaw had said in the preface to The Millionairess, had fallen into such contempt that "ballot papers were less esteemed than toilet papers" (page 268), and the war had not changed anything: "the New World proved the same as the old one, with the same fundamental resistance to change of habits and the same dread of government interference surviving in the adult voter like the child's dread of a policeman" (page 296). This was hardly fair on the Labour government elected in 1945, which, under Prime Minister Clement Attlee, quickly implemented the most radical—and Socialist—political agenda of the twentieth century, including the nationalization of health services, major industries, and transportation. Nonetheless, Shaw continued to agitate for more political reform. In 1947 he wrote a postscript for a collection of Fabian essays in which he insisted that even though the Attlee cabinet might well be "crammed with ex-Fabians," much remained to be done: a "basic income... to abolish poverty and ignorance," the creation of a "democratic aristocracy" to replace "haphazard mobocracy," and electoral reform (through a "coupled vote") to ensure gender equality in the House of Commons, and more (page 301).

Was this the "obsolete Old Pioneer" dismissed by future Labour Party leader Michael Foot as an embarrassment who "stopped thinking" in the early 1930s (Holroyd III:484)? Hardly. Then and now, Shaw's provocative engagement with political events, movements, and ideologies, encompassing local government to world war, not only merits but demands attention. He made modest claims about what he was trying to achieve in his political writings—"I... try to open my readers' eyes to the political facts under which they live. I cannot change their minds; but I can increase their knowledge" (preface to *Geneva*, *Bodley Head* VII:30)—and as James Alexander (11) and others have argued he could make no claim to being a great political theorist. Perhaps, as well, as his friend Gilbert Murray said, Shaw was sometimes possessed with "the damnable vice of preferring rhetoric to truth" (*Platform and Pulpit* xiv), and Shaw unapologetically confessed to "habitually and deliberately" overstating his case "to make people sit up and listen to it, and to frighten them into acting on it" (*Everybody's Political What's What?* 49). Eric Bentley has suggested that while Shaw should always be taken seriously, "he cannot always be taken literally," and we should understand that as "an exasperated idealist" he was driven to make some "dubious declarations" (Bentley 16–17). Most people would include Shaw's support of Stalin among those dubious declarations, though putting that down to "exasperation" (with Democracy) doesn't wash with a more recent critic, Matthew Yde, who is adamant that Shaw was "in deadly earnest in his defense of Stalin's liquidation policies" (Yde 12).

Whatever position one takes on Shaw's stand on particular issues — few were uncontroversial — we remain deeply in his debt for his willingness to speak frankly and fearlessly about the great national and international political issues of his time, striving as he constantly was, says Gareth Griffith, "to understand, to explain, to delight and outrage, to extend the intellectual consciousness of his time" (Griffith 3).

The modest selection in this book from Shaw's voluminous writings cannot possibly do full justice to the range and depth of his political opinions, but if the selection provokes the same response as Oliver Twist's to his meagre portion of workhouse gruel, it will have served its purpose. (For "more," please consult Sources and Further Reading, page 305.)

Bernard Shaw and His Times: A Chronology

[This chronology is common to all five volumes in the Critical Shaw series, and reflects the topics of the series: Politics, Theater, Literature, Music, and Religion. For a comprehensive and detailed chronology of Shaw's life and works, see A. M. Gibbs, A Bernard Shaw Chronology (Basingstoke: Palgrave, 2001).]

1856 Shaw born in Dublin (26 July).

1859 Charles Darwin publishes *On the Origin of Species by Means of Natural Selection*.

1864 Herbert Spencer publishes *Principles of Biology* (and coins the phrase "survival of the fittest").

1865 The Salvation Army is founded by Methodist preacher William Booth.

1870 The doctrine of papal infallibility is defined as dogma at the First Vatican Council.

1876 Shaw moves from Dublin to London. He begins ghostwriting music reviews for Vandeleur Lee for *The Hornet*.

1879 Shaw begins writing music reviews for *The Saturday Musical Review*, *The Court Journal*, and other publications. He writes his first novel, *Immaturity*, quickly followed by four others: *The Irrational Knot* (1880), *Love Among the Artists* (1881), *Cashel Byron's Profession* (1882), and *An Unsocial Socialist* (1883).

1883 Shaw reads Karl Marx's *Das Kapital* (in a French translation) in the British Museum Reading Room.

1884 The Fabian Society is founded; Shaw joins in the same year. He publishes his first book review in *The Christian Scientist*.

1885 Shaw begins publishing book reviews regularly in *The Pall Mall Gazette*.

1886 Eleanor Marx, daughter of Karl Marx, organizes a reading of Ibsen's *A Doll's House*; Shaw reads the part of Krogstad.

1889 Having written music reviews for over a decade, Shaw becomes a full-time critic for *The Star*, and then (in 1890) *The World*.

1891 Shaw publishes *The Quintessence of Ibsenism* (revised and updated in 1922).

1892 Shaw's first play, *Widowers' Houses*, is performed.

1893 Founding of the Independent Labour Party, a socialist advocacy group.

1894 Shaw resigns from *The World* and henceforth writes only occasional music reviews. *Arms and the Man* is first performed. Shaw becomes acquainted with aspiring theatre critic Reginald Golding Bright.

1895 Shaw becomes full-time drama critic for *The Saturday Review*. He publishes a lengthy review column almost every week for the next two and a half years.

1897 Shaw is elected a member of the Vestry of the Parish of St Pancras (until 1903).

1898 Shaw marries Charlotte Payne-Townshend and resigns as *The Saturday Review* drama critic. He publishes *The Perfect Wagnerite* and *Plays: Pleasant and Unpleasant*. One of the "unpleasant" plays, *Mrs Warren's Profession*, is refused a performance licence by the Lord Chamberlain; the ban will stay in effect until 1924.

1901 *Caesar and Cleopatra* is first performed, with music written by Shaw. Queen Victoria dies.

1904 J. E. Vedrenne and Harley Granville Barker begin their management of the Court Theatre (until 1907), with Shaw as a principal playwright. Eleven Shaw plays are performed in three seasons.

1905 *Man and Superman* is first performed. Albert Einstein publishes his theory of relativity.

1906 Founding of the Labour Party. *Major Barbara* and *The Doctor's Dilemma* are first performed.

1908 *Der tapfere Soldat*, an unauthorized operetta loosely based on *Arms and the Man*, with music by Oscar Straus and libretto by Rudolf Bernauer and Leopold Jacobson, is first performed in Vienna. It is later staged (1910) in translation as *The Chocolate Soldier*.

1909 *The Shewing-up of Blanco Posnet* is refused a licence by the Lord Chamberlain. W. B. Yeats and Lady Gregory stage it at the Abbey Theatre in Dublin. Shaw appears as a witness before the Joint Select Committee of the House of Lords and the House of Commons on Stage Plays (Censorship).

1911 Shaw joins the managing council of the Royal Academy of Dramatic Art. His strong support of RADA's programs will include bequeathing RADA a third of his royalties. Shaw writes an introduction for the Waverley edition of Dickens's *Hard Times*.

1913 *Pygmalion* is first performed.

1914 Beginning of the First World War. Shaw publishes *Common Sense About the War*.

1916 Easter Rising in Dublin against British rule of Ireland.

1917 The Russian Revolution overthrows the imperialist government and installs a communist government under Vladimir Ilyich Lenin. The United States joins the war against Germany. On 17 July Czar Nicholas II and his family are executed.

1918 Representation of the People Act gives the vote to all men over twenty-one, and to women over thirty if they meet certain qualifications (e.g., property owners, university graduates). End of the First World War.

1920 *Heartbreak House* is first performed. Shaw completes *Back to Methuselah*, a five-play cycle on evolutionary themes. League of Nations formed.

1921 The Irish Free State gains independence from Britain. Shaw writes the preface to *Immaturity*.

1922 Joseph Stalin becomes general secretary of the Communist Party Central Committee. Benito Mussolini becomes Italian prime minister.

1923 *Saint Joan* is first performed, with music written by Shaw.

1924 Ramsay MacDonald becomes the first Labour prime minister, in a Labour-Liberal coalition government.

1925 Adolf Hitler publishes *Mein Kampf* [*My Struggle*].

1926 General strike in Great Britain, 4–13 May. Shaw is awarded the 1925 Nobel Prize for Literature.

1928 Representation of the People (Equal Franchise) Act gives the vote to all women over twenty-one. Shaw publishes *The Intelligent Woman's Guide to Socialism and Capitalism*. *The Apple Cart* is first performed.

1929 The Wall Street Crash, 28–29 October, which signalled the beginning of the Great Depression. Shaw speaks as a delegate to the third International Congress of the World League for Sexual Reform. Sir Barry Jackson establishes the Malvern Festival, dedicated to Shaw's plays.

1931 Shaw visits Russia. He celebrates his seventy-fifth birthday on 26 July in Moscow's Concert Hall of Nobles with two thousand guests. He meets Stalin on 29 July.

1932 Unemployment reaches 3.5 million in Great Britain. South Wales and the industrial north experience mass unemployment and poverty. *Too True to Be Good* receives its English première at the Malvern Festival.

1933 Shaw makes his first visit to the United States. He speaks to an audience of thirty-five hundred at the Metropolitan Opera House (11 April). Hitler becomes German chancellor.

1934 *The Six of Calais* is first performed.

1936 Shaw makes his second (and last) visit to the United States. *The Millionairess* is first performed.

1938 *Geneva* is first performed. Shaw rejects a proposal from producer Gabriel Pascal for a musical version of *Pygmalion*.

1939 Beginning of the Second World War.

1941 The United States enters the Second World War.

1943 Charlotte Shaw dies.

1944 Shaw publishes *Everybody's Political What's What?*

1945 End of the Second World War. United Nations formed. The UK Labour Party wins its first majority government. Clement Atlee becomes prime minister. His government implements an extensive nationalization program of British industry and services.

1947 Discovery of the Dead Sea Scrolls in Qumran Caves, West Bank.

1948 World Council of Churches founded in Amsterdam.

1950 Shaw publishes his last book review in *The Observer* (26 March). He dies in Ayot St Lawrence, Hertfordshire (2 November).

A Note on the Text

Sources for the selections of Shaw's political writings are given in the heading for each selection. Full bibliographical details for the sources, when not included in the heading, are provided in Sources and Further Reading, where secondary sources on Shaw's political writings are also listed. Shaw's original spelling and punctuation have been retained. All ellipses inserted in the text are editorial unless otherwise noted. Brief explanatory notes are included in square brackets. In cases where there are multiple references to the same person or event, the note is given only for the first reference.

Part I: Fabian Socialist

Shaw's belief in and commitment to social democracy were expressed many times in the early years of his political activism, nearly always under the auspices of the Fabian Society, an organization founded in January 1884 with the objective, through peaceful and democratic means, of transforming Great Britain into a Socialist state. Shaw joined the Fabian Society in September 1884 and quickly became one of its most influential and active members. He took a leading role in defining the goals and strategies of the society and in planning its development into a significant force within the established British political structure. Given the power of the well-entrenched political parties (Liberal and Conservative), divisions within the Fabian Society itself, the influence of other political groups with conflicting agendas (e.g., the Anarchists), and, as Shaw perceived it, the political apathy of the British working class, it proved to be a huge task, but it eventually led to the founding of the Labour Party in 1906 and the election of a Labour Government in 1929.

1. A Manifesto. Fabian Tracts, no. 2. London: The Fabian Society, 1884.

[In the second of the Fabian Society's famous tracts, Shaw defined its core political principles and objectives.]

The Fabians are associated for the purpose of spreading the following opinions held by them, and discussing their practical consequences.

That, under existing circumstances, wealth cannot be enjoyed without dishonour, or foregone without misery.

That it is the duty of each member of the State to provide for his or her wants by his or her own Labour.

That a life-interest in the Land and Capital of the nation is the birth-right of every individual born within its confines; and that access to this birth-right should not depend upon the will of any private person other than the person seeking it.

That the most striking result of our present system of farming out the national Land and Capital to private individuals has been the division of Society into hostile classes, with large appetites and no dinners at one extreme, and large dinners and no appetites at the other.

That the practice of entrusting the land of the nation to private persons in the hope that they will make the best of it has been discredited by the consistency with which they have made the worst of it; and that the Nationalization of the Land in some form is a public duty.

That the pretensions of Capitalism to encourage Invention, and to distribute its benefits in the fairest way attainable, have been discredited by the experience of the nineteenth century.

That, under the existing system of leaving the National Industry to organize itself, Competition has the effect of rendering adulteration, dishonest dealing, and inhumanity compulsory.

That since Competition among producers admittedly secures to the public the most satisfactory products, the State should compete with all its might in every department of production.

That such restraints upon Free Competition as the penalties for infringing the Postal monopoly, and the withdrawal of workhouse and prison labour from the markets, should be abolished.

That no branch of Industry should be carried on at a profit by the central administration.

That the Public Revenue should be raised by a direct Tax; and that the central administration should have no legal power to hold back for the replenishment of the Public Treasury any portion of the proceeds of the Industries administered by them.

That the State should compete with private individuals—especially with parents—in providing happy homes for children, so that every child may have a refuge from the tyranny or neglect of its natural custodians.

That Men no longer need special political privileges to protect them against Women; and that the sexes should henceforth enjoy equal political rights.

That no individual should enjoy any Privilege in consideration of services rendered to the State by his or her parents or other relations.

That the State should secure a liberal education and an equal share in the National Industry to each of its units.

That the established Government has no more right to call itself the State than the smoke of London has to call itself the weather.

That we had rather face a Civil War than such another century of suffering as the present one has been.

2. The Manifesto of the Fabian Parliamentary League, 1887. [Essays in Fabian Socialism, pp. 139–40]

[*At a meeting of the Fabian Society on 17 September 1886, at which Shaw was present, the following motion was debated and passed: "That it is advisable that Socialists should organize themselves as a political party for the purpose of transferring into the hands of the whole working community full control over the soil and the means of production, as well as over the production and distribution of wealth." The outcome was the formation of the Fabian Parliamentary League. Its manifesto, which Shaw helped draft, was published in 1887.*]

The Fabian Parliamentary League is composed of Socialists who believe that Socialism may be most quickly and most surely realized by utilizing the political power already possessed by the people. The progress of the Socialist party in the German Reichstag, in the Legislature of the United States, and in the Paris Municipal Council, not only proves the possibility of a Socialist party in Parliament, but renders it imperative on English Socialists to set energetically about the duty of giving effect in public affairs to the growing influence of Socialist opinion in this country.

The League will endeavor to organize Socialist opinion, and to bring it to bear upon Parliament, municipalities, and other representative bodies; it will, by lectures and publications, seek to deal with the political questions of the day, analysing the ultimate tendencies of measures as well as their immediate effects, and working for or against proposed measures of social reform according as they tend towards, or away from, the Socialist ideal.

The League will take active part in all general and local elections. Until a fitting opportunity arises for putting forward Socialist candidates to form the nucleus of a Socialist party in Parliament, it will confine itself to supporting those candidates who will go furthest in the direction of Socialism. It will not ally itself absolutely with any political party; it will jealously avoid being made use of for party purposes; and it will be guided in its action by the character, record, and pledges of the candidates before the constituencies. In Municipal, School Board, Vestry, and other local elections, the League will, as it finds itself strong enough, run candidates of its own, and by placing trustworthy Socialists on local representative bodies it will endeavor to secure the recognition of the Socialist principle in all the details of local government.

It will be the duty of members of the League, in every borough, to take active part in the public work of their districts; and to this end they should organize themselves into a Branch of the League. They should appoint a secretary to keep lists of all annual and other elections in his district and of all candidates; to attend to the registration of Socialists; to watch the public conduct of all officials, and keep a record thereof for guidance at future elections; to enlist volunteers for special work, and generally to act as a centre of the organization. Individual members should write to their Parliamentary representatives on any Bill on which the League takes action; should take every opportunity of defending and advocating Socialism in their local press; should visit the workhouses of their neighborhood; and should exercise a careful supervision of local funds. By steady work on these and similar lines, Socialists will increase their power in the community, and will before long be able to influence effectively the course of public opinion.

3. From "The Transition to Social Democracy." An Address at Bath on 7 September 1888 to the Economic Section of the British Association. [*Essays in Fabian Socialism*, pp. 33–61]

[*The Fabian Parliamentary League never became a political force in its own right, in part because it lacked full support from the Fabian Society itself. Many Fabians believed that the necessary compromises involved in the established democratic process undermined its commitment to the basic principles of Socialism. Shaw, however, accepted the need for compromise.*]

...Before I recite the steps of the transition, I will, as a matter of form, explain what Social Democracy is, though doubtless nearly all of my hearers are already conversant with it.

What the achievement of Socialism involves economically is the transfer of rent from the class which now appropriates it to the whole people. Rent being that part of the produce which is individually unearned, this is the only equitable method of disposing of it. There is no means of getting rid of economic rent. So long as the fertility of land varies from acre to acre, and the number of persons passing by a shop window per hour varies from street to street, with the result that two farmers or two shopkeepers of exactly equal intelligence and industry will reap unequal returns from their year's work, so long will it be equitable to take from the richer farmer or shopkeeper the excess over his fellow's gain which he owes to the bounty of Nature or the advantage of situation, and divide that excess or rent equally between the two. If the pair of farms or shops be left in the hands of a private landlord, he will take the excess, and, instead of dividing it between his two tenants, live on it himself idly at their expense. The economic object of Socialism is not, of course, to equalize farmers and shopkeepers in couples, but to carry out the principle over the whole community by collecting all rents and throwing them into the national treasury. As the private proprietor has no reason for clinging to his property except the legal power to take the rent and spend it on himself—the legal power being in fact what really constitutes him a proprietor—its abrogation would mean his expropriation. The socialization of rent would mean the socialization of the sources of production by the expropriation of the present private proprietors, and the transfer of their property to the entire nation. The transfer, then, is the subject matter of the transition to Socialism, which began some forty-five years ago, as far as any phase of social evolution can be said to begin at all.

It will be at once seen that the valid objections to Socialism consist wholly of practical difficulties. On the ground of abstract justice, Socialism is not only unobjectionable, but sacredly imperative. I am afraid that in the ordinary middle-class opinion Socialism is flagrantly dishonest, but could be established off-hand tomorrow with the help of the guillotine, if there were no police, and the people were wicked enough. In truth, it is as honest as it is inevitable; but all the mobs and guillotines in the world can no more establish it than police coercion can avert it. The first practical difficulty is raised by the idea of the entire people collectively owning land, capital, or anything else. Here is the rent arising out of the people's industry: here are the pockets of the private proprietors. The problem is to drop the rent, not into those private pockets, but into the people's pocket. Yes; but where is the people's pocket? Who is the people? What is the people? Tom we know, and Dick: also Harry; but solely and separately as individuals: as a trinity they have no existence. Who is their trustee, their guardian, their man of business, their manager, their secretary, even their stakeholder? The Socialist is stopped dead at the threshold of practical action by this difficulty until he bethinks himself of the State as the representative and trustee of the people. Now if you will just form a hasty picture of the governments which called themselves States in Ricardo's day [i.e., British economist David Ricardo, 1772–1823], consisting of rich proprietors legislating either by divine right or by the exclusive suffrage of the poorer proprietors, and filling the executives with the creatures of their patronage and favoritism; if you look beneath their oratorical parliamentary discussions, conducted with all the splendor and decorum of an expensive sham fight; if you consider their class interests, their shameless corruption, and the waste and mismanagement which disgraced all their bungling attempts at practical business of any kind, you will understand why Ricardo, clearly as he saw the economic consequences of private appropriation of rent, never dreamt of State appropriation as a possible alternative. The Socialist of that time did not greatly care: he was only a benevolent Utopian who planned model communities, and occasionally carried them out, with negatively instructive and positively disastrous results. When his successors learned economics from Ricardo, they saw the difficulty quite as plainly as Ricardo's vulgarizers, the Whig doctrinaires who accepted the incompetence and corruption of States as permanent inherent State qualities, like the acidity of lemons. Not that the Socialists were not doctrinaires too; but outside economics they were pupils of [German philosopher Georg Wilhelm Friedrich] Hegel [1770–1831], whilst the Whigs were pupils of [British philosopher and social reformer Jeremy] Bentham [1748–1832] and [British legal philosopher John] Austin [1790–1859]. Bentham's was not the school in which men learned to solve problems to which history alone could give the key, or to form conceptions which belonged to the evolutional order. Hegel, on the other hand, expressly taught the conception of the perfect State, if not absolutely perfect, at least practically trustworthy. They contemplated the insolent and inefficient government official of their day without rushing to the conclusion that the State uniform had a magic property of extinguishing all business capacity, integrity, and common civility in the wearer. When State officials obtained their posts by favoritism and patronage, efficiency on their part was an accident, and politeness a condescension. When they retained their posts without any effective responsibility to the public, they naturally defrauded the public by making their posts sinecures, and insulted the public when, by personal inquiry, it made itself troublesome. But every successfully conducted private establishment in the kingdom was an example of the ease with which public ones could be reformed as soon as there was the effective will to find out the way. Make the passing of a sufficient examination an indispensable preliminary to entering the executive; make the executive responsible to the government and the government responsible to the people; and State departments will be provided with all the guarantees for integrity and efficiency that private money-hunting pretends to. Thus the old bugbear of State imbecility did not terrify the Socialist: it only made him a Democrat. But to call himself so simply would have had the effect of classing him with the ordinary destructive politician who is a Democrat without ulterior views for the sake of formal Democracy—one whose notion of Radicalism is the pulling up of aristocratic institutions by the roots—who is, briefly, a sort of Universal Abolitionist. Consequently, we have the distinctive term Social Democrat, indicating the man or woman who desires through Democracy to gather the whole people into the State, so that the State may be trusted with the rent of the country, and finally with the land, the capital, and the organization of the national industry—with all the sources of production, in short, which are now abandoned to the cupidity of irresponsible private individuals.

 The benefits of such a change as this are so obvious to all except the existing private proprietors and their parasites, that it is very necessary to insist on the impossibility of effecting it suddenly. The young Socialist is apt to be catastrophic in his views—to plan the revolutionary program as an affair of twenty-four lively hours, with Individualism in full swing on Monday morning, a tidal wave of the insurgent proletariat on Monday afternoon, and Socialism in complete working order on Tuesday. A man who believes that such a happy despatch is possible will naturally think it absurd and even inhuman to stick at bloodshed in bringing it about. He can prove that the continuance of the present system for a year costs more suffering than could be crammed into any Monday afternoon, however sanguinary. This is the phase of conviction in which are delivered those Socialist speeches which make what the newspapers call "good copy," and which are the only ones they as yet report. Such speeches are encouraged by the hasty opposition they evoke from thoughtless persons, who begin by tacitly admitting that a sudden change is feasible, and go on to protest that it would be wicked. The experienced Social Democrat converts his too ardent follower by first admitting that if the change could be made catastrophically it would be well worth making, and then proceeding to point out that as it would involve a readjustment of productive industry to meet the demand created by an entirely new distribution of purchasing power, it would also involve, in the application of labor and industrial machinery, alterations which no afternoon's work could effect. You cannot convince any man that it is impossible to tear down a government in a day; but everybody is convinced already that you cannot convert first and third class carriages into second class; rookeries [slums] and palaces into comfortable dwellings; and jewellers and dressmakers into bakers and builders, by merely singing the Marseillaise. No judicious person, however deeply persuaded that the work of the court dressmaker has no true social utility, would greatly care to quarter her idly on the genuinely productive worker pending the preparation of a place for her in their ranks. For although she is to all intents and purposes quartered on them at present, yet she at least escapes the demoralization of idleness. Until her new place is ready, it is better that her patrons should find dressmaking for her hands to do, than that Satan should find mischief. Demolishing a Bastille with seven prisoners in it is one thing: demolishing one with fourteen million prisoners is quite another. I need not enlarge on the point: the necessity for cautious and gradual change must be obvious to everyone here, and could be made obvious to everyone elsewhere if only the catastrophists were courageously and sensibly dealt with in discussion.

What then does a gradual transition to Social Democracy mean specifically? It means the gradual extension of the franchise; and the transfer of rent and interest to the State, not in one lump sum, but by instalments. Looked at in this way, it will at once be seen that we are already far on the road, and are being urged further by many politicians who do not dream that they are touched with Socialism—nay, who would earnestly repudiate the touch as a taint.

[Shaw goes on to review progress in social and political reform throughout the nineteenth century, embedded in legislation such as the 1832 and 1867 Reform Acts, the 1842 Income Tax Act, the 1847 Factory Act, and the 1880 Education Act. He also draws attention to the growing Trade Union movement and its role in "awakening the social conscience" of the work force. As a model of a "socialized" organization working in the national interests rather than the interests of private owners, he cites the British Post Office.]

In the meantime the extraordinary success of the post office, which, according to the teaching of the [influential free trade and *laissez faire*] Manchester school [of economic thought], should have been a nest of incompetence and jobbery, had not only shown the perfect efficiency of State enterprise when the officials are made responsible to the class interested in its success, but had also proved the enormous convenience and cheapness of socialistic or collectivist charges over those of private enterprise. For example, the Postmaster-General charges a penny for sending a letter weighing an ounce from Kensington to Bayswater [adjacent districts of London]. Private enterprise would send half a pound the same distance for a farthing, and make a handsome profit on it. But the Postmaster-General also sends an ounce letter from Land's End to John o' Groat's House [870 miles] for a penny. Private enterprise would probably demand at least a shilling, if not five, for such a service; and there are many places in which private enterprise could not on any terms maintain a post office. Therefore a citizen with ten letters to post saves considerably by the uniform socialistic charge, and quite recognizes the necessity for rigidly protecting the Postmaster's monopoly.

[Shaw comments on the enthusiasm and naivety of the early Socialist movement, eager for a rapid implementation of radical thinking.]

Numbers of young men, pupils of [John Stuart] Mill [1806–73], [Herbert] Spencer [1820–1903], [Auguste] Comte [1798–1857], and [Charles] Darwin [1809–82], roused by Mr Henry George's *Progress and Poverty* [1879], left aside evolution and freethought; took to insurrectionary economics; studied Karl Marx; and were so convinced that Socialism had only to be put clearly before the working classes to concentrate the power of their immense numbers in one irresistible organization, that the Revolution was fixed for 1889—the anniversary of the French Revolution—at latest. I remember being asked satirically and publicly at that time how long I thought it would take to get Socialism into working order if I had my way. I replied, with a spirited modesty, that a fortnight would be ample for the purpose. When I add that I was frequently complimented on being one of the more reasonable Socialists, you will be able to appreciate the fervour of our conviction, and the extravagant levity of our practical ideas. The opposition we got was uninstructive: it was mainly founded on the assumption that our projects were theoretically unsound but immediately possible, whereas our weak point lay in the case being exactly the reverse. However, the ensuing years sifted and sobered us. "The Socialists," as they were called, have fallen into line as a Social Democratic party, no more insurrectionary in its policy than any other party. But I shall not present the remainder of the transition to Social Democracy as the work of fully conscious Social Democrats. I prefer to ignore them altogether—to suppose, if you will, that the Government will shortly follow the advice of the *Saturday Review*, and, for the sake of peace and quietness, hang them.

First, then, as to the consummation of Democracy. Since 1885 every man who pays four shillings a week rent can only be hindered from voting by anomalous conditions of registration which are likely to be swept away very shortly. This is all but manhood suffrage. However, I may leave adult suffrage out of the question, because the outlawry of women, monstrous as it is, is not a question of class privilege, but of sex privilege. To complete the foundation of the democratic State, then, we need manhood suffrage, abolition of all poverty disqualifications, abolition of the House of Lords, public payment of candidature expenses, public payment of representatives, and annual elections. These changes are now inevitable, however unacceptable they may appear to those of us who are Conservatives. They have been for half a century the commonplaces of Radicalism. We have next to consider that the state is not merely an abstraction: it is a machine to do certain work; and if that work be increased and altered in its character, the machinery must be multiplied and altered too. Now, the extension of the franchise does increase and alter the work very considerably: but it has no direct effect on the machinery. At present the State machine has practically broken down under the strain of spreading democracy, the work being mainly local, and the machinery being mainly central. Without efficient local machinery the replacing of private enterprise by State enterprise is out of the question; and we shall presently see that such replacement is one of the inevitable consequences of Democracy. A democratic State cannot become a *Social*-Democratic State unless it has in every centre of population a local governing body as thoroughly democratic in its constitution as the central Parliament. This matter is also well in train. In 1888 a Government avowedly reactionary passed a Local Government Bill which effected a distinct advance towards the democratic municipality [by establishing elected county councils and county borough councils]. It was furthermore a Bill with no single aspect of finality anywhere about it. Local Self-Government remains prominent within the sphere of practical politics. When it is achieved, the democratic State will have the machinery for Socialism.

And now, how is the raw material of Socialism—otherwise the Proletarian man—to be brought to the Democratic State machinery? Here again the path is easily found. Politicians who have no suspicion that they are Socialists are advocating further instalments of Socialism with a recklessness of indirect results which scandalizes the conscious Social Democrat. The phenomenon of economic rent has assumed prodigious proportions in our great cities. The injustice of its private appropriation is glaring, flagrant, almost ridiculous. In the long suburban roads about London, where rows of exactly similar houses stretch for miles countrywards, the rent changes at every few thousand yards by exactly the amount saved or incurred annually in travelling to and from the householder's place of business. The seeker after lodgings, hesitating between Bloomsbury and Tottenham, finds every advantage of situation skimmed off by the landlord with scientific precision. As lease after lease falls in, houses, shops, goodwills of businesses which are the fruits of the labor of lifetimes, fall into the maw of the ground landlord. Confiscation of capital, spoliation of households, annihilation of incentive, everything that the most ignorant and credulous fundholder ever charged against the Socialist, rages openly in London, which begins to ask itself whether it exists and toils only for the typical duke and his celebrated jockey and his famous racehorse. Lord Hobhouse and his unimpeachably respectable committee for the taxation of ground values [the royal commission for the implementation of the 1869 Land Transfer Act] are already in the field claiming the value of the site of London for London collectively; and their agitation receives additional momentum from every lease that falls in. Their case is unassailable; and the evil they attack is one that presses on the ratepaying and leaseholding classes as well as upon humbler sufferers. This economic pressure is reinforced formidably by political opinion in the workmen's associations. Here the moderate members are content to demand a progressive Income Tax, which is virtually Lord Hobhouse's proposal; and the extremists are all for Land Nationalization, which is again Lord Hobhouse's principle. The cry for such taxation cannot permanently be resisted. And it is very worthy of remark that there is a new note in the cry. Formerly taxes were proposed with a specific object—as to pay for a war, for education, or the like. Now the proposal is to tax the landlords in order to get some of *our* money back from them—take it from them first and find a use for it afterwards. Ever since Mr Henry George's book reached the English Radicals, there has been a growing disposition to impose a tax of twenty shillings in the pound on obviously unearned income: that is, to dump four hundred and fifty millions a year down on the Exchequer counter; and then retire with three cheers for the restoration of the land to the people.

The results of such a proceeding, if it actually came off, would considerably take its advocates aback. The streets would presently be filled with starving workers of all grades, domestic servants, coach builders, decorators, jewellers, lacemakers, fashionable professional men, and numberless others whose livelihood is at present gained by ministering to the wants of these and of the proprietary class. "This," they would cry, "is what your theories have brought us to! Back with the good old times, when we received our wages, which were at least better than nothing." Evidently the Chancellor of the Exchequer would have three courses open to him. (1) He could give the money back again to the landlords and capitalists with an apology. (2) He could attempt to start State industries with it for the employment of the people. (3) Or he could simply distribute it among the unemployed. The last is not to be thought of: anything is better than *panem et circenses* ["bread and circuses"]. The second (starting State industries) would be far too vast an undertaking to get on foot soon enough to meet the urgent difficulty. The first (return with an apology) would be a *reductio ad absurdum* ["reduction to the absurd"] of the whole affair—a confession that the private proprietor, for all his idleness and his voracity, is indeed performing an indispensable economic function—the function of capitalizing, however wastefully and viciously, the wealth which surpasses his necessarily limited power of immediate personal consumption. And here we have checkmate to Henry Georgism, or State appropriation of rent without Socialism. It is easy to show that State is entitled to the whole income of the Duke of Westminster [Hugh Grosvenor, 1825–99, 1st Duke of Westminster, a major London landowner], and to argue therefrom that he should straightaway be taxed twenty shillings in the pound. But in practical earnest the State has no right to take five farthings of capital from the Duke or anybody else until it is ready to invest them in productive enterprise. The consequences of withdrawing capital from private hands merely to lock it up unproductively in the treasury would be so swift and ruinous, that no statesman, however fortified with the destructive resources of abstract economics, could persist in it. It will be found in the future as in the past that governments will raise money only because they want it for a specific purpose, and not on *a priori* ["from what is before," i.e., based on theoretical deduction] demonstrations that they have a right to it. But it must be added that when they *do* want it for a specific purpose, then, also in the future as in the past, they will raise it without the slightest regard to *a priori* demonstrations that they have no right to it.

Here then we have got to a deadlock. In spite of democrats and land nationalizers, rent cannot be touched unless some pressure from quite another quarter [than government on its own initiative] forces productive enterprise on the State. Such pressure is already forthcoming. The quick starvation of the unemployed, the slow starvation of the employed who have no relatively scarce special skill, the unbearable anxiety or dangerous recklessness of those who are employed today and unemployed tomorrow, the rise in urban rents, the screwing down of wages by pauper immigration and home multiplication, the hand-in-hand advance of education and discontent, are all working up to explosion point.... But whilst we are pointing the moral and adorning the tale according to our various opinions, an actual struggle is beginning between the unemployed who demand work and the local authorities appointed to deal with the poor. In the winter, the unemployed collect round red flags, and listen to speeches for the want of anything else to do. They welcome Socialism, insurrectionism, currency craze—anything that passes the time and seems to express the fact that they are hungry. The local authorities, equally innocent of studied economic views, deny that there is any misery; send leaders of deputations to the Local Government Board, who promptly send them back to the guardians; try bullying; try stone-yards; try bludgeoning; and finally sit down helplessly and wish it were summer again or the unemployed at the bottom of the sea. Meanwhile the charity fund, which is much less elastic than the wages fund, overflows at the Mansion House [official residence of the Lord Mayor of London] only to run dry at the permanent institutions. So unstable a state of things cannot last. The bludgeoning, and the shocking clamor for bloodshed from the anti-popular newspapers, will create a revulsion among the humane section of the middle class. The section which is blinded by class prejudice to all sense of social responsibility dreads personal violence from the working class with a superstitious terror that defies enlightenment or control. Municipal employment must be offered at last. This cannot be done in one place alone: the rush from other parts of the country would swamp an isolated experiment. Wherever the pressure is, the relief must be given on the spot. And since public decency, as well as consideration for its higher officials, will prevent the County Council from instituting a working day of sixteen hours at a wage of a penny an hour or less, it will soon have on its hands not only the unemployed, but also the white slaves of the sweater [i.e., an industrial employer paying meagre wages for work in crowded and unhygienic conditions such as cotton mills] who will escape from their den and appeal to the municipality for work the moment they become aware that municipal employment is better than private sweating. Nay, the sweater himself, a mere slave driver paid "by the piece," will in many instances be as anxious as his victims to escape from his hideous trade. But the municipal organization of the industry of these people will require capital. Where is the municipality to get it? Raising the rates is out of the question: the ordinary tradesmen and householders are already rated and rented to the limit of endurance: further burdens would almost [certainly] bring them into the street with a red flag.

PART I: FABIAN SOCIALIST

Dreadful dilemma!, in which the County Council, between the devil and the deep sea, will hear Lord Hobhouse singing a song of deliverance, telling a golden tale of ground values to be municipalized by taxation. The land nationalizers will swell the chorus: the Radical progressive income taxers singing together, and the ratepaying tenants shouting for joy. The capital difficulty thus solved—for we need not seriously anticipate that the landlords will actually fight, as our President [Lord Bramwell, President of the Economic Section of the British Association] once threatened—the question of acquiring land will arise. The nationalizers will declare for its annexation by the municipality without compensation; but that will be rejected as spoliation, worth only of revolutionary Socialists. The no-compensation cry is indeed a piece of unpractical catastrophic insurrectionism; for whilst compensation would be unnecessary and absurd if every proprietor were expropriated simultaneously, and the proprietary system replaced by full-blown Socialism, yet when it is necessary to proceed by degrees, the denial of compensation would have the effect of singling out individual proprietors for expropriation whilst the others remained unmolested, and depriving them of their private means long before there was suitable municipal employment for them. The land, as it is required, will therefore be honestly purchased; and the purchase money, or the interest thereon, will be procured, like the capital, by taxing rent. Of course this will be at bottom an act of expropriation just as much as the collection of Income Tax today is an act of expropriation. As such, it will be denounced by the landlords as merely a committing of the newest sin the oldest kind of way. In effect, they will be compelled at each purchase to buy out one of their body and present his land to the municipality, thereby distributing the loss fairly over their whole class, instead of placing it on one man who is no more responsible than the rest. But they will be compelled to do this in a manner that will satisfy the moral sense of the ordinary citizen as effectively as that of the skilled economist.

We now foresee our municipality equipped with land and capital for industrial purposes. At first they will naturally extend the industries they already carry on, road making, gas works, tramways, building, and like. It is probable that they will for the most part regard their action as a mere device to meet a passing emergency. The Manchester School will urge its Protectionist theories as to the exemption of private enterprise from the competition of public enterprise, in one supreme effort to practise for the last time on popular ignorance of the science which it has consistently striven to debase and stultify. For a while the proprietary party will succeed in hampering and restricting municipal enterprise; in attaching the stigma of pauperism to its service; in keeping the lot of its laborers as nearly as possible down to private competition level in point of hard work and low wages. But its power will be broken by the disappearance of that general necessity for keeping down the rates which now hardens local authority to humane appeals. The luxury of being generous at someone else's expense will be irresistible. The ground landlord will be the municipal milch cow; and the ordinary ratepayers will feel the advantage of sleeping in peace, relieved at once from the fear of increased burdens and of having their windows broken and their premises looted by hungry mobs, nuclei of all the socialism and scoundrelism of the city. They will have just as much remorse in making the landlord pay as the landlord has had in making them pay—just as much and no more. And as the municipality becomes more democratic, it will find landlordism losing power, not only relatively to democracy, but absolutely....

[Shaw goes on to insist that a minimum wage must be paid to municipal employees—"at first, to avoid an overwhelming rush of applicants for employment, it must be made too small to tempt

any decently employed laborer to forsake his place and run to the municipality, still, it will not be the frankly infernal competition wage"—and that educational standards for the working classes must be raised. *"Now the tendency of private property is to keep the masses mere beasts of burden. The tendency of Social Democracy is to educate them."]*

This, then, is the humdrum program of the practical Social Democrat today. There is not one new item in it. All are applications of principles already admitted, and extensions of practices already in full activity. All have on them that stamp of the vestry [i.e., local government] which is so congenial to the British mind. None of them compel the use of the words Socialism or Revolution: at no point do they involve guillotining, declaring the Rights of Man, swearing on the altar of the country, or anything else that is supposed to be essentially un-English. And they are all sure to come—landmarks on our course already visible to far-sighted politicians even of the [Conservative] party which dreads them.

Let me, in conclusion, disavow all admiration for this inevitable, but sordid, slow, reluctant, cowardly path to justice. I venture to claim your respect for those enthusiasts who still refuse to believe that millions of their fellow creatures must be left to sweat and suffer in hopeless toil and degradation, whilst parliaments and vestries grudgingly muddle and grope towards paltry instalments of betterment. The right is so clear, the wrong so intolerable, the gospel so convincing, that it seems to them that it *must* be possible to enlist the whole body of workers—soldiers, policemen, and all—under the banner of brotherhood and equality; and at one great stroke to set Justice on her rightful throne. Unfortunately, such an army of light is no more to be gathered from the human product of nineteenth century civilization than grapes are to be gathered from thistles. But if we feel glad of that impossibility; if we feel relieved that the change is to be slow enough to avert personal risk to ourselves; if we feel anything less than acute disappointment and bitter humiliation at the discovery that there is yet between us and the promised land a wilderness in which many must perish miserably of want and despair: then I submit to you that our institutions have corrupted us to the most dastardly degree of selfishness. The Socialists need not be ashamed of beginning as they did by proposing militant organization of the working classes and general insurrection. The proposal proved impracticable; and it has now been abandoned—not without some outspoken regrets—by English Socialists. But it still remains as the only finally possible alternative to the Social Democratic program which I have sketched today.

4. From "What Socialism Is," *Fabian Tract no. 13*. London: The Fabian Society, 1890.

[This succinct explanation of Shaw's understanding of Socialism rests on a belief in the validity and effectiveness of a reformed parliamentary democracy (Parliament "will govern in the interest of the people when the majority is selected from the wage-earning class"), a belief that was to be sorely tested over the coming years.]

Socialism is a plan for securing equal rights and opportunities for all. The Socialists are trying to have the land and machinery gradually "socialized," or made the property of the whole people, in order to do away with idle owners, and to win the whole product for those whose labor produces it. The establishment of Socialism, when once the people are resolved upon it, is not so difficult as might be supposed. If a man wishes to work on his own account, the rent of his place of business, and the interest on the capital needed to start him, can be paid to the County Council of his district just as easily as to the private landlord and capitalist. Factories are already largely regulated by public inspectors, and can be conducted by the local authorities just as gas-works, water-works and tramways are now conducted by them in various towns. Railways and mines, instead of being left to private companies, can be carried on by a department under the central government, as the postal and telegraph services are carried on now. The Income Tax collector who today calls for a tax of a few pence in the pound on the income of the idle millionaire, can collect a tax of twenty shillings in the pound [i.e., 100 percent] on every unearned income in the country if the State so orders. Remember that Parliament, with all its faults, has always governed the country in the interest of the class to which the majority of its members belonged. It governed in the interest of the country gentlemen in the old days when they were in a majority in the House of Commons; it has governed in the interests of the capitalists and employers since they won a majority by the Reform Bill of 1832; and it will govern in the interest of the people when the majority is selected from the wage-earning class. Inquirers will find that Socialism can be brought about in a perfectly constitutional manner, and that none of the practical difficulties which occur to everyone in his first five minutes' consideration of the subject have escaped the attention of those who have worked at it for years. Few now believe Socialism to be impracticable except those with whom the wish is father to the thought.

5. From "The Impossibilities of Anarchism," 1891. [*Essays in Fabian Socialism*, pp. 65–99]

[*Resistance to the democratic process came not only from within the Fabian Society, but, with far more passion and determination, from anarchist groups who, throughout Europe, the United States, and Great Britain were a significant political presence. In the name of individual liberty, anarchists demanded rapid and uncompromising dismantling of the established social and political order, but not* through established democratic means. However much he respected the anarchists' objectives, Shaw firmly rejected their methods. In a paper read to the Fabian Society on 16 October 1891 he explained his position. Shaw based his criticism of anarchism on an essay by a leading American anarchist, Benjamin Tucker (1854–1939), who had founded an anarchist magazine, Liberty, in Boston in 1881. The March 1888 issue of Liberty included Tucker's essay "State Socialism and Anarchism: How Far They Agree, and Wherein They Differ." Shaw refers to, and quotes from, this essay through his rejection of anarchism.]

Anarchists and Socialists

Some years ago, as the practical policy of the Socialist party in England began to shape itself more and more definitely into the program of Social Democracy, it became apparent that we could not progress without the greatest violations of principles of all sorts. In particular, the democratic side of the program was found to be incompatible with the sacred principle of the Autonomy of the Individual. It also involved a recognition of the State, an institution altogether repugnant to the principle of Freedom. Worse than that, it involved compromise at every step; and principles, as [Liberal statesman] Mr John Morley [1838–1923] once eloquently showed, must not be compromised. The result was that many of us fell to quarrelling; refused to associate with one another; denounced each other as trimmers [compromisers] or Impossibilists, according to our side in the controversy; and finally succeeded in creating a considerable stock of ill-feeling. My own side in the controversy was the unprincipled one, as Socialism to me has always meant, not a principle, but certain definite economic measures which I wish to see taken. Indeed, I have often been reproached for limiting the term Socialism too much to the economic side of the great movement towards equality. That movement, however, appears to me to be as much an Individualist as a Socialist one; and though there are Socialists, like Sir William Harcourt [1827–1904], to whom Socialism means the sum total of humanitarian aspiration, in which the transfer of some millions of acres of property from private to public ownership must seem but an inessential and even undesirable detail, this sublimer shade of Socialism suffers from such a lack of concentration upon definite measures, that, but for the honor and glory of the thing, its professors might as well call themselves Conservatives. Now what with Socialists of this sort, and persons who found that the practical remedy for white slavery was incompatible with the principle of Liberty, and the practical remedy for despotism incompatible with the principle of Democracy, and the practical conduct of politics incompatible with the principle of Personal Integrity (in the sense of having your own way in everything), the Practical men were at last driven into frank Opportunism. When, for instance, they found national and local organization of the working classes opposed by Socialists on the ground that Socialism is universal and international in principle; when they found their Radical and Trade Unionist allies ostracized by Socialists for being outside the pale of the Socialist faith one and indivisible; when they saw agricultural laborers alienated by undiscriminating denunciations of allotments as "individualistic"; then they felt the full force of the saying that Socialism would spread fast enough if it were not for the Socialists. It was bad enough to have to contend with the conservative forces of the modern unsocialist State without also having to fight the seven deadly virtues in possession of the Socialists themselves. The conflict between ideal Socialism and practical Social Democracy destroyed the Chartist organization half a century ago, as it destroyed the Socialist League only the other day. But it has never gone so far as the conflict between Social Democracy and Anarchism. For the Anarchists will recommend abstention from voting and refusal to pay taxes in cases where the Social Democrats are strenuously urging the workers to organize their votes so as to return candidates pledged to contend for extension of the franchise and for taxation of unearned incomes, the object of such taxation being the raising of State capital for all sorts of collective purposes, from the opening of public libraries to the municipalization and nationalization of our industries. In fact, the denunciation of Social Democratic methods by the Anarchists is just as much a matter of course as the denunciation of Social Democratic aims by Conservatives. It is possible that some of the strangers present may be surprised to hear this, since no distinction is made in the newspapers which support the existing social order between Social Democrats and Anarchists, both being alike hostile to that order. In the columns of such papers all revolutionists are Socialists; all Socialists are Anarchists; and all Anarchists are incendiaries, assassins, and thieves. One result of this is that the imaginative French or Italian criminal who reads the papers sometimes declares, when taken red-handed in the commission of murder or burglary, that he is an Anarchist acting on principle. And in all countries the more violent and reckless temperaments among the discontented are attracted by the name Anarchist merely because it suggests desperate, thorough, uncompromising implacable war on existing injustices. It is therefore necessary to warn you that there are some persons abusively called Anarchists by their political opponents, and others ignorantly so described by themselves, who are nevertheless not Anarchists at all within the meaning of this paper. On the other hand, many persons who are never called Anarchists either by themselves or others take Anarchist ground in their opposition to Social Democracy just as clearly as the writers with whom I shall more particularly deal.... They distrust State action, and are jealous advocates of the prerogative of the individual, proposing to restrict the one and to extend the other as far as is humanly possible, in opposition to the Social Democrat, who proposes to democratize the State and throw upon it the whole work of organizing the national industry, thereby making it the most vital organ in the social body. Obviously there are natural limits to the application of both views; and the Anarchists and Social Democrats are alike subject to the fool's argument that since neither collective provision for the individual nor individual freedom from collective control can be made complete, neither party is thoroughly consistent. No dialectic of that kind will, I hope, be found in the following criticism of Anarchism. It is confined to the practical measures proposed by Anarchists, and raises no discussion as to aims or principles. As to those we are all agreed. Justice, Virtue, Truth, Brotherhood, the highest interests of the people, moral as well as physical: these are dear not only to Social Democrats and Anarchists, but also to Tories, Whigs, Radicals, and probably also to Moonlighters and Dynamitards....

Democracy

[Tucker asserts] that "Under the system of State Socialism, which holds the community responsible for the health, wealth, and wisdom of the individual, the community, through its majority expression, will insist more and more on prescribing the conditions of health, wealth, and wisdom. Thus impairing and finally destroying individual independence and with it all sense of individual responsibility."

"Whatever, then, the State Socialists may claim or disclaim, their system, if adopted, is doomed to end in a State religion, to the expense of which all must contribute and at the altar of which all must kneel; a State school of medicine, by whose practitioners the sick must invariably be treated; a State system of hygiene, prescribing what all must and must not eat, drink, wear, and do; a State code of morals, which will not content itself with punishing crime, but will prohibit what the majority decide to be vice; a State system of instruction, which shall do away with all private schools, academies, and colleges; a State nursery, in which all children must be brought up in common at the public expense; and, finally, a State family, with an attempt to stirpiculture, or scientific breeding, in which no man or woman can refuse to have children if the State orders them. Thus will Authority achieve its acme and Monopoly be carried to its highest power."

In reading this, one is reminded of Mr Herbert Spencer's habit of assuming that whatever is not white must be black. Mr Tucker, on the ground that "it has ever been the tendency of power to add to itself, to enlarge its sphere, to encroach beyond the limits set for it," admits no alternative to the total subjection of the individual, except the total abolition of the State. If matters really could and did come to that I am afraid the individual would have to go under in any case; for the total abolition of the State in this sense means the total abolition of the collective force of Society, to abolish which it would be necessary to abolish Society itself. There are two ways of doing this. One, the abolition of the individuals composing society, could not be carried out without an interference with their personal claims much more serious than that required, even on Mr Tucker's showing, by Social Democracy. The other, the dispersion of the human race into independent hermitages over the globe at the rate of twenty-five to the square mile, would give rise to considerable inequality of condition and opportunity as between the hermits of Terra del Fuego or the Arctic regions and those of Florida or the Riviera, and would suit only a few temperaments. The dispersed units would soon re-associate; and the moment they did so, good-bye to the sovereignty of the individual. If the majority believed in an angry and jealous God, then, State or no State, they would not permit an individual to offend that God and bring down his wrath upon them; they would rather stone and burn the individual in propitiation. They would not suffer the individual to go naked among them; and if he clothed himself in an unusual way which struck them as being ridiculous or scandalous, they would laugh at him; refuse him admission to their feasts; object to be seen talking with him in the streets; and perhaps lock him up as a lunatic. They would not allow him to neglect sanitary precautions which they believed essential to their own immunity from zymotic [contagious] disease. If the family were established among them as it is established among us, they would not suffer him to intermarry within certain degrees of kinship. Their demand would so rule the market that in most places he would find no commodities in the shops except those preferred by a majority of the customers; no schools except those conducted in accordance with the ideas of the majority of parents; no experienced doctors except those whose qualifications inspired confidence in a whole circle of patients. This is not "the coming slavery" of Social Democracy: it is the slavery already come. What is more, there is nothing in the most elaborately negative practical program yet put forward by Anarchism that offers the slightest mitigation of it. That in comparison with ideal irresponsible absolute liberty it is slavery, cannot be denied. But in comparison with the slavery of Robinson Crusoe, which is the most Anarchistic alternative Nature, our taskmistress allows us, it is pardonably described as "freedom."...

...Democracy does not give majorities absolute power, nor does it enable them to reduce minorities to ciphers. Such limited power of coercing minorities as majorities must possess, is not given to them by Democracy any more than it can be taken away from them by Anarchism. A couple of men are stronger than one: that is all. There are only two ways of neutralizing this natural fact. One is to convince men of the immorality of abusing the majority power, and then to make them moral enough to refrain from doing it on that account. The other is to realize [Edward Bulwer] Lytton's fancy of *vril* [a supernatural force in Lytton's 1871 novel *Vril: The Power of the Coming Race*] by inventing a means by which each individual will be able to destroy all his fellows with a flash of thought, so that the majority may have as much reason to fear the individual as he to fear the majority. No method of doing either is to be found in Individualistic of Communist Anarchism: consequently these systems, as far as the evils of majority tyranny are concerned, are no better than the Social-Democratic program of adult suffrage with maintenance of representatives and payment of polling expenses from public funds—faulty devices enough, no doubt, but capable of accomplishing all that is humanly possible at present to make the State representative of the nation; to make the administration trustworthy; and to secure the utmost power to each individual and consequently to minorities. What better can we have whilst collective action is inevitable? Indeed, in the mouths of the really able Anarchists, Anarchism means simply the utmost attainable thoroughness of Democracy. [Russian anarchist Peter] Kropotkin [1842–1921], for example, speaks of free development from the simple to the composite by "the free union of free groups"; and his illustrations are "the societies for study, for commerce, for pleasure and recreation" which have sprung up to meet the varied requirements of the individual of our age. But in every one of these societies there is government by a council elected annually by a majority of voters; so that Kropotkin is not at all afraid of the democratic machinery and the majority power. Mr Tucker speaks of "voluntary association," but gives no illustrations, and indeed avows that "Anarchists are simply unfettered Jeffersonian Democrats." [After Thomas Jefferson, 1743–1826, third President of the United States, 1801–09.] He says, indeed, that "if the individual has a right to govern himself, all external government is tyranny"; but if governing oneself means doing what one pleases without regard to the interests of neighbors, then the individual has flatly no such right. If he has no such right, the interference of his neighbors to make him behave socially, though it is "external government," is not a tyranny; and even if it were they would not refrain from it on that account. On the other hand, if governing oneself means compelling oneself to act with due regard to the interests of the neighbors, then it is a right which men are proved incapable of exercising without external government. Either way, the phrase comes to nothing; for it would be easy to show by a little play upon it, either that altruism is really external government or that democratic State authority is really self-government.

Mr Tucker's adjective, "voluntary," as applied to associations for defence or the management of affairs, must not be taken as implying that there is any very wide choice open in these matters. Such association is really compulsory, since if it be foregone affairs will remain unmanaged and communities defenceless. Nature makes short work of our aspirations towards utter impunity. She leaves communities in no wise "free" to choose whether they will labor and govern themselves. It is either that or starvation or chaos. Her tasks are inexorably set: her penalties are inevitable: her payment is strictly "payment by results." All the individual can do is to shift and dodge his share of the task on to the shoulders of others, or filch some of "natural wage" to add to his own. If they are fools enough to suffer it, that is their own affair so far as Nature is concerned. But it is the aim of Social Democracy to relieve these fools by throwing on all an equal share in the inevitable labor imposed by the eternal tyranny of Nature, and so secure to every individual no less than his equal quota of the nation's product in return for no more than his equal quota of the nation's labor. These are the best terms humanity can make with its tyrant. In the eighteenth century it was easy for the philosophers and for [Scottish philosopher] Adam Smith [1723–90] to think of this rule of Nature as being "natural liberty" in contrast to the odious and stupid oppression of castes, priests, and kings—the detested "dominion of man over man." But we, in detecting the unsoundness of

Adam Smith's private property and *laisser-faire* recipe for natural liberty, begin to see that though there is political liberty, there is no natural liberty, but only natural law remorselessly enforced. And so we shake our heads when we see LIBERTY on the title-page of Mr Tucker's paper just as we laugh when we see THE COMING SLAVERY on Mr Herbert Spencer's *Man and the State* [i.e., *The Man Versus the State*, 1884].

We can now begin to join the threads of our discussion. We have seen that private appropriation of land in any form, whether limited by Individualistic Anarchism to occupying owners or not, means the unjust distribution of a vast fund of social wealth called rent, which can by no means be claimed as due to the labor of any particular individual or class of individuals. We have seen that Communist Anarchism, though it partly—and only partly—avoids the rent difficulty, is, in the condition of morals developed under existing Unsocialism, impracticable. We have seen that the delegation of individual powers by voting; the creation of authoritative public bodies; the supremacy of the majority in the last resort; and the establishment and even endowment, either directly and officially or indirectly and unconsciously, of conventional forms of practice in religion, medicine, education, food, clothing, and criminal law, are, whether they be evils or not, inherent in society itself, and must be submitted to with the help of such protection against their abuse as democratic institutions more than any others afford. When Democracy fails, there is no antidote for intolerance save the spread of better sense. No form of Anarchism yet suggested provides any escape. Like bad weather in winter, intolerance does much mischief; but as, when we have done our best in the way of overcoats, umbrellas, and good fires, we have to put up with the winter, so, when we have done our best in the way of Democracy, decentralization, and the like, we must put up with the State.

PART I: FABIAN SOCIALIST

The Anarchist Spirit

I suppose I must not leave the subject without a word as to the value of what I will call the Anarchist spirit as an element in progress. But before I do so, let me disclaim all intention of embarrassing our Anarchist friends who are present by any sympathy which I may express with that spirit. On the Continent the discussion between Anarchism and Social Democracy is frequently threshed out with the help of walking-sticks, chair-legs, and even revolvers. In England this does not happen, because the majority of an English audience always declines to take an extreme position, and, out of an idle curiosity to hear both sides, will, on sufficient provocation, precipitately eject theorists who make a disturbance, without troubling itself to discriminate as to the justice of their views. When I had the privilege some time ago of debating publicly with [British journalist] Mr G.W. Foote [1850–1915] on the Eight Hours question [i.e., limiting the standard working day to eight hours], a French newspaper which dealt with the occasion at great length devoted a whole article to an expression of envious astonishment at the fact that Mr Foote and I abstained from vilifying and finally assaulting one another, and that our partisans followed our shining example and did not even attempt to prevent each other's champions from being heard. Still, if we do not permit ourselves to merge Socialism, Anarchism, and all the other isms into rowdyism, we sometimes debate our differences, even in the eminently respectable Fabian Society, with considerable spirit. Now far be it from me to disarm the Anarchist debater by paying him compliments. On the contrary, if we have here any of those gentlemen who make it their business to denounce Social Democrats as misleaders of the people and trimmers; who declaim against all national and municipal projects, and clamor for a desperate resistance to rent, taxes, representative government and organized collective action of every sort: then I invite them to regard me as their inveterate opponent—as one who regards such doctrine, however sincerely it may be put forward, as at best an encouragement to the workers to neglect doing what is possible under pretext of waiting for the impossible, and at worst as furnishing the reactionary newspapers in England, and the police agents on the Continent, with evidence as to the alleged follies and perils of Socialism. But at the same time, it must be understood that I do not stand here to defend the State as we know it. [Russian anarchist Mikhail] Bakounin's [1814–76] comprehensive aspiration to destroy all States and Established Churches, with their religious, political, judicial, financial, criminal, academic, economic, and social laws and institutions, seems to me perfectly justifiable and intelligible from the point of view of the ordinary "educated man," who believes that institutions make men instead of men making institutions. I fully admit and vehemently urge that the State at present is simply a huge machine for robbing and slave-driving the poor by brute force. You may, if you are a stupid or comfortably-off person, think that the policeman at the corner is the guardian of law and order—that the gaol, with those instruments of torture, the treadmill, plank bed, solitary cell, cat-o'-nine-tails, and gallows, is a place to make people cease to do evil and learn to do well. But the primary function of the policeman, and that for which his other functions are only blinds, is to see that you do not lie down to sleep in this country without paying an idler for the privilege; that you do not taste bread until you have paid the idler's toll in the price of it; that you do not resist the starving blackleg who is dragging you down to his level for the idler's profit by offering to do your work for a starvation wage. Attempt any of these things, and you will be hauled off and tortured in the name of law and order, honesty, social equilibrium, safety of property and person, public duty, Christianity, morality, and what not, as a vagrant, a thief, and a rioter. Your soldier, ostensibly a heroic and patriotic defender of his country, is really an unfortunate man driven by destitution to offer himself as food for powder for the sake of regular rations, shelter, and clothing; and he must, on pain of being arbitrarily imprisoned, punished with petty penances like a naughty child, pack-drilled, flogged, or shot, all in the blessed name of "discipline," to do anything he is ordered to, from standing in his red coat in the hall of an opera house as a mere ornament, to flogging his comrade or committing murder. And *his* primary function is to come to the rescue of the policeman when the latter is overpowered. Members of Parliament whose sole qualifications for election were £1000 loose cash, and "independent" income, and a vulgar strain of ambition; parsons quoting scripture for the purposes of the squire; lawyers selling their services to the highest bidder at the bar, and maintaining the supremacy of the moneyed class on the bench; juries of employers masquerading as the peers of the proletarians in the dock; University professors elaborating the process known as the education of a gentleman; artists striving to tickle the fancy or flatter the vanity of the aristocrat or plutocrat; workmen doing their work as badly and slowly as they dare so as to make the most of their job; employers starving and overworking their hands and adulterating their goods as much as *they* dare: these are the actual living material of those imposing abstractions known as the State, the Church, the Law, the Constitution, Education, the Fine Arts, and Industry. Every institution, as Bakounin saw, religious, political, financial, judicial, and so on, is corrupted by the fact that the men in it either belong to the propertied classes themselves or must sell themselves to it in order to live. All the purchasing power that is left to buy men's souls with after their bodies are fed is in the hands of the rich; and everywhere, from the Parliament which wields the irresistible coercive forces of the bludgeon, bayonet, machine gun, dynamite, shell, prison, and scaffold, down to the pettiest centre of shabby-genteel social pretension, the rich pay the piper and call the tune. Naturally, they use their power to steal more money to continue paying the piper; and thus all society becomes a huge conspiracy and hypocrisy. The ordinary man is insensible to the fraud just as he is insensible to the taste of water, which, being constantly in contact with his mucous membrane, seems to have no taste at all. The villainous moral conditions on which our social system is based are necessarily in constant contact with our moral mucous membrane, so we lose our sense of their omnipresent meanness and dishonour....

...It is easy to say [as the Anarchists do], Abolish the State; but the State will sell you up, lock you up, blow you up, knock you down, bludgeon, shoot, stab, hang—in short, abolish you, if you lift your hand against it. Fortunately, there is, as we have seen, a fine impartiality about the policeman and the soldier, who are the cutting edge of the State power. They take their wages and obey their orders without asking questions. If those orders are to demolish the homestead of every peasant who refuses to take the bread out of his children's mouths in order that his landlord may have money to spend as an idle gentleman in London, the soldier obeys. But if his orders were to help the police to pitch his lordship into Holloway Gaol until he had paid an Income Tax of twenty shillings on every pound of his unearned income [i.e., 100 percent tax], the soldier would do that with equal devotion to duty, and perhaps with a certain private zest that might be lacking in the other case. Now these orders come ultimately from the State—meaning, in this country, the House of Commons. A House of Commons consisting of 660 gentlemen and 10 workmen will order the soldier to take money from the people for the landlords. A House of Commons consisting of 660 workmen and 10 gentlemen will probably, unless the 660 are fools, order the soldier to take money from the landlords for the people. With this hint I leave the matter, in the full conviction that the State, in spite of the Anarchists, will continue to be used against the people by the [propertied] classes until it is used by the people against the classes with equal ability and equal resolution.

6. From the *Fabian Election Manifesto 1892*. London: The Fabian Society, 1892.

[The General Election of 1892 was the first opportunity the Fabian Society had to play an active role in Parliamentary elections. The Conservative Party, led by Lord Salisbury (1830–1903), held office in the previous Parliament (1886–92). In the 1892 election Salisbury was opposed by Liberal leader William Ewart Gladstone (1809–98), who had held the office of Prime Minister on three previous occasions. The Conservatives gained the largest number of seats in the election, but fell short of a majority. Salisbury stayed on as Prime Minister, but resigned after losing a vote of confidence in the House of Commons. Gladstone then became Prime Minister again, leading a minority government with the support of the Irish Parliamentary (Home Rule) Party led by Justin McCarthy (1830–1912). Shaw wrote the 1892 Fabian Election Manifesto, which, among other things, attacked both the Conservatives and the Liberals for failing to undertake fundamental social and economic reform, demanded electoral reform to break the "tyranny" of two-party rule, and outlined the case for the formal creation of a political party whose main purpose would be to represent the interests of the working class. Shaw's commitment to the democratic process is absolute, though his impatience with what he perceived as the political apathy of the working class is unambiguously expressed.]

The Conspiracy of Hypocrisy

In both parties alike [Conservative and Liberal], the conspiracy of silence on the fundamental question of how to alter our outrageously unjust system of distributing the wealth of the country has remained unbroken. During the present Government's term of office, there have been constant complaints as to the extravagance of public expenditure. We have had clamour in the name of ratepayers against spending the paltriest of sums on pianofortes for Board Schools, and in the name of the taxpayers against every new ironclad [warship]. Meanwhile, nearly three thousand million pounds sterling have been wasted on the propertied classes in rent and in that particular form of interest which costs its recipient no more labor than the cashing of a dividend warrant or the cutting off of a coupon. Out of this legalized plunder probably a thousand millions has been capitalized by the "abstinence" of the plunderers so as to increase the tax on future labor: the rest has been squandered in the endowment of idleness. Yet both Liberals and Conservatives agree that whatever other expenditures we can retrench in or dispense with, this endowment must be left untouched. They are willing to economise in the army, the navy, the schools, the housing of the poor, sanitation, smoke prevention, river embankments, harbors, in anything and everything that is of national importance, sooner than touch one penny of the unearned incomes of the idle rich, or even take the simplest step to forestall their increase. Every budget is drawn up on the principle that all devices for screwing the revenue out of the poor must be exhausted before the idle rich are touched. The country postman has to walk excessive distances for miserable wages in order that the profit on the Post Office may be filched from the employees and from the public by the Chancellor of the Exchequer in order to keep down the Income Tax; and with the same object taxes on the food of the people are maintained in defiance of every sound canon of political economy and common sense. Ministers are ready to moralize on every subject but this authorised spoilation of the industrious by the idle; to point out every social evil except the root of all social evils; to insist on every reform except its reform. Whenever they allude to it, they imply that it does not exist; that the class which lives on rent and dividends, and spends them in the manner revealed by the Tranby Croft gambling case [in which a senior army officer was accused of cheating at baccarat at a country house party attended by the future Edward VII in September 1890], is an industrious and deserving class; that the poor are poor because of their improvidence and vice; and that all assertions to the contrary are direct incitements to Anarchy. During the recent trial of [French Anarchist François] Ravachol [1859–92] in Paris, the Press advertised the exploits and spread the arguments of the assassin and dynamiter throughout Europe without an attempt to controvert them, because it would have been impossible to do so without calling attention to the social injustices which he made the excuse for his crimes.

The Tyranny of Our Party System

Under these circumstances [i.e., the lack of working-class representation in Parliament], it is not surprising that we hear from all quarters a demand for a new party devoted singly to the interests of Labor. Unfortunately, the difficulties which hamper the beginnings of a third political party in England can only be appreciated by those who have learnt them from practical electioneering experience. By our method of deciding parliamentary elections, the seat is given to the candidate who obtains the highest number of votes at the first ballot, although double as many may be divided among his competitors; so that the majority in the House of Commons may easily represent a minority of the nation. It therefore becomes of the utmost consequence to the majority in any constituency that its vote should not be "split": that is, divided between two or more rival candidates on the same side. Consequently, if a third candidate comes forward in a one-member constituency he is at once accused of a treacherous design to split the vote in the interests of the party which he professes to oppose; and he is boycotted at the polls by all who are sufficiently experienced and disciplined in politics to understand that nothing but a solid party vote can win a closely contested election. This state of things, whilst it is fatal to Independent candidates, suits the two established political parties so well that they both, when in office, ignore the demand of the advanced sections for the introduction of the Continental system of the Second Ballot, which assures the final victory at the polls to the majority, whether the vote has been split at the first ballot or not. Pending the introduction of this reform, the tyranny of our party system is complete. This was strikingly shown at the recent elections for the London County Council, where the necessity for presenting a united front to the enemy compelled the voters to boycott all the Independent candidates without regard to their programs or past services.

The practical conclusion is that until we get the Second Ballot all candidates who are not the nominees of an organized party may be left out of account; and it is a waste of time and votes to put them forward except when the object is, not to win the seat, but either to advertise their opinions or to defeat some other candidate by splitting the vote of his side. When a candidate is run to win, he must come forward either as the nominee of one of the two established parties, or as the nominee of a new and advanced party which has made sufficient headway in the constituency to have disestablished and taken the place of the Liberal party in local politics.

Need for an Independent Labor Party

...[T]he process of swamping the Liberal Associations with Socialists and Radicals, though it can, when adroitly managed, considerably quicken the pace of political reform, is yet but a paltry substitute for the straightforward action of a genuine Working Class party, supported by Working Class subscriptions and completely independent of both Liberal and Conservative aid. The fact that no such party exists is disgraceful to the Working Classes. A subscription of only three half-pence a year from every male worker in the kingdom would bring in a parliamentary fund of £50,000 a year. If the wage workers of both sexes and of all ages subscribed one penny a year, the result would be an annual fund of nearly £60,000. If we confine ourselves to that section of the Working Class which has been organized and brought under discipline by Trade Unions... we find that the members could have maintained a parliamentary fund of £130,000 a year by paying a penny a week per member. The bricklayers, who have just decided to vote £3 a week from the funds of their Trade Union to maintain their representative in the London County Council, might do as much for a delegate of their own in the House of Commons; and the four Unions of Railway Workers could at least support one member in Parliament, even if they had to do it by a special levy. The poverty of the workers is therefore no excuse for their slavish political apathy. They make greater sacrifices to support legions of publicans and sporting bookmakers than free political institutions would cost them; and there is no escaping the inference that they care more for drinking and gambling than for freedom. The same workman who pleads want of education and opportunity as an excuse for not understanding party politics is at no loss when the subject is football, or racing, or pigeon-flying, or any subject, however complicated, that he really wants to understand. Under such circumstances it is useless to discuss what a Labor party might do at the election now upon us. There is no Labor party; and there is no possibility of forming one in time for the dissolution. It is true that in every constituency plenty of men will applaud any orator who advocates a Labor party. But the Labor candidate who depends on them for his election expenses or for two pounds a week to support him whilst he is working for them on the County Council or in Parliament, soon finds that it is one thing to make people shout and another to make them pay. As for Labor Associations sufficiently numerous and powerful to make the voters feel that all Progressive votes not given to the Labor candidate would be wasted, there are not a dozen such bodies in England, even if we include the Parliamentary Committee of the Trade Union Congress, the representatives of which usually vote as the Liberal whips direct on all occasions in Parliament except when the regulation of factories and mines, or the liability of employers for accidents to their employees, come up for settlement.... The test of the political capacity of a class is shown by its power to make the most of ordinary circumstances; and under ordinary circumstances the Working Class does nothing at all, whereas the upper and middle classes organize their forces and put forward and support their candidates just as regularly in the most obscure constituencies as they do in Midlothian, where they have Mr Gladstone to rouse them to enthusiasm. It is easy to account for this state of things by pointing out that the poverty and drudgery in which the workers are plunged leaves them no means and no energy to spare for political work. But to account for facts is not to alter them; and poverty or no poverty, drudgery or no drudgery, the workers must make up their minds that no power on earth can make free men and women of people who will not spend a shilling a year on their political business. During the present year the workers of London suffered themselves to be shamefully defeated at the School Board election because not more than one in four of them would take the pains to walk to the polling station on a rainy evening. Gentlemen who had openly sneered at the children of the working classes as "gutter children" were returned at the top of the poll in constituencies where excellent Labor candidates were defeated; and the Board Schools of the capital will consequently remain for the next two years in the hands of the party which, under cover of sparing the rates, ran in the interests of the ground landlords as against those of the children. Later on, the defeat was supposed to be redeemed by a great triumph for the Working Classes at the County Council election. The Fabian Society admittedly contributed largely to that success by collecting all the facts and figures relating to the great London monopolies, and printing and distributing over 500,000 leaflets, besides organizing and delivering several courses of lectures in all parts of London before the election. But the Working Classes did not pay for the leaflets or for the lectures. Everything had to be "free," which means that the 470 members of the London Fabian Society had to find the time and money; and the Society would be hopelessly bankrupt at this moment in consequence but for the liberality of a few comparatively rich friends who came to the rescue. The same story can be told by the other bodies, Socialist and Radical, which helped to organize the victory. The ordinary working man seemed to take it quite as a matter of course that all this trouble and expense should be incurred for his sake by somebody else, and to feel that he had shown sufficient public spirit in listening to the canvasser's instructions instead of turning him out of the house as an intruder. In the face of these facts the Fabian Society, though convinced of the need of a new political party devoted solely to the interests of the Working Class, would be trifling with the public if it pretended that there was any such thing yet in existence as a Labor Party, or that the present movement of popular feeling in that direction is worth sufficient pounds, shillings, pence and votes, to run twenty genuine Labor candidates without middle-class support successfully at the forthcoming election.

7. From "What Socialism Will be Like." A Lecture to the Hammersmith (London) Socialist Society, 12 July 1896. Published in *The Labour Leader*, 19 December 1896. [*Platform and Pulpit*, pp. 23–31]

[*It is rare for Shaw to say "I don't know," an indication in this instance of his early efforts to understand how Socialism would work in practice. The balance between the best interests of the community, which, Shaw argues, necessarily require State interventions and controls, and individual freedoms, including artistic freedoms, is difficult to determine, but he comes down on the side of giving ample scope for free enterprise to flourish under Socialism.*]

My lecture will be very short. It consists of three words—*I don't know*. Having delivered it, by way of opening a discussion, I will proceed to make a few remarks....

I am afraid we get a great many converts because Socialism is supposed to favor the idea that the socialization of the sources of production by the expropriation people will then have got at the back of their work—a sort of kingdom of heaven on earth, when something will cease from troubling. The other day, at a meeting of the Fabian Society—of the very able executive of which I happen to be a member—when we proposed that the society should present to the International Congress some sort of affirmation of our views on Socialism, one Socialist—a most self-sacrificing and stalwart worker for the cause—was driven almost to a frenzy by the very plain statement that, instead of Socialism proposing to abolish the wage system, the only object of Socialism was to secure that everybody should be paid wages—absolutely steady wages, in the employment of the community—wages regulated by the general convenience and moral sense of the community. Under Socialism we shall require policemen. Possibly their duties will not be exactly the same as now, but then, probably, everybody will ride a bicycle, and will anybody tell me that we shall not want some representative of the community to look after citizens in the street? Having got your policeman, then, how are you going to pay him the "entire product" of his labor? Whatever you pay him will be wages, so our sole object will be to proceed steadily to pay everybody wages.

We shall proceed to make the shopkeeper a municipal official, to sell goods at a price to be determined in the interests of the whole community—generally with regard to the cost of production, although it might be desirable to put a high price on gin, for example, and a very low price on some other commodity. Our municipal shopkeeper will have a definite status and a pension to look forward to when he retires. Many people look forward to Socialism as a system where everybody will get what they want without having to pay for it. One cannot do that now (except when the shopkeeper is not looking), but our present system of society does it under the names of Rent and Interest, by means of which an idle rich man gets his goods for nothing. But under Socialism we want our shops or stores having customers with not a penny to spend without having earned it by their own labor. But there would be modifications of this. We have already found out that it is bad public economy to have a toll-keeper for roads and bridges, and the cost of these is now defrayed out of the rates. So when we have a good Socialist system well in work, and people have lost the habit of imagining that anybody was going to live for nothing, the towns would make the same arrangement about bread. We would come to the conclusion that it would save a lot of trouble and bookkeeping to turn into the stores an ascertained required amount of bread, and let everybody take as much as they wanted, and they would pay for it out of their rates. Of course, you would have a certain number of individuals who under no system of society could be induced to work at all, and you would lose a little bread in that way, but you would save the policeman's labor and the community would in the end gain more than it lost.

But it would damp my ardor for Socialism very considerably if I thought that everything would be done by the County Council. There is no reason to believe we shall ever sanction any law which would prevent a man working for himself, or from hiring another man to work for him for wages if he chooses. Suppose London were socialized tomorrow: then, of course, the County Council would be equipped entirely with Socialists. The public want newspapers, and we will suppose the County Council ran them. I imagine they would be bad newspapers, but that would not matter—they would be all the more popular. But a certain section of the public would like good literature and independent criticism. But if the County Council produced a newspaper which told the truth boldly, every councillor would lose his seat in a week. So all such undertakings would have to be carried on by individuals. Do you suppose that at my age I would go and earn my livelihood in the municipal shop in any "honest" way? I would not do it. I earn my livelihood by my pen, mostly in writing criticisms which people—especially those criticized—for the most part do not like. Am I to understand that any Socialist contemplates that when someone had got a little money or credit in an honest way—say enough to start a newspaper—some Socialist authority would say: "No; that would be private capitalism: we will not allow you"? If so, I would start a revolution against Socialism the very next day. The man who wanted to employ me might be foolish enough—or grasping—but since Socialism would have guaranteed me a comfortable livelihood, a private individual could only secure me by offering at least as good terms as the community.

So there could be no wage slavery practised. If the private individual were able to give a man better terms than the community it could not be by monopoly of land and capital. It would be that he had beaten the public authority in supplying the public need with some new invention, want, or organization which the public were willing to pay him for. Under such circumstances I fail to see any reason for interference. On the contrary, nothing more fatal to human progress than such interference can be imagined. The public bodies under Socialism could watch the results of private enterprize. To the enterprizing man who had invented something—say the bicycle, the typewriter, or the electric light—and made a success if it, the State would step in and say: "Very kind of you to show us. We will take on that business." Then the private enterprizer would have to turn and invent something else. Under the present system we pay the successful enterprizer too well, and thus rob him of incentive to renewed ingenuity! In point of fact, however, a great deal of so-called private enterprize is in no sense such. For example, owing to increase of population a village grows to a town. Thirty miles distant another village does the same. It is desirable, in the interests of the community, that a railway should be made between the two places. Will anyone say that the making of such a railway involves "enterprize" or "initiative"? But under the present system, instead of its being done on the public incentive, we leave it to a number of individuals who want to get dividends. So under Socialism "private enterprize and initiative" would necessarily be limited to something which really was new. No man would have a chance of getting outside the public routine unless he had found out a new public want and was willing to take on himself the risk of working it out.

What we really want done is to have all the large industries of the country—about which there is no "enterprize"—organized by the public authorities, and also, of course, to have all rent of land and capital—all the economic rents (which have the effect of putting unearned money into private pockets)—put into the hands of the State. No one now supposes that £17,000,000 should every year go into the pockets of half-a-dozen private gentleman in London as "rent." We are agreed that every farthing of that should go to the London public authorities, in so far as it arises from a monopoly of situation. Suppose a man wanted to go into business for himself under Socialism. Since no man would have discovered a new method of making land, he would have to pay, for the land he occupied, its full economic rent to the community. If he hadn't capital himself I presume he would borrow from the State, and would pay interest for it. And by the "State" I mean the nearest authority representing the people.

Now, suppose a man found out something so much wanted—which the State could not supply and the public were willing to pay for—that he became thunderingly rich. Suppose another man—say, a dentist—did the same. Suppose this dentist were exceedingly clever. It would be all very well to say to him: You shall be the town dentist, and we will pay you good wages." He would say: "No, thank you; I don't need my labor organized by the community. I will pay you rent for the premises I wish to occupy, and put up a brass plate. Here we are—free citizens—I will charge you what I like!" If the carrying out of our views leads to increased prosperity, every member of the community would have more to spend on their teeth, and they would bid against each other for the services of this extraordinarily clever dentist.

Then you have your artist. I grant that if he painted very great pictures he would not make much money. But suppose he painted popular pictures, like [French artist] Gustave Doré [1833–83], for example. It was found possible to put them all into one room, erect a turnstile at the door, and charge a shilling for leave to pass it. I do not see how, under Socialism, the community could interfere with that! I see no Socialist ground of public policy for doing so, although under such circumstances a man might become very rich. A man painting a picture is not the same thing as a man making a loaf of bread. The man who buys the loaf consumes it, but the man who pays to consume a shillingworth of the picture leaves it intact, and the sight of the picture is something which can be continually sold, and it becomes, not less, but more valuable. 'Tis true the average man does not go to look at a picture because he likes it, but because many other men have gone to see it.

Again, take four musicians who play string quartets. By constant practice together they at last acquire extraordinary skill in playing chamber music very beautifully. Everybody wants to hear them, and people are quite willing to pay to hear them. What is to prevent them, under Socialism, agreeing with an organizer and putting up a turnstile like the artist? And, bear in mind, chamber music cannot be properly played and appreciated in a big building like St James's Hall. If you have not heard a string quartet played in a small room you have never heard chamber music played and heard at all properly. Now we, as good Socialists, having the community's good at heart, let in, say, fifty persons and exclude the remainder. How are we to ascertain who the people are who should hear it? Our musicians would put the fifty seats up to auction, and it is appalling to imagine how much they might fetch! The organizing agent would probably get much more than he would pay the instrumentalists—although he would pay more than the London County Council bandmen get.

Then take the drama. I do not know whether, under Socialism, people will still want to hear Shakespeare. I doubt it—I hope somebody more up to date will turn up. So let us suppose you had a small body of persons who had extraordinary skill in producing Ibsen's dramas. [Norwegian playwright Henrik Ibsen, 1828–1906, was a major influence on Shaw.] A gentleman [Charles Charrington] who has produced *A Doll's House* in every quarter of the globe tells me that the most successful performance he had ever given took place in an ordinary house. It is impossible to present Ibsen properly in a big theatre. Well, suppose this gentleman organized exceedingly fine performances of *A Doll's House* under Socialism, and said: "I will not have them produced in your big theatres, because it is not possible to produce them with the proper effect there. So I will produce the play in my own house, and put the seats up for auction." Well, I reckon that under Socialism I should be in a position to give ten guineas for a ticket—and I would give it straight away! And so, again, our extraordinarily clever producer of Ibsen would get enormously rich. Not to multiply examples, I see no reason why any man should be interfered with in the spontaneous pursuit of his plans, and so it might be possible for certain individuals to be considerably richer than others.

'Tis true, Socialism looks with suspicion on inequality of wealth, but that does not contradict the equality Socialism aims at. And it is impossible to form any Socialist system whatever without assuming equality of condition. There might be, as under the feudal system, various strata—men in one grade being superior to those in another; but within the particular grade and rank it is impossible to proceed on any basis save equality—that is to say, equality before the law and equal political rights. There is one mechanical inequality to which we Socialists have a great objection—that is, a large inequality of purchasing power. For instance, tomorrow morning a certain number of young persons will begin to work for the first time, being just grown up. It is the interest of the community that the work they start on should be that which is most needed for the wellbeing of the community. But owing to the unequal distribution of wealth what happens is that numbers of these new workers will start working for rich men, as flunkeys or building barges and yachts, for instance—things the community is not in want of. So it must always be a matter of public policy to prevent any large class of men becoming enormously richer than their fellows. To prevent this you have nothing to do but go at them with a progressive income tax. An income tax is an exceedingly Socialistic institution. In fact, that is one of the objections of the upper class to it. But I do not think any such danger would arise. By the very terms of the case such instances as I have mentioned would be exceptional. A painter would only be able to get people to pay to look at his pictures on condition that they are very exceptional. So would the quartet party. From my knowledge of the general musical amateur I should say it would generally be better for him to listen to anybody but himself. And in regard to dramatic companies, I am not sure you would not have private theatricals under Socialism in every second house. But you may depend upon it the professional actor would have to be very good indeed. So would the great surgeon-dentist. Exceptional skill only would avail.

Nevertheless, I think it would be not only not dangerous, but very desirable, to have a few persons with a little extra money to spend. They could not spend it on themselves. A man with a gigantic fortune, let him try his utmost, cannot live more expensively than the richest *class* of the community. If a millionaire wants to buy a loaf of bread he doesn't go into a baker's shop and find special loaves made with gilt tops. He buys the same kind of bread you and I buy—perhaps he buys a bit better suit of clothes than mine! Under Socialism there would be a general level of prosperity, and everybody would be able to buy good bread and good clothes. So, beyond the point of general prosperity your enormously rich man would be forced to have a hobby of some kind. Take our friend William Morris, for instance. [Morris, 1834–96, was a leading decorative craftsman in furnishing, textiles, and book binding (and a Socialist).] He is now doing a very useful thing, recklessly spending large sums of money in collecting specimens of the finest printed books in Europe. Our comrade is an artist. He is buying these old books because they are worth looking at. Here he is, spending his superfluity of income on something no government could do. No doubt, Morris's collection will some time find itself in public hands, and will be enjoyed by the community. Of course, we Socialists are given to talk art, but how many of us who speak with enthusiastic admiration of Morris have even spent half-a-crown on art in our lives!

8. From "The Illusions of Socialism," *The Home Journal* (New York), 21 and 28 October 1896. [*Selected Non-Dramatic Writings of Bernard Shaw*, pp. 406–26]

[*Shaw's frustration with various illusionary and idealistic proponents of Socialism is reflected in his own pragmatic approach to the implementation of Socialist objectives. To be successful, he insists, Socialism "must come into the field as political science and not as sentimental dogma."*]

...Now... if I say flatly that Socialism as it appears to ninety-nine out of every hundred of the ardent young Socialists who will read this book, is an illusion, I do not say that there is no reality behind the illusion, nor that the reality will not be much better than the illusion. Only, I do say, very emphatically, that if the Socialist future were presented in its reality to those who are devoting all the energy they have to spare after their day's work, and all the enthusiasm of which they are capable, to the "Cause," many of them would not lift a finger for it, and would even disparage and loathe it as a miserably prosaic "bourgeois" development and extension of the middle class respectability of today. When any part of Socialism presents itself in the raw reality of a concrete proposal, capable of being adopted by a real Government, and carried out by a real Executive, the professed Socialists are the last people in the country who can be depended on to support it. At best, they will disparage it as "a palliative," and assure the public that it will do no good unless the capitalist system is entirely abolished as well. At worst, they will violently denounce it, and brand its advocates as frauds, traitors, and so on. This natural antagonism between the enthusiasts who conceive Socialism and the statesmen who have to reduce it to legislative and administrative measures, is inevitable. Every man, enthusiast or realist, has more or less power of self-criticism; and the more he is reasoned with, the more reasonable he is likely to be in his attitude.

First, let me carefully insist on the fact that the cheerful view I have put forward of illusions as useful incentives to men to strive after still better realities, is not true of all illusions. If a man sets his heart on being a millionaire, or a woman on becoming the spouse of Christ, and attaining to eternal beatitude by living a nun and dying a saint, there is not the smallest likelihood that the results will be worth exchanging for the lot of a decent railway porter or factory girl. Similarly, if a Socialist is merely a man crying out for the millennium because he wants unearned happiness for himself and the world, not only will he not get it, but he will be just as dissatisfied with what he will get as with his present condition. There are foolish illusions as well as wise ones; and a man may be opposed to our existing social system because he is not good enough for it just as easily as because it is not good enough for him....

Now it will not be questioned that Socialism, if it is to gain serious attention nowadays, must come into the field as political science and not as sentimental dogma. It is true that it is founded on sentimental dogma, and is quite unmeaning and purposeless apart from it. But so are all modern democratic political systems. The American constitution affirms, quite accurately and inevitably, that every man has a natural right to life, liberty, and the pursuit of happiness. This is the formal expression of the fact that a democratic political system must start from the assumption of an absolutely dogmatic, unreasonable, unaccountable, in short, "natural" determination on the part of every citizen to live, do, and say as he pleases, and to use his powers to make himself happy in his own way. Moralizers have proved again and again that life, estimated on the rational basis of a comparison of its pleasures with its pains, anxieties, and labours, is not worth living. High Tories have proved, and can still prove, that slaves purchase freedom at the exorbitant cost of guaranteed subsistence, good government, peace, order, and security. Philosophers have warned us that the pursuit of happiness is of all pursuits the most wretched, and that happiness has never yet been found except on the way to some other goal. Every man's reason assents to these propositions; and every man's will utterly ignores them. Mankind is, by definition, unreasonable on these subjects; and we affirm our unreason by claiming what we call natural rights, and agitating for political recognition of these rights as postulates from which all legislation must start, and to the practical satisfaction and enlargement of which it must all be directed. Every political document in which these rights find a fuller and more conscious expression, however ineffectual it may be practically, becomes a historic landmark, as, for example, Magna Charta [i.e., Magna Carta, 1215], the Petition of Rights [1628], the Habeas Corpus Act [1679], and the American Constitution [1787]. The final recognition of "natural rights" for every man in the Declaration of Independence [1776], in spite of the practical exclusion of women and blacks from the definition, was the formal inauguration of modern Democracy on its firm dogmatic basis.

But it is one thing to ascertain what you want to secure, and quite another to ascertain the right method of securing it. The American Constitution is often such an exasperating obstruction to life, liberty, and pursuit of happiness of the American nation, that American reformers long to tear it up; and every gentleman who has been mentally disabled at a

University explains that natural rights cannot exist because they are illogical—as if that were not the whole point of them. A nation making its first attempts to secure its natural rights is like a lady trying to relieve the thirsty discomfort of a very hot day by eating ices. The most obvious steps are not merely ineffectual: they defeat their own object. The early democrats, having become accustomed, under oligarchical or autocratic systems, to associate the denial of their natural rights with governmental action, began by systematically attempting to extend the power of the individual and to curtail that of the State. Hence we get, as the first fruits of Democracy, the triumph of the Whig and his principles of Freedom of Contract, Laissez-faire, and so on, with the Manchester School in his van, and the Anarchists as his extreme left wing, just as [Oliver] Cromwell [1599–1658, soldier and statesman, Lord Protector of Great Britain, 1653–58] had his left wing of Levellers [a radical group supporting religious toleration, extension of the franchise, and abolition of the monarchy and the House of Lords]. But a brief experience of Whig Anarchism, as a safeguard for natural rights, shows that the problem of securing their fullest practicable exercise is much more complicated than it once seemed. It is perceived that just as science throws no light on the dogmatic foundation of Democracy, so the natural right dogmas throw no light on the science of politics. The most immediate and obvious inferences from these dogmas have produced a state of things which, at its worst, is a perfect hell of slavery, misery, and destruction of life in the factory and mine, and at its best, though better, on the whole, than anything that has gone before, is out of the question as a permanently satisfactory social adjustment. It has been discovered that the dominant factor in human society is not political organization, but industrial organization; and that to secure to the people control of political organization, whilst letting the industrial organization slip through the fingers, is to intensify slavery under the political forms and pretensions of freedom and equality. In short, unless the Government controls industry, it is useless for the people to control the Government.

When this became plain, the Manchester School was superseded by the Collectivist or Socialist School; and Democracy became Social Democracy, their objects being the regulation, and finally the proprietorship, organization, and control of industry by the State. Now it is to be observed that we have here no recantation or revision of the dogmas of the American constitution. Democracy still pursues happiness, and strains after wider life and liberty; and it still disregards the teaching of Asceticism and Pessimism. And Socialism is quite on the side of Democracy—quite agrees that the system it proposes must stand or fall by its success in making the people livelier, freer, and happier than they can be without it. Consequently Socialism is not distinguishable on its dogmatic side from the older-fashioned Democracy, Republicanism, Radicalism or Liberalism, or even from English Conservatism, which no longer pretends to be the organ of a class as against the people, and which is, in fact, more advanced practically than German Social-Democracy. The sole distinction lies in its contention that industrial Collectivism is the true political science of Democracy. The Socialists do not say to the Manchesterists, "Your humanitarian objects are misinterpretations of Man's will," but "Your methods of fulfilling our common object are mistaken, because your social science is erroneous. In your induction you have missed the greater part of the facts, because your interest and class prejudices have turned your attention exclusively towards the lesser part. You have relied too much on deduction and too little on historical research and contemporary investigation. You have ludicrously underrated the complexity of the problem to be solved, and have allowed yourselves to be hampered and stopped in your reasoning by old associations of ideas which you have mistaken for principles. To the politicians, as the engineers who must work the political machine, and the artificers who must repair and enlarge it, you have given and are giving bad advice and impracticable directions. We therefore propose to persuade the people to dismiss you and elect us in your place."

The whole question at issue, then, is one of political science and practice, and of them alone. Just as the introduction of the screw-steamer, or the cutting of the Suez Canal [constructed 1859–69, linking the Red Sea and the Mediterranean], did not affect the emigrant's desire to go to America or Ceylon [Sri Lanka], but simply provided him with a better method of getting there, so Socialism does not affect the goal of Democracy, but simply offers a better means of reaching it. There is no disposition to question this—at least verbally—on the Socialist side. Ever since Marx and Engels, in the Communist Manifesto [1848], declared that all other human institutions have been and still are and ever must be only the reflection, in politics, art, religion, and what not, of industrial institutions, we have had the utmost ostentation of the scientific character of Socialism, first as against the Utopian Socialism of [French philosopher Charles] Fourier [1772–1837], and more recently as against the pure Opportunism of the established political parties. Manchesterism was the first modern political system that came into the field with absolute integrity as an application of pure political and industrial science, and not of supernatural religion or duty. Socialism is equally secular, and more materialistic and fatalistic, because it attributes more importance to circumstances as a factor in personal character and to industrial organization as a factor in society. The data of Collectivism are to be found in [British government statistical] Blue Books, statistical abstracts, reports, records and observations of the actual facts and conditions of industrial life, not in dreams, ideals, prophecies and revelations. In theorizing from these data, Socialists have blundered often enough—Marx, for instance, was as faulty in his abstract economics as Adam Smith—but the blunder has never been due to any intentional vitiation of the secularity of the argument by unscientific considerations.

And now, what faces us as to the consequence of this scientific character of Socialism? Clearly, it must obey the law to which all science bows when it requires the support of the people. It must be popularized by being first dramatized and then theorized. It must be hidden under a veil of illusions embroidered with promises, and provided with a simple mental handle for the grasp of the common mind. I do not propose to attempt an account of all these illusions and carpenterings: in demonstrating their necessity I have done as much as I can do with profit. What follows is by way of illustration merely.

The dramatic illusion of Socialism is that which presents the working-class as a virtuous hero and heroine in the toils of a villain called "the capitalist," suffering terribly and struggling nobly, but with a happy ending for them, and a fearful retribution for the villain, in full view before the fall of the curtain on a future of undisturbed bliss. In this drama, the proletarian finds somebody to love, to sympathize with, and to champion, whom he identifies with himself; and somebody to execrate and feel indignantly superior to, whom he can identify with the social tyranny from which he suffers. Socialism is thus presented on the platform exactly as life is presented on the stage of the Adelphi Theatre [famous for its Victorian melodramas], quite falsely and conventionally, but in the only way in which the audience can be induced to take an interest in it.

Closely allied to the dramatic illusion, and indeed at bottom the same thing, is the religious illusion. This illusion presents Socialism as consummating itself by a great day of wrath, called "The Revolution," in which capitalism, commercialism, competition, and all the lusts of the Exchange, shall be brought to judgment and cast out, leaving the earth free for the kingdom of heaven on earth, all of which is revealed in an infallible book by a great prophet and leader. In this illusion the capitalist is not a stage villain, but the devil; Socialism is not the happy ending of a drama, but heaven; and Karl Marx's *Das Kapital* is "the Bible of the working-classes." The working-man who has been detached from the Established Church or the sects by the Secularist propaganda, and who, as an avowed Agnostic or Atheist, strenuously denies or contemptuously ridicules the current beliefs in heavens and devils and bibles will, with the greatest relief and avidity, go back to his old habits of thought and imagination when they reappear in this secular form. The Christian who finds the supernatural aspect of his faith slipping away from him, recaptures it in what seems to him a perfectly natural aspect as Christian Socialism.

A popular drama must have plenty of sensational incidents—combats, trials, plots, hair-breadth escapes, and so forth. They are copiously supplied by the history of revolutionary Socialism, which has been as romantically told as any history in the world. What incidents are to a drama, persecutions and salvational regenerations are to a religion. Accordingly we have, in the religious illusion of Socialism, a profuse exploitation of the calamities of martyrs exiled, imprisoned, and brought to the scaffold for "The Cause"; and we are told of the personal change, the transfigured, lighted-up face, the sudden accession of self-respect, the joyful self-sacrifice, the new eloquence and earnestness of the young working man who has been rescued from a purposeless, automatic loafing through life, by the call of the gospel of Socialism.

In describing the dramatic and the religious illusions separately, I do not lose sight of the fact that most men are subject to both, just as most civilized men go both to the theatre and the church, though some go to one and not to the other. But, mixed or apart, they are the chief means by which Socialism has laid hold of its disciples. Cruder and narrower dramatic and religious versions of the social problem still hold the field against them; but the wider, humaner, more varied and interesting character of the Socialist version, its optimism, its power of bringing happiness and heaven from dreamland and from beyond the clouds down into living, breathing reach, and the power it gains from its contact with and constant reference to contemporary fact and experience, give it an appearance of immense modernity and practicability as compared to the more barbarous and imaginary conceptions which it is superseding. But it is none the less illusory; and the more the Socialist leaders yield to the temptation to wallow recklessly in the enthusiasm and applause it creates, the more certain they are, when the moment for action arrives, to find themselves thwarted by its wrongheadedness. For when the reality at last comes to the men who have been nursed on dramatizations of it, they do not recognize it. Its prosaic aspect revolts them; and since it must necessarily come by penurious instalments, each maimed in the inevitable compromise with powerful hostile interests, its advent has neither the splendid magnitude nor the absolute integrity of principle dramatically and religiously necessary to impress them. Hence they either pass it by contemptuously or join the forces of reaction by opposing it vehemently. Worse still, to prevent the recurrence of such scandals, and maintain the purity of their faith, they begin to set up rigid tests of orthodoxy; to excommunicate the genuinely scientific Socialists; to entrust the leadership of their organizations to orators and preachers: in short, to develop all the symptoms of what the French call Impossibilism.

The first condition of an illusion is, of course, that its victim should mistake it for a reality. The dramatic and religious illusions of Socialism, in their extreme forms, are too gross, to mercilessly and insistently contradicted by experience to impose on a capable man when once he is confronted with practical political work and responsibility. Though very few Socialists gain sufficient practical experience to be completely cured of Impossibilism, partial cures occur every day. The invaluable habit of mind which we modern Socialists have learnt from our Jevonian economics [political economist William Stanley Jevons, 1835–82] should therefore save us from the error of regarding Socialists as either out-and-out Possibilists or out-and-out Impossibilists. Neither in Socialism or anything else is it true that whatever is not white is black. Every gradation of credulity, from the crudest dreaming to the most sceptical practicality, is represented in the Socialist movement. In the extreme sections of the Socialist-Democratic Federation, in the Communist-Anarchist side of the Independent Labour Party, and in the Anarchist groups, the dramatic and religious illusions will be found just as I have described them. At the other extremity you have the typical Fabian, who flatly declares that there will be no revolution; that there is no class war; that the wage earners are far more conventional, prejudiced, and "bourgeois," than the middle class; that there is not a single democratically constituted authority in England, including the House of Commons, that would not be much more progressive if it were not restrained by fear of the popular vote; that Karl Marx is no more infallible than [Greek philosopher] Aristotle [384–322 BCE] or [English philosopher Francis] Bacon [1561–1626], [English political economist David] Ricardo [1772–1823] or [English historian Henry Thomas] Buckle [1821–62], and, like them, made mistakes which are now plain to any undergraduate; that a professed Socialist is neither better nor worse morally than a Liberal or Conservative, nor a working-man than a capitalist; that the working-man can alter the present system if he chooses, whereas the capitalist cannot because the working-man will not let him; that it is perverse stupidity to declare in one breath that the working-classes are starved, degraded, and left in ignorance by a system which heaps victuals, education, and refinement on the capitalist, and to assume in the next that the capitalist is a narrow, sordid scoundrel, and the working-man a high-minded, enlightened, magnanimous philanthropist; that Socialism will come by prosaic instalments of public regulation and public administration enacted by ordinary parliaments, vestries, municipalities, parish councils, school boards, and the like; and that not one of these instalments will amount to a revolution, or will occupy a larger place in the political program of its day than a Factory Bill or a County Government Bill now does; all this meaning that the lot of the Socialist is to be one of dogged political drudgery, in conflict, not with the wicked machinations of the capitalist, but with the stupidity, the narrowness, in a word the idiocy (using the word in its precise and original meaning) of all classes, and especially of the class which suffers most by the existing system.

Taking these as the two extremes between which all avowed and conscious Socialists, and a good many unavowed and unconscious ones, are to be found, we see that the scale is apparently one of diminishing illusion. But the real scale is one of acuteness of intellect, political experience, practical capacity, the strength of character which gives a man power to look unpleasant facts in the face, and doubtless also the comfortable circumstances which enable clever professional men, with fair incomes, to be more philosophical than poor and worried ones. This is why a very crude illusion will impose on the men at one end of the scale, whilst it requires a comparatively very subtle one to impose on the men at the other....

My reader must now beware of the illusion that other Socialists do not recognize this scale. On the contrary, all Socialists do; but each considers himself as being at the sensible, hard-headed end of it. And the more completely a Socialist is the dupe of the dramatic and religious illusions in their crudest form, the more positively is he convinced that he is founded on a triple rock of "scientific political economy," history, and social evolution. The way in which a man, out of the abyss of an ignorance of the subject ten times deeper than any ordinary honest unconsciousness of it, will expound to you such blurred notions as he has been able to pick up of "surplus value," over-production, commercial crises, the imminent breakdown of the capitalist system by the laws of its own development, and so on, is quite as funny as the way in which the man who opposes him will retort with scraps from the economic prophets of the Manchester school—supply and demand, the population question, the law of diminishing return, and what not.

And here we come to the second line of illusion—that which supplies the demand for a theory, not only as a sort of trapeze for the intellect, but as a scientific basis for faith. The demand is now a thoroughly popular one: even the narrowest chapel-goer likes to hear that fossils have been discovered on the tops of mountains (showing that the Deluge is scientifically proved), and that the name of Nebuchadnezzar [630–562 BCE, King of Babylon 605–562 BCE], has been deciphered on Babylonian bricks. But the popularization of genuine scientific theories is becoming daily more impossible among people who have not had an elaborate secondary education—that is, the vast majority of citizens—because the theories, as they are followed up, lose their original crude and simple forms, and become not only complex in themselves, but unintelligible without reference to other theories. For example, the old theory of light, which had the great authority of [English physicist and mathematician Isaac] Newton [1642–1727] to recommend it, presented the solar spectrum (popularly, the rainbow) as consisting of three primary colours, with three secondary ones produced by the overlapping and mixing of the primaries. This was a very easy explanation: every child could take his penny paints, red, blue and yellow, and mix them into purple, green, and orange. But the modern theory of the spectrum which has prevailed since [English scientist Thomas] Young's [1773–1829] time, is no such simple matter: it cannot be made intelligible to anyone who does not know something of the whole theory of light. The result is that to this day the notion of primary and secondary colours remains the popular theory....

[Shaw then discusses outmoded and modern Socialist theories of Rent and Value.]

However, a Socialist is a Socialist; and whichever theory he adopts, he arrives at the same conclusion: the advocacy of a transfer of "the means of production, distribution, and exchange" from private to collective ownership. If he could be persuaded that the old theory did not support this "principle," as he calls it, he would give up the old theory, even if Jevons were still too hard for him. And thereby comes the cherished illusion that all Socialists are agreed in principle though they may differ as to tactics. This is perhaps the most laughable of all the illusions of Socialism, so outrageously is it contradicted by the facts. It is quite true that the Socialists are in perfect agreement with one another except on those points on which they happen to differ. They can claim that happy understanding not only among themselves, but with the Liberals and Conservatives as well. But the notion that their differences are at present any less fundamental than their agreements is an illusion, as the following examination will show.

With the Socialists who are under the religious illusion in its most Calvinistic mode, the formula about the means of production represents a principle to be carried out to its logical extreme in unbroken integrity—Man, from their point of view, being made for Socialism and not Socialism for Man. The toleration of even such a convenient infraction of the principle as allowing an individual to keep a typewriter or a bicycle for his own exclusive use without some very explicit and constant affirmation of the fact that it was common property, would be resisted by them as determinedly as an old-fashioned New England Methodist resists the introduction of an organ into his meeting house. Other Socialists—the Fabians, for instance—openly and expressly treat the question of private property as one of pure convenience, and declare that as long as the livelihood of the people is made independent of private capital and enterprise, the more private property and individual activity we have the better. Here, clearly, far from the Calvinistic Socialist being agreed with the Fabian Socialist in principle, it is just on the question of principle that they are irreconcilable, though circumstances may at any moment bring them to an agreement as to tactics. I myself am firmly persuaded that Socialism will not prove worth carrying out in its integrity—that long before it has reached every corner of the political and industrial organization, it will have so completely relieved the pressure to which it owes its force that it will recede before the next great movement in social development, leaving relics of untouched Individualist Liberalism in all directions among the relics of feudalism which Liberalism itself has left. I believe that its dissolution of the petty autocracies and oligarchies of private landlordism and capitalism will enormously stimulate genuine individual enterprise instead of suppressing it; and I strongly suspect that Socialist States will connive at highly undemocratic ways of leaving comparatively large resources in the hands of certain persons, who will thereby become obnoxious as a privileged class to the consistent levellers.... This, of course, is not my "principle": it is my practical view of the situation; but the fact that I do not think it wrong to take that view, and should unhesitatingly vote for a man who took it as against a man who took what I have called the Calvinist view [i.e., of John Calvin, 1509–1604, French Protestant reformer] appears to the Calvinist mind to be conclusive evidence either that I am no Socialist, or else that I am so cynically indifferent to "principle" in the abstract that I cannot properly be said to be anything at all. To settle the matter, let us again apply the Jevonian method. Instead of asking "Are you a Socialist or not?" let us say, "How much are you a Socialist?" or, more practically still, "What do you want to Socialize [nationalize]; and how much and when do you propose to Socialize it?" The moment the case is put this way, all pretence of agreement vanishes. Let me suggest a few detailed questions. Do you advocate the socialization of the cotton industry, of shipbuilding, of railways, of coalmines, of building, of food supply, and of the clothing trades? If so, do you contemplate the socialization of the book industry?... Do you advocate the socialization of the church, the chapel, the "hall of science," the services of the Ethical Society, and of the Salvation Army? If so, do you advocate the socialization of the theatre and the concert room? Do you propose merely to extend State enterprise to industry, or to enforce State monopoly in some cases and not in others, according to circumstances? For instance, if you socialized surgery and painting, would you punish a dentist for making a private contract with a citizen to extract his tooth for a guinea, or fine [English artist and designer] Sir Edward Burne Jones [1833–98] for painting his daughter's portrait out of office hours for nothing?

I might devise pages of such questions; but the above are quite sufficient to divide Socialists into two sections: first, the fanatics who are prepared to sacrifice all considerations of human welfare and convenience sooner than flinch from the rigorous application of "their principles," even to the point of burlesquing their own creed; and, second, the more or less practical men, among whom there would be as much diversity of opinion on each particular point as there is on any ordinary question in the House of Commons. Thus the unity of Socialism, and the existence of definite boundary lines between it and Progressivism, prove to be mere illusions. Notwithstanding which, the battle cry of the Communist Manifesto, "Proletarians from every land, unite!" still inspires us; and we gain a foolish but effective courage from the imaginary tread of millions of workers joining the mighty columns of the Revolution....

Up to a certain point, illusion—or, as it is commonly called by Socialists, "enthusiasm"—is, more or less, precious and indispensable; but beyond that point it gives more trouble than it is worth: in Jevonese language, its utility becomes disutility. There are some Socialists who, to put it plainly, are such fools that they do more harm than good, even in the roughest sort of preliminary propaganda. Others, more sensible, do excellent work as preachers and revivalists, but are nuisances when the work of formal political organization begins. Others, who can get as far as organizing an election without being disqualified by the vehemence of their partisanship, would, if elected themselves, be worse than useless as legislators and administrators. Others are good parliamentary orators and debaters, but bad committee men. As the work requires more and more ability and temper, it requires more freedom from the cruder illusions, especially those which dramatize one's opponents as villains and fiends, and more and more of that quality which is the primal republican material—that sense of sacredness of life which makes a man respect his fellow without regard to his social rank or intellectual class, and recognizes the fool of Scripture only in those persons who refuse to be bound by any relations except the personally luxurious ones of love, admiration, and identity of political opinion and religious creed. Happily, none of us is quite without this republican quality; for it is not a question of having it or not, but of having it more or less (the inevitable Jevons again, you see): and it is certain that unless it is so strong in a man that he is habitually at least a little conscious of it, he is hardly good enough for the world as it is, much less for the Socialist world to come. To such a man alone can Equality have any sense or validity in a society where men differ from one another through an enormous compass of personal ability, from the peasant to the poet and philosopher. Perhaps to such a one alone will it be plain that a Socialist may, without offence or arrogance, or the least taint of intentional cynicism, discourse as freely as I have done on the illusions of his own creed.

Part II: Resolute Socialist, Disillusioned Democrat

There are strong traces throughout Shaw's early political writings of his doubts about the viability of transforming British society into a Socialist Democracy. With divisions among proponents of Socialism, and in the face of entrenched political structures (including limited male franchise and women entirely excluded from the franchise), Shaw began to explore alternatives to the democratic process. While his commitment to the objectives of Socialism (the elimination of poverty, for example) remained resolute, his skepticism about Democracy itself, and, indeed, humanity's capacity to make any progress at all, rapidly increased.

1. From "The Revolutionist's Handbook and Pocket Companion," *Man and Superman*, 1903. [*The Bodley Head Bernard Shaw*, II: 737–80]

[Shaw's disillusionment with Democracy was expressed forcefully in an appendix to Man and Superman, *"The Revolutionist's Handbook and Pocket Companion," attributed to a character from the play, John Tanner MIRC (Member of the Idle Rich Class). At this point in his career Shaw was neither idle nor especially rich, but in all other respects Tanner is the authentic voice of Shaw's evolving political opinions. It is here that Shaw explores the concept of social and political progress being dependent not on men, but supermen, created through genetic engineering, or, as he puts it, "intelligent breeding." In the published edition of* Man and Superman *"The Revolutionist's Handbook" is followed by a series of "Maxims for Revolutionists," one of which is that "Democracy substitutes election by the incompetent many for appointment by the corrupt few."]*

The Political Need for the Superman

The need for the Superman is, in its most imperative aspect, a political one. We have been driven to Proletarian Democracy by the failure of all the alternative systems; for these depended on the existence of Supermen acting as despots or oligarchs; and not only were these Supermen not always or even often forthcoming at the right moment and in an eligible social position, but when they were forthcoming they could not, except for a short time and by morally suicidal coercive methods, impose superhumanity on those whom they governed; so by mere force of "human nature," government by consent of the governed has supplanted the old plan of governing the citizen as a public-schoolboy is governed.

Now we have yet to see the man who, having any practical experience of Proletarian Democracy, has any belief in its capacity for solving great political problems, or even for doing ordinary parochial work intelligently and economically. Only under despotisms and oligarchies has the Radical faith in "universal suffrage" as a political panacea arisen. It withers the moment it is exposed to practical trial, because Democracy cannot rise above the level of the human material of which its voters are made. Switzerland seems happy in comparison with Russia; but if Russia were as small as Switzerland, and had her social problems simplified in the same way by impregnable natural fortifications and a population educated by the same variety and intimacy of international intercourse, there might be little to choose between them. At all events Australia and Canada, which are virtually protected democratic republics, and France and the United States, which are avowedly independent democratic republics, are neither healthy, wealthy, nor wise; and they would be worse instead of better if their popular ministers were not experts in the art of dodging popular enthusiasms and duping popular ignorance. The politician who once had to learn how to flatter Kings has now to learn how to fascinate, amuse, coax, humbug, frighten, or otherwise strike the fancy of the electorate; and though in advanced modern States, where the artizan is better educated than the King, it takes a much bigger man to be a successful demagogue than to be a successful courtier, yet he who holds popular convictions with prodigious energy is the man for the mob, whilst the frailer sceptic who is cautiously feeling his way towards the next century has no chance unless he happens by accident to have the specific artistic talent of the mountebank as well, in which case it is as a mountebank that he catches votes, and not as a meliorist. Consequently the demagogue, though he professes (and fails) to readjust matters in the interests of the majority of the electors, yet stereotypes mediocrity, organizes intolerance, disparages exhibition of uncommon qualities, and glorifies conspicuous exhibitions of common ones. He manages a small job well: he muddles rhetorically through a large one.

When a great political movement takes place, it is not consciously led nor organized: the unconscious self in mankind breaks its way through the problem as an elephant breaks through a jungle; and the politicians make speeches about whatever happens in the process which, with the best intentions, they do all in their power to prevent. Finally, when social aggregation arrives at a point demanding international organization before the demagogues and electorate have learnt how to manage even a country parish properly much less internationalize Constantinople, the whole political business goes to smash; and presently we have Ruins of Empires, New Zealanders sitting on a broken arch of London Bridge, and so forth.

To that recurrent catastrophe we shall certainly come again unless we can have a Democracy of Supermen; and the production of such a Democracy is the only change that is now hopeful enough to nerve us to the effort that Revolution demands.

Progress an Illusion

Unfortunately the earnest people get drawn off the track of evolution by the illusion of progress. Any Socialist can convince us easily that the difference between Man as he is and Man as he might become, without further evolution, under millenial conditions of nutrition, environment, and training, is enormous. He can show that inequality and iniquitous distribution of wealth and allotment of labor have arisen through an unscientific economic system, and that Man, faulty as he is, no more intended to establish any such ordered disorder than a moth intends to be burnt when it flies into a candle flame. He can show that the difference between the grace and strength of the acrobat and the bent back of the rheumatic field laborer is a difference produced by conditions, not by nature. He can show that many of the most detestable human vices are not radical, but are mere reactions of our institutions on our very virtues. The Anarchist, the Fabian, the Salvationist, the Vegetarian, the doctor, the lawyer, the parson, the professor of ethics, the gymnast, the soldier, the sportsman, the inventor, the political programmaker, all have some prescription for bettering us; and almost all their remedies are physically possible and aimed at admitted evils. To them the limit of progress is, at worst, the completion of all the suggested reforms and the levelling up of all men to the point attained already by the most highly nourished and cultivated in mind and body.

Here, then, as it seems to them, is an enormous field for the energy of the reformer. Here are many noble goals attainable by many of those paths up the Hill Difficulty [an allusion to John Bunyan's *Pilgrim's Progress*, 1678, one of Shaw's favorite novels] along which great spirits love to aspire. Unhappily, the hill will never be climbed by Man as we know him. It need not be denied that if we all struggled bravely to the end of the reformers' paths we should improve the world prodigiously. But there is no more hope in that If than in the equally plausible assurance that if the sky falls we shall all catch larks. We are not going to tread those paths: we have not sufficient energy. We do not desire the end enough: indeed in most cases we do not effectively desire it at all. Ask any man would he like to be a better man; and he will say yes, most piously. Ask him would he like to have a million of money; and he will say yes, most sincerely. But the pious citizen who would like to be a better man goes on behaving just as he did before. And the tramp who would like the million does not take the trouble to earn ten shillings: multitudes of men and women, all eager to accept a legacy of a million, live and die without having ever possessed five pounds at one time, although beggars have died in rags on mattresses stuffed with gold which they accumulated because they desired it enough to nerve them to get it and keep it....

At the present time we have... the Fabian Society, with its peaceful, constitutional, moral, economical policy of Socialism, which needs nothing for its bloodless and benevolent realization except that the English people shall understand it and approve of it. But why are the Fabians well spoken of in circles where thirty years ago the word Socialist was understood as equivalent to cut-throat incendiary? Not because the English have the smallest intention of studying or adopting the Fabian policy, but because they believe that the Fabians, by eliminating the element of intimidation from the Socialist agitation, have drawn the teeth of insurgent poverty and saved the existing order from the only method of attack it really fears. Of course, if the nation adopted the Fabian policy, it would be carried out by brute force exactly as our present property system is. It would become the law; and those who resisted it would be fined, sold up, knocked on the head by policemen, thrown into prison, and in the last resort "executed" just as they are when they break the present law. But as our proprietary class has no fear of that conversion taking place, whereas it does fear sporadic cut-throats and gunpowder plots, and strives with all its might to hide the fact that there is no moral difference whatever between the methods by which it enforces its proprietary rights and the method by which the dynamitard asserts his conception of natural human rights, the Fabian Society is patted on the back just as the Christian Social Union is, whilst the Socialist who says bluntly that a Social evolution can be made only as all other revolutions have been made, by the people who want it killing, coercing, and intimidating the people who don't want it, is denounced as a misleader of the people, and imprisoned with hard labor to show him how much sincerity there is in the objection of his captors to physical force.

Are we then to repudiate Fabian methods, and return to those of the barricader, or adopt those of the dynamitard and the assassin? On the contrary, we are to recognize that both are fundamentally futile. It seems easy for the dynamitard to say "Have you not just admitted that nothing is ever conceded except to physical force? Did not Gladstone admit that the Irish Church was disestablished, not by the spirit of Liberalism, but by the explosion which wrecked Clerkenwell prison [carried out by the Fenian Irish Republican Brotherhood in 1867]?" Well, we need not foolishly and timidly deny it. Let it be fully granted. Let us grant, further, that all this lies in the nature of things; that the most ardent Socialist, if he owns property, can by no means do otherwise than Conservative proprietors until property is forcibly abolished by the whole nation; nay, that ballots and parliamentary divisions, in spite of their vain ceremony of discussion, differ from battles only as the bloodless surrender of an outnumbered force in the field differs from Waterloo or Trafalgar [decisive English victories over Napoleon, 1815 and 1805]. I make a present of all these admissions to the Fenian who collects money from thoughtless Irishmen in America to blow up Dublin Castle; to the detective who persuades foolish young workmen to order bombs from the nearest ironmonger and then delivers them up to penal servitude; to our military and naval commanders who believe, not in preaching, but in an ultimatum backed by plenty of lyddite; and, generally, to all whom it may concern. But of what use is it to substitute the way of the reckless and bloodyminded for the way of the cautious and humane? Is England any the better for the wreck of Clerkenwell prison, or Ireland for the disestablishment of the Irish Church? Is there the smallest reason to suppose that the nation which sheepishly let Charles and Laud and Strafford coerce it, gained anything because it afterwards, still more sheepishly, let a few strongminded Puritans, inflamed by the masterpieces of Jewish revolutionary literature, cut off the heads of the three? [English King Charles I was publicly tried and executed in 1649; Archbishop of Canterbury William Laud was executed in 1645 after a long trial; Thomas

Wentworth, Earl of Strafford, was executed in 1641.] Suppose the Gunpowder plot had succeeded, and set a Fawkes dynasty permanently on the throne, would it have made any difference to the present state of the nation? [Guy Fawkes, 1570–1606, was executed after a failed attempt to blow up the Houses of Parliament.]....

[Shaw goes on to give other examples—including the French and American Revolutions—of what he considered to be the futility of political change caused by violent (rather than rational) means.]

...Nothing can save society then except the clear head and the wide purpose: war and competition, potent instruments of selection and evolution in one epoch, become ruinous instruments of degeneration in the next. In the breeding of animals and plants, varieties which have arisen by selection through many generations relapse precipitously into the wild type in a generation or two when selection ceases; and in the same way a civilization in which lusty pugnacity and greed have ceased to act as selective agents and have begun to obstruct and destroy, rushes downwards and backwards with a suddenness that enables an observer to see with consternation the upwards steps of many centuries retraced in a single lifetime. This has often occurred even within the period covered by history; and in every instance the turning point has been reached long before the attainment, or even the general advocacy on paper, of the levelling-up of the mass to the highest point attainable by the best nourished and cultivated normal individuals.

We must therefore frankly give up the notion that Man as he exists is capable of net progress. There will always be an illusion of progress, because wherever we are conscious of an evil we remedy it, and therefore always seem to ourselves to be progressing, forgetting that most of the evils we see are the effects, finally become acute, of long-unnoticed retrogressions; that our compromising remedies seldom fully recover the lost ground; above all, that on the lines along which we are degenerating, good has become evil in our eyes, and is being undone in the name of progress precisely as evil is undone and replaced by good on the lines along which we are evolving. This is indeed the Illusion of Illusions; for it gives us infallible and appalling assurance that if our political ruin is to come, it will be effected by ardent reformers and supported by enthusiastic patriots as a series of necessary steps in our progress. Let the Reformer, the Progressive, the Meliorist then reconsider himself and his eternal ifs and ands which never become pots and pans. Whilst Man remains what he is, there can be no progress beyond the point already attained and fallen headlong from at every attempt at civilization; and since even that point is but a pinnacle to which few people cling in giddy terror above an abyss of squalor, mere progress should no longer charm us.

The Verdict of History

...Enough, then, of this goose-cackle about Progress: Man, as he is, never will nor can add a cubit to his stature by any of its quackeries, political, scientific, educational, religious, or artistic. What is likely to happen when this conviction gets into the minds of the men whose present faith in these illusions is the cement of our social system, can be imagined only by those who know how suddenly a civilization which has long ceased to think (or, in the old phrase, to watch and pray) can fall to pieces when the vulgar belief in its hypocrisies and impostures can no longer hold out against is failures and scandals. When religious and ethical formulae become so obsolete that no man of strong mind can believe them, they have also reached the point at which no man of high character will profess them; and from that moment until they are formally disestablished, they stand at the door of every profession and every public office to keep out every able man who is not a sophist or a liar. A nation which revises its parish councils once in three years, but will not revise its articles of religion once in three hundred, even when those articles avowedly began as a political compromise dictated by Mr Facing-Both-Ways, is a nation that needs remaking.

Our only hope, then, is evolution. We must replace the man by the superman. It is frightful for the citizen, as the years pass him, to see his own contemporaries so exactly reproduced by the younger generation, that his companions of thirty years ago have their counterparts in every city crowd, where he has to check himself repeatedly in the act of saluting as an old friend some young man to whom he is only an elderly stranger. All hope of advance dies in his bosom as he watches them: he knows that they will do just what their fathers did, and that the few voices which will still, as always before, exhort them to do something else and be something better, might as well spare their breath to cool their porridge (if they can get any). Men like [art critic John] Ruskin [1819–1900] and [historian Thomas] Carlyle [1795–1881] will preach to Smith and Brown for the sake of preaching, just as St Francis preached to the birds and St Anthony to the fishes. But Smith and Brown, like the fishes and birds, remain as they are: and the poets who plan Utopia and prove that nothing is necessary for their realization but that Man should will them, perceive at last, like [German composer] Richard Wagner [1813–83, much admired by Shaw], that the fact to be faced is that Man does not effectively will them. And he never will until he becomes Superman.

And so we arrive at the end of the Socialist's dream of "the socialization of the means of production and exchange," of the Positivist's dream of the moralizing of the capitalist, and of the ethical professor's, legislator's, educator's dream of putting commandments and codes and lessons and examination marks on a man as harness is put on a horse, ermine on a judge, pipeclay [for whitening uniforms] on a soldier, or a wig on an actor, and pretending that his nature has been changed. The only fundamental and possible Socialism is the socialization of the selective breeding of Man: in other terms, of human evolution. We must eliminate the Yahoo [a brutish race in Jonathan Swift's *Gulliver's Travels* (1726)], or his vote will wreck the commonwealth.

The Method

As to the method, what can be said as yet except that where there is a will, there is a way? If there be no will, we are lost. That is a possibility for our crazy little empire, if not for the universe; and as such possibilities are not to be entertained without despair, we must, whilst we survive, proceed on the assumption that we have still energy enough to not only will to live, but to will to live better. That may mean that we must establish a State Department of Evolution, with a seat in the Cabinet for its chief, and a revenue to defray the cost of direct State experiments, and provide inducements to private persons to achieve successful results. It may mean a private society or a chartered company for the improvement of human live stock. But for the present it is far more likely to mean a blatant repudiation of such proposals as indecent and immoral, with, nevertheless, a general secret pushing of the human will in the repudiated direction; so that all sorts of institutions and public authorities will under some pretext or other feel their way furtively towards the Superman.... One thing at least is clear to begin with. If a woman can, by careful selection of a father, and nourishment of herself, produce a citizen with efficient senses, sound organs, and a good digestion, she should clearly be secured a sufficient reward for that natural service to make her willing to undertake and repeat it. Whether she be financed in the undertaking by herself, or by the father, or by a speculative capitalist, or by a new department of, say, the Royal Dublin Society, or (as at present) by the War Office maintaining her "on the strength" and authorizing a particular soldier to marry her, or by a local authority under a by-law directing that women may under certain circumstances have a year's leave of absence on full salary, or by the central government, does not matter provided the result be satisfactory.

It is a melancholy fact that as the vast majority of women and their husbands have, under existing circumstances, not enough nourishment, no capital, no credit, and no knowledge of science or business, they would, if the State would pay for birth as it now pays for death, be exploited by joint stock companies for dividends, just as they are in ordinary industries. Even a joint stock human stud farm (piously disguised as a reformed Foundling Hospital or something of that sort) might well, under proper inspection and regulation, produce better results than our present reliance on promiscuous marriage. It may be objected that when an ordinary contractor produces stores for sale to the Government, and the Government rejects them as not up to the required standard, the condemned goods are either sold for what they will fetch or else scrapped: that is, treated as waste material; whereas if the goods consisted of human beings, all that could be done would be to let them loose or send them to the nearest workhouse. But there is nothing new in private enterprise throwing its human refuse on the cheap labor market and the workhouse; and the refuse of the new industry would presumably be better bred than the staple product of ordinary poverty. In our present happy-go-lucky industrial disorder, all the human products, successful or not, would have to be thrown on the labor market; but the unsuccessful ones would not entitle the company to a bounty and so would be a dead loss to it. The practical commercial difficulty would be the uncertainty and the cost in time and money of the first experiments. Purely commercial capital would not touch such heroic operations during the experimental stage; and in any case the strength of mind needed for so momentous a new departure could not be fairly expected from the Stock Exchange. It will have to be handled by statesmen with character enough to tell our democracy and plutocracy that statecraft does not consist in flattering their follies or applying their suburban standards of propriety to the affairs of four continents. The matter must be taken up either by the State or by some organization strong enough to impose respect upon the State.

The novelty of any such experiment, however, is only in the scale of it. In one conspicuous case, that of royalty, the State does already select the parents on purely political grounds; and in the peerage, though the heir to a dukedom is legally free to marry a dairymaid, yet the social pressure on him to confine his choice to politically and socially eligible mates is so overwhelming that he is really no more free to marry the dairymaid than George IV [1762–1830, King of Great Britain 1820–30] was to marry Mrs Fitzherbert [his mistress, to whom he was secretly but illegally married]; and such a marriage could only occur as a result of extraordinary strength of characters on the part of the dairymaid acting upon extraordinary weakness on the part of the duke. Let those who think the whole conception of intelligent breeding absurd and scandalous ask themselves why George IV was not allowed to choose his own wife whilst any tinker could marry whom he pleased? Simply because it did not matter a rap politically whom the tinker married, whereas it mattered very much whom the king married. The way in which all considerations of the king's personal rights, of the claims of the heart, of the sanctity of the marriage oath, and of romantic morality crumpled up before this political need shows how negligible all these apparently irresistible prejudices are when they come into conflict with the demand for quality in our rulers....

Well, nowadays it is not the King that rules, but the tinker. Dynastic wars are no longer feared, dynastic alliances no longer valued. Marriages in royal families are becoming rapidly less political, and more popular, domestic, and romantic. If all the kings in Europe were made as free tomorrow as King Cophetua [who, in African legend, married a beggar maid], nobody but their aunts and chamberlains would feel a moment's anxiety as to the consequences. On the other hand a sense of the social importance of the tinker's marriage has been steadily growing. We have made a public matter of his wife's health in the month after her confinement. We have taken the minds of his children out of his hands and put them into those of our State schoolmaster. We shall presently make their bodily nourishment independent of him. But they are still riff-raff; and to hand the country over to riff-raff is national suicide, since riff-raff can neither govern nor will let anyone else govern except the highest bidder of bread and circuses. There is no public enthusiast alive of twenty years' practical democratic experience who believes in the political adequacy of the electorate or of the bodies it elects. The overthrow of the aristocrat has created the necessity for the Superman....

2. From "Why All Women are Peculiarly Fitted to be Good Voters." A speech to the National Union of Women's Suffrage Societies, Queens Hall, London, 26 March 1907. *New York American*, 21 April 1907. [Weintraub, *Fabian Feminist*, pp. 248–54]

[*Although he was subsequently disappointed by what little positive impact (in his view) women voters and women Members of Parliament had on government policies, Shaw's support of extending the franchise to all adult women was unequivocal. The 1884 Manifesto of the Fabian Society had called for equal political rights for men and women, and at the end of the speech given here Shaw refutes the* notion "that any social problem will ever be satisfactorily solved," unless "women have their due share of getting it solved." It was not, however, until 1928 that women were given equal voting rights.]

I do not wish to be considered in this article as the supporter or representative of any political party. England has a Liberal party; it has a Conservative party; it has a Labor party; it has an Irish party. Unfortunately it has not yet got a Shaw party. If it had, that party would be uncompromisingly on the side of giving the suffrage to women, and I can promise that should they get it the House of Commons will be quite the most amusing Legislature on the face of the globe.

I think I must take my stand as a representative more or less of literature, a profession in which there is no question about the ability of women to stand side by side in all branches of the art with men. I have purposely brought in the subject of literature because I want to explain one literary utterance which I am sure has been greatly misunderstood.

When Mr Dickinson's bill [Willoughby Dickinson's unsuccessful March 1907 Women's Suffrage Bill] was about to be discussed in the House of Commons *The Times*, suddenly feeling that the masculine opposition to that bill was not quite so convincing as it might be, appealed to a very eminent literary woman to come to the rescue of *The Times*.... [British novelist] Mrs Humphry Ward [Mary Augusta Ward, 1851–1920] wrote an extremely amusing letter, in which she pointed out that the best arguments for men to use against giving the suffrage to women were the political ignorance of women, their restriction to their own affairs, their narrow outlook on life.

Now, Mrs Humphry Ward is one of the most able public women in London. Mrs Humphry Ward has enlarged the whole sphere of her national life by inventing the vacation school [summer school], which no man apparently had ever thought of, and which is going to be in the future really the only important part of school life.

She did that by an extremely able piece of public organization, by which she eventually imposed her ideas on the whole of London. Well. Mrs Humphry Ward quite clearly cannot have meant seriously that women were incapable of public affairs. The question is, what did she mean and what was she doing?

I will tell you. She was getting at my sex. Every single thing that Mrs Humphry Ward said in that letter about women was equally true of men, and I am bound to say that the letter made such an impression on me that I began seriously to consider whether I had any right to advocate the extension of the suffrage to women, instead of endeavoring to form an active society for the purpose of taking it away from men.

I have decided on the whole not to take that course. If you do not give the suffrage to men or to women I do not exactly see whom you are going to give it to. I quite grant that men and women are very little capable of governing either their own affairs or the affairs of a nation, and if I could find any superior class of beings to entrust the government to I would entrust the government to it. As it is, I think we must put up with what we have got, and that is human nature.

And human nature is human nature. It is not masculine nature or feminine nature. It is human nature. The country is not governed and never will be governed by the mass of its population. What is meant by modern democracy is not the government of the country by the whole people, but the government of the country by the consent of the whole people. You give a man a vote, not because you believe that he is a very politically able person, but because you believe he has intelligence to know when he is uncomfortable.

And, therefore, you may make up your minds that exactly the same arguments that go to give the suffrage for men go to give the suffrage for women.

Now I am sorry to say that the opposition to women's suffrage has brought into existence in England the most entirely disgraceful, the most absolutely contemptible form of conservatism.

I am not now speaking against the Conservative party. I am just as much against conservatism as I am against liberalism. Many conservative positions I can respect. But there is a new sort of conservatism coming in which is quite new to me and which is absolutely dastardly beyond anything I can express, because the new sort of conservative does not come forward frankly and say that he opposes such and such a measure of reform, but he says, "I will hear nothing of that measure of reform."

I go further than that. If that sort of conservative had existed in the year 1832 when the great Reform Bill [which significantly extended the male franchise] was passed, what would that man have said? Would he have taken the side of the old Tories who believed in the government of England by their country gentlemen, who were with [British essayist Thomas] De Quincey [1785–1859] when he said boldly: "What nobler class can you have to govern than your country gentlemen?" He would have said: "No, I am an advocate not of this miserable half and half measure which enfranchises the middle class. I am in favor of adult suffrage, and until you bring in a bill for adult suffrage, I shall not vote for this reform. I shall stand uncompromisingly against this with my exalted and extreme principles."

And if he had lived in 1887 [the reference is to the 1884 Third Reform Act] when a further extension of the franchise was granted, he would have been in exactly the same position. He would have said, "Don't give it to the working class. Why should you enfranchise certain members of the working class? Why should you enfranchise two-thirds, when you know one-third would be left out in the cold? Let us have down-to-the-bottom adult suffrage or nothing."

Now, I am going to tell you what these new Conservatives will say when you offer them adult suffrage. They will say, "Adult suffrage! Are the children not to have votes? Look at the sufferings of children! Look at the number in industrial employment! Are not children the most important part of the community? Are they not at least as politically intelligent as the majority of grown-up persons in this country?" "Adult suffrage," they will say. "Perish the thought! We will oppose it tooth and nail until you give us humanity suffrage."

And if you took them at their word and offered them humanity suffrage they would complain because you did not give a vote to the cat. Don't be taken in by the trick. No single political measure in England or in any other country can ever be passed that goes right to the logical extremity of the theory which it represents. The thing is entirely impossible and every honest politician knows it.

The man who won't give you an instalment does not mean to pay you at all.

I offer this test of the really honest supporter of giving the franchise to women: Ask him or ask her, "If a bill were brought in tomorrow giving the vote only to one woman in the country and that woman a member of the highest and most exclusive class, that woman the Queen, would you vote for the bill?"

I would vote for that bill, and anybody who would not vote for that bill, whether it was to give one vote for the Queen or one vote to one washerwoman, will never be a practical politician unless he or she is really not in favor of extending the franchise at all, which I am afraid is the real reason at the bottom of this opposition.

There are a great number of questions, which I have not time to deal with in this article, which absolutely do not exist in England, because women have no direct political existence at all. There is a whole range of things which have never been mentioned in any newspaper, which are not referred to in any programme, which people have not got in their minds, and are not related to politics at all, but which are of vital importance, which would spring into life and spring into the very front of political warfare if only the influence of women began to be felt directly through the vote.

[Shaw then compares the situation in Great Britain unfavourably with that in New Zealand, where the 1893 Electoral Act gave all women the right to vote.]

...[What] you have not realized [is] that the vote is withheld from woman because she is said to be an inferior person, a person who is said to be unworthy of the vote.

I know that many men frankly take up that position. I have a great appreciation of the man who stands up solidly and who says: "I am a man. I am a broad-chested manly man. I am a lord of creation. I claim my divine right to govern this petticoated thing, this inferior person, with no mind, no knowledge of politics, and of very little use in the world except to make my home comfortable." I can understand that man, and I can enjoy a man who is really a gorgeous idiot.

I like men to be thorough in their absurdity and folly. I have even a sort of liking for the man who comes up to me and says: "After all, you know, think of Michael Angelo and Beethoven. Has any woman ever produced great works of art like them?"

I reply: "My friend, have you ever produced any great works of art?"

I think there is a great deal of sense in the position he takes up. If any government will bring in a bill tomorrow restricting the franchise to persons who have produced great works of art, then I think I shall support that bill. A great many women will have votes under that and the majority of the ladies and gentlemen who are now opposing the franchise for women will be disenfranchised by that bill.

Now, the last thing I want to say to you is something which, perhaps, may not have occurred to Englishmen and Englishwomen. They belong to a free country, and what I am going to say to you now is something that would, perhaps, occur only to a man who, like myself, belongs to a country which is not free. [Ireland did not gain independence from Great Britain until 1921.] The real curse of the nation which is not politically free is that all its deepest spiritual energies, all its political activity, all its philosophic activity—all the very best that it has of human activity—is taken up in the struggle to regain that political liberty which never should be denied to any country or to any nation.

If you want to know why in a country so clever as Ireland you find such a terrible behind-handedness with regard to all those great waves of the human spirit which sweep from time to time over Europe and over the whole world—why things that you are discussing and exciting yourselves about have not yet been heard of in Ireland—I shall tell you the reason.

It is because all the men in Ireland, all the best spirit in Ireland, are together occupied in the struggle to obtain the political freedom of Ireland: and all that energy which might be placed at the service of the world, and might be placed at the service of England, is being taken up with the mere question of political freedom. Now I do not ask you to agree with me on that subject, but I am going to ask you to make an application. Remember that there is in England at present a very wonderful contingent of women of extraordinary ability, of women who are at present doing first rate work on royal commissions, who in all sorts of social movements have been showing what women can do when they lay their mind to it.

Remember, there is a theory in England that the House of Commons consists of 670 of the cleverest and best men in the country. Well, let me tell you that the House of Commons never will consist of the 670—never as long as it consists exclusively of men—absolutely the best and cleverest people in the country, for some of its best are women.

I will undertake if any government approaches me on the subject and asks me whether, if it empties its benches a little under what they are at present, the seats could be replaced with better women—I will undertake to do it. But the difficulty is that almost all that talent that women have now, instead of being applied to the solution of our social problems—those problems which concern both sexes alike—is wasted in this agitation—an agitation which ought to be utterly unnecessary, because women are struggling to get the franchise.

By giving them the franchise England will set free an immense and beneficial flood of political and social energy which is now being taken up by this question. It will get that question off their minds—a question which in any really intelligent country ought to have been settled a century ago.

Sweep that one difficulty away. Give women, particularly able women, something else to do than going about on platforms clamoring for this right, which should never have been withheld or denied them, and then you will get a united force of both sexes tackling these social problems, without the solution of which we shall be plunged in the ruin that has overtaken other civilizations in history which have towered in the past. You want the help of women in that.

As far as I have been working on these problems in my lifetime, I have always been working with women, on the same objects as women, and I have always found that their help, their assistance and point of view were absolutely indispensable.

I deny that any social problem will ever be satisfactorily solved unless women have their due share of getting it solved.

Let us get this obstacle of the political slavery of women out of the way and then we shall see all set to work on the problems—both sexes together with a will.

3. "The Crime of Poverty." A speech delivered at the War Against Poverty demonstration, Albert Hall, London, 11 October 1912. [*Platform and Pulpit*, pp. 93–96]

[*The elimination of poverty was a constant objective throughout Shaw's political life. In this 1912 speech he uses some of his strongest language ever to describe poverty—"an abominable disease and a very horrible crime"—and urges the audience to emulate the suffragettes in taking militant action to achieve results.*]

I have received many letters during the last few days from gentlemen who, seeing that I was advertized to take part in a meeting for the abolition of poverty, suggested that I might make a modest beginning in the form of pecuniary accommodation to themselves privately. But all these gentlemen made the mistake of representing themselves as being miserably poor. I am present at this meeting because there is nothing in the world I hate more than a poor man. I should be a Conservative if I had sympathy for the poor.

It happened that when I was a small child my nurse used to take me out for exercise in the open air. She did not exercise me in the open air; she took me to visit her friends. Her friends were mostly poor people. I thought them most horrible people. I simply detested them, and I still detest them. I think such people ought not to exist.

I am perfectly determined not to be poor if I can help it. I don't want to be rich. I would be content with, say, four or five thousand pounds a year. But I am not content to have four or five thousand a year and to be surrounded by dirty, ignorant people who have only a pound a week.

I am not content to have a nice house myself. I want everybody else to have a nice house; I have got to look at those houses. The only reason why I like my drawing room to be nice is that I have to look at it. I don't eat it. For the same

PART II: RESOLUTE SOCIALIST, DISILLUSIONED DEMOCRAT

reason I want other people's houses to look nice—on the outside, at any rate. If I thought your houses were beautiful inside, you might have the inestimable favor of hearing my brilliant conversation, which is celebrated throughout Europe.

I want to cure poverty as an abominable disease and as a very horrible crime. I never had any sort of enthusiasm for the ordinary movements for the suppression of crime. If a man is by disposition a murderer you cannot make him a philanthropist. You cannot turn a real, genuine, congenital thief into an honest man. He may be a very pleasant man—I have known many charming thieves—but you cannot change him fundamentally. We are always clamoring to do the impossible.

You can, however, take a dirty man and you can clean him. You can take an ignorant man and you can teach him. You can take a poor man and you can give him money. Then he won't be a poor man any longer.

Therefore, in standing on this platform I claim to be standing upon the only practical platform that exists in England. All the other parties are setting out to do something which cannot be done. That is how the governing classes occupy themselves. They imagine it will keep the people quiet.

Our method of proceeding by demanding a minimum [income] is really the method by which all civilizations have advanced. The law imposes upon everyone in this hall a minimum of clothes. I am sorry the law does not go further and impose a minimum as to the quality of the clothes. I strongly object to the quality of clothes worn in London today. It is foolish to say that everyone should be dressed if you do not say that they shall be well dressed.

In the same way we must insist on a minimum of honesty. We allow a man to be a large shareholder, but we prevent him from being a pickpocket. We insist on that minimum of honesty even for millionaires. But a pickpocket is nowhere nearly so harmful to the community as the poor man. The poor man breeds disease and casts a blight over the people. The first thing to do, therefore, is to insist on a minimum of money in everyone's pockets.

We have gone so far in this direction as to give a man five shillings a week when he is seventy years of age [under the 1908 Old-Age Pensions Act]. I defy you to give one reason for giving a man [women were also eligible] of seventy five shillings a week, which is not a far better reason for giving a man of twenty-seven £500 a year [i.e., just under ten shillings a week]. The thing can be done. There is no difficulty in producing a higher standard of life. You are stupid enough to waste your opportunities. With the exception of a few ladies and gentlemen, everyone who is working is producing more than he consumes. Roughly, he is producing twice as much. What should we, if we were reasonable beings (which I know you are not), expect to follow as a consequence of that extraordinary fact? Would you not expect this country to be getting richer and richer from one generation to another? Would you not expect the children to be healthier and heavier, the men and women stronger and more beautiful? Would you not expect its slums to be disappearing by magic, its diseases to be passing away, the necessity for working long hours to be ceasing? Would you not be expecting this earth to be fulfilling its real destiny, to be transforming itself into the Kingdom of Heaven?

What are we actually doing with this enormous surplus of wealth? We are throwing it into the pockets of people who use it, not for the improvement of the country, but for its degradation. When are you going to stop it?

Some enthusiasts tonight have asked, "When are you going to turn out the Government?" They know very well that we have not the heart nor the power to turn out even the people who interrupt us in this audience. Turn out the Government? We have not the strength in the House of Commons to turn anybody out; it is as much as we can do to keep ourselves in. [The first Labour Government was not formed until 1924.]

The task before us is to turn out a whole epoch of civilization, to turn out a generation which has become entirely corrupt by worn-out traditions and prejudices, to inaugurate and bring in a new epoch. It can only be done by the spreading of a great conception among the people, of a higher conception of life. You, who are here, are a picked and chosen few. I wish you would go amongst those who think they are money-making, and who are really grinding each other down, and break their windows. Other movements besides the Suffrage movement need to be militant. We want a conviction of sin and of salvation, a wave of intense shame at existing conditions which shall make them intolerable to those who imagine that they profit by it.

The hammer of public opinion is needed and, I repeat, a genuine conviction of sin. The greatest curse of poverty is that it destroys the will power of the poor until they become the most ardent supporters of their own poverty. We have to talk to these people, and, if possible, talk sense.

I am not sure that the interrupters tonight have not set us a good example. I suggest that you go to other political meetings, and when someone says, "Bulgaria," or "Ireland," or "Land Reform," you say, "What about Poverty?" Such action will begin by you being turned out. I hope it will end in a bad epoch being turned out.

Part III: War and Revolution

By the outbreak of the First World War in 1914 Shaw had become Britain's most prominent playwright, with an international as well as domestic reputation. *Mrs Warren's Profession, Caesar and Cleopatra, Man and Superman, John Bull's Other Island, Major Barbara, The Doctor's Dilemma, Pygmalion*: these and other plays had been performed throughout Europe, North America, and Asia. As a political activist, however, Shaw's success was not nearly so apparent. The Fabian Society continued to publish its tracts, Shaw was still writing and lecturing extensively on political subjects, and he also used his plays to provoke political discussion. The Labour Party had been founded (1906), and the suffragette movement, supported by Shaw, was constantly at the forefront of public attention. But for all that there was precious little evidence of progress toward the social and political reforms that Shaw had been advocating by now for some thirty years. And then came the catastrophe of the First World War.

1. From *Common Sense About the War*, 1914. First published as a supplement to the *New Statesman*, 14 November 1914. Reprinted in *What I Really Wrote About the War*, pp. 22–110.

[Shaw's opposition to the war prompted one of his most courageous political essays. His refusal to embrace patriotism, coupled with his advice to soldiers on both sides of the conflict to shoot their officers "and go home to gather in their harvests in the villages and make revolution in the towns," provoked widespread contempt and vilification throughout Great Britain. The essay, Shaw said, "had a shocking effect on the most amiable and innocent of our people." He was accused of "passionate pro-Germanism, Defeatism, and Pacifism"; "if the amiable people [of England] had not been too amiable to lynch me, I should have been lynched." Some of Shaw's other views on the war, while not quite as inflammatory as his "shoot their officers" entreaty, were also received with dismay by government and military alike: unionize the troops, guarantee them employment before discharge, pay civilian volunteers, and maintain civil liberties in wartime.]

The time has now come to pluck up courage and begin to talk and write soberly about the war. At first the mere horror of it stunned the more thoughtful of us; and even now only those who are not in actual contact with or bereaved relation to its heartbreaking wreckage can think sanely about it, or endure to hear others discuss it cooly. As to the thoughtless, well, not for a moment dare I suggest that for the first few weeks they were all scared out of their wits; for I know too well that the British civilian does not allow his perfect courage to be questioned: only experienced soldiers and foreigners are allowed the infirmity of fear. But they certainly were—shall I say a little upset? They felt in that solemn hour that England was lost if only one single traitor in their midst let slip the truth about anything in the universe. It was a perilous time for me.

PART III: WAR AND REVOLUTION

I do not hold my tongue easily; and my inborn dramatic faculty and professional habit as a playwright prevent me from taking a one-sided view even when the most probable result of taking a many-sided one is prompt lynching. Besides, until [Irish] Home Rule emerges from its present suspended animation, I shall retain my Irish capacity for criticizing England with something of the detachment of a foreigner, and perhaps with a certain slightly malicious taste for taking the conceit out of her. [Secretary for War] Lord Kitchener [1850–1916] made a mistake the other day in rebuking the Irish volunteers for not rallying faster to the defence of "their country." They do not regard it as their country yet. He should have asked them to come forward as usual and help poor old England through a stiff fight. Then it would have been all right.

Having thus frankly confessed my bias, which you can allow for as a rifleman allows for the wind, I give my views for what they are worth. They will be of some use; because, however blinded I may be by prejudice or perversity, my prejudices in this matter are not those which blind the British patriot, and therefore I am fairly sure to see some things that have not yet struck him.

And first, I do not see this war as one which has welded Governments and peoples into complete and sympathetic solidarity as against the common enemy. I see the people of England united in a fierce detestation and defiance of the views and acts of Prussian Junkerism [aristocratic authoritarianism]. And I see the German people stirred to the depths by a similar antipathy to English Junkerism, and angered by the apparent treachery and duplicity of the attack made on them by us in their extremist peril from France and Russia. I see both nations duped, but alas! not quite unwillingly duped, by their Junkers and Militarists into wreaking on one another the wrath they should have spent in destroying Junkerism and Militarism in their own country. And I see the Junkers and Militarists of England and Germany jumping at the chance they have longed for in vain for many years of smashing one another and establishing their own oligarchy as the dominant military power in the world. No doubt the heroic remedy for this tragic misunderstanding is that both armies should shoot their officers and go home to gather in their harvests in the villages and make a revolution in the towns: and though this is not at present a practicable solution, it must be frankly mentioned because it or something like it is always a possibility in a defeated conscript army if its commanders push it beyond human endurance when its eyes are opening to the fact that in murdering its neighbors it is biting off its nose to vex its face, besides riveting the intolerable yoke of Militarism and Junkerism more tightly than ever on its own neck. But there is no chance—or, as our Junkers would put it, no danger—of our soldiers yielding to such an ecstasy of commonsense. They have enlisted voluntarily; they are not defeated nor likely to be; their communications are intact and their meals reasonably punctual; they are as pugnacious as their officers; and in fighting Prussia they are fighting a more deliberate, conscious, tyrannical, personally insolent, and dangerous Militarism than their own. Still, even for a voluntary professional army, that possibility exists, just as for the civilian there is a limit beyond which taxation, bankruptcy, privation, terror, and inconvenience cannot be pushed without revolution or a social dissolution more ruinous than submission to conquest. I mention all this, not to make myself wantonly disagreeable, but because military persons, thinking naturally that there is nothing like leather, are now talking of this war as likely to become a permanent institution like the Chamber of Horrors at Madame Tussaud's, forgetting, I think, that the rate of consumption maintained by modern military operations is much greater relatively to the highest possible rate of production maintainable under the restrictions of war time than it has ever been before.

PART III: WAR AND REVOLUTION

The European settlement at the end of the war will be effected, let us hope, not by a regimental mess of fire-eaters sitting round an up-ended drum in a vanquished Berlin or Vienna, but by some sort of Congress in which all the Powers (including, very importantly, the United States of America) will be represented. Now I foresee a certain danger of our being taken by surprise at that Congress, and making ourselves unnecessarily difficult and unreasonable, by presenting ourselves to it in the character of Injured Innocence. We shall not be accepted in that character. Such a Congress will most certainly regard us as being, next to the Prussians (if it makes even that exception), the most quarrelsome people in the universe. I am quite conscious of the surprise and scandal this anticipation may cause among my more highminded (*hochnäsig*, the Germans call it) readers. Let me therefore break it gently by expatiating for a while on the subject of Junkerism and Militarism generally, and on the history of the literary propaganda between England and Potsdam [traditional home of German and Prussian royalty] which has been going on openly for the last forty years on both sides.

[Shaw then argues that Junkerism and Militarism are rife in both Prussia and England, and goes on to describe anti-German propaganda in England leading up to the First World War. Prominent in the propaganda was an anonymous 1871 novel—the author was George Tomkyns Chesney (1830–95), a British army general—called The Battle of Dorking: Reminiscences of a Volunteer, *which describes an invasion of Britain by a German army.]*

...*The Battle of Dorking* had an enormous sale; and the wildest guesses were current as to its authorship. And its moral was "To arms; or the Germans will besiege London as they besieged Paris" [in 1871 during the Franco-Prussian War]. From that time until the present, the British propaganda of war with Germany has never ceased. The lead given by *The Battle of Dorking* was taken up by articles in the daily press and the magazines.... Throughout all these agitations the enemy, the villain of the piece, the White Peril, was Prussia and her millions of German conscripts. At first, in *The Battle of Dorking* phase, the note was mainly defensive. But from the moment when the Kaiser began to copy our Armada policy by building a big fleet, the anti-German agitation became openly aggressive; and the cry that the German fleet or ours must sink, and that a war between England and Germany was bound to come some day, speedily ceased to be merely a cry with our Militarists and became axiom with them. And what our Militarists said our Junkers echoed and our Junker diplomatists played for. The story of how they manoeuvred to hem Germany and Austria in with an Anglo-Franco-Russian combination will be found told with soldierly directness and with proud candor of a man who can see things from his own side only in the article by Lord Roberts [Field Marshal Frederick Roberts, 1832–1914] in the current number of *The Hibbert Journal* (October 1914). There you shall see also, after the usual nonsense about [German philosopher Friedrich] Nietzsche [1844–1900], the vision of "British administrators bearing the White Man's Burden," of "young men, fresh from the public schools of Britain, coming eagerly forward to carry on the high traditions of Imperial Britain in each new dependency which comes under our care," of "our fitness as an Imperial race," of "a great task committed to us by Providence," of "the will to conquer that has never failed us," and of "assuming control of one fifth of the earth's surface and the care of one in five of all the inhabitants of the world." Not a suggestion that the inhabitants of the world are perhaps able to take care of themselves. Not even a passing recollection when that White Man's Burden is in question that the men outside the British Empire, and even inside the German Empire, are by no means exclusively black. Only the *sancta simplicitas* [holy simplicity] that glories in "the proud position of England," the "sympathy, tolerance, prudence, and benevolence of our rule" in the east (as shown, the Kaiser is no doubt sarcastically remarking, in the Delhi sedition trial [in June 1913, for alleged conspiracy against British rule]), the chivalrous feeling that it is our highest duty to save the world from the horrible misfortune of being governed by anybody but those young men fresh from the public schools of Britain. Change the words Britain and British to Germany and German, and the Kaiser will sign the article with enthusiasm. *His* opinion, *his* attitude (subject to that merely verbal change) word for word.

Now, please observe that I do not say that the agitation was unreasonable. I myself steadily advocated the formation of a formidable armament, and ridiculed the notion that we, who are wasting hundreds of millions annually on idlers and wasters [i.e., the idle rich], could not easily afford double, treble, quadruple our military and naval expenditure. I advocated the compulsion of every man to serve his country, both in war and peace. The idlers and wasters, perceiving dimly that I meant the cost to come out of their pockets, and meant to use the admission that riches should not exempt a man from military service as an illustration of how absurd it is to exempt him from civil service, did not embrace my advocacy with enthusiasm; so I must reaffirm it now lest it should be supposed that I am condemning those whose proceedings I am describing. Though often horribly wrong in principle, they were quite right in practice as far as they went. But they must stand to their guns now that the guns are going off. They must not pretend that they were harmless Radical lovers of peace, and that the propaganda of Militarism and of inevitable war between England and Germany is a Prussian infamy for which the Kaiser must be severely punished. That is not fair, not true, not gentlemanly. We began it; and if they met us half-way, as they certainly did, it is not for us to reproach them. When the German fire-eaters drank to

The Day (of Armageddon) they were drinking to the day of which our Navy League fire-eaters had first said "It's bound to come." Therefore let us have no more nonsense about the Prussian Wolf and the British Lamb, the Prussian Machiavelli and the English Evangelist. We cannot shout for years that we are boys of the bulldog breed, and then suddenly pose as gazelles. No. When Europe and America come to settle the treaty that will end this business (for America is concerned in it as much as we are) they will not deal with us as the lovable and innocent victims of a treacherous tyrant and a savage soldiery. They will have to consider how these two incorrigibly pugnacious and inveterately snobbish peoples, who have snarled at one another for forty years with bristling hair and grinning fangs, and are now rolling over with their teeth in one another's throats, are to be tamed into trusty watchdogs of the peace of the world. I am sorry to spoil the saintly image with a halo which the British Jingo journalist sees just now when he looks in the glass; but it must be done if we are to behave reasonably in the imminent day of reckoning....

And now I proceed from general considerations to the diplomatic history of the present case, as I must in order to make our moral position clear. But first, lest I should lose all credit by the startling incompatibility between the familiar personal characters of our statesmen and the diplomacy for which they are officially responsible, I must say a word about the peculiar psychology of English statesmanship, not only for the benefit of my English readers, who do not know that it is peculiar just as they do not know that water has any taste (because it is always in their mouths), but as a plea for more charitable construction from the wider world.

We know by report, however unjust it may seem to us, that there is an opinion abroad, even in the quarters most friendly to us, that our excellent qualities are marred by an incorrigible hypocrisy. To France we have always been Perfidious Albion. In Germany, at this moment, that epithet would be

PART III: WAR AND REVOLUTION

scorned as far too flattering to us. [French novelist] Victor Hugo [1802–85] explained the relative unpopularity of *Measure for Measure* among Shakespeare's plays on the ground that the character of the hypocrite Angelo was a too faithful dramatization of our national character. Pecksniff [in Dickens's novel *Martin Chuzzlewit*] is not considered so exceptional an English gentleman in America as he is in England.

Now we have not acquired this reputation for nothing. The world has no greater interest in branding England with this particular vice of hypocrisy than in branding France with it; yet the world does not cite Tartuffe [in Molière's play *Tartuffe*] as a typical Frenchman as it cites Angelo and Pecksniff as typical Englishmen. We may protest against it as indignantly as the Prussian soldiers protest against their equally universal reputation for ferocity in plunder and pillage, sack and rapine; but there is something in it. If you judge an English statesman by his conscious intentions, his professions, and his personal charm, you will often find him an amiable, upright, humane, anxiously truthful man. If you judge him, as a foreigner must, solely on the official acts for which he is responsible, and which he has to defend in the House of Commons for the sake of his party, you will often be driven to conclude that this estimable gentleman is, in point of being an unscrupulous superprig and fool, worse than [ruthless Italian statesman] Caesar Borgia [1475–1507] and [Prussian general and military historian] General Von Bernhardi [1849–1930] rolled into one, and in foreign affairs a Bismarck [Prussian statesman, 1815–98; Chancellor of the German Empire 1871–90] in everything except commanding ability, blunt common sense, and freedom from illusion as to the nature and object of his own diplomacy. And the permanent officials in whose hands he is will probably deserve all this and something to spare. Thus you will get the amazing contrast that confronts us now between the Machiavellian [British foreign secretary] Sir Edward Grey [1862–1933] of the Berlin newspapers and the amiable and popular Sir Edward Grey we know in England. In England we are all prepared to face any world Congress and say "We know that Sir Edward Grey is an honest English gentleman, who meant well as a true patriot and friend of peace; we are quite sure that what he did was fair and right; and we will not listen to any nonsense to the contrary." The Congress will reply, "We know nothing about Sir Edward Grey except what he did [i.e., lead England into the war]; and as there is no secret and no question as to what he did, the whole story being recorded by himself, we must hold England responsible for his conduct, whilst taking your word for the fact, which has no importance for us, that his conduct has nothing to do with his character."

The general truth of the situation is, as I have spent so much of my life in trying to make the English understand, that we are cursed with a fatal intellectual laziness, an evil inheritance from the time when our monopoly of coal and iron made it possible for us to become rich and powerful without thinking or knowing how: a laziness which is becoming highly dangerous to us now that our monopoly is gone or superseded by new sources of mechanical energy. We got rich by pursuing our own immediate advantage instinctively: that is, with a natural childish selfishness; and when any question of our justification arose, we found it easy to silence it with any sort of plausible twaddle (provided it flattered us, and did not imply any trouble or sacrifice) provided by our curates at £70 a year, or by journalists employed by commercial moralists with axes to grind. In the end we have become fat-headed, and not only lost all intellectual consciousness of what we were doing, and with it all power of objective self-criticism, but stacked up a lumber of pious phrases for ourselves which not only satisfied our corrupted and half-atrophied consciences, but gave us a sense that there is something extraordinarily ungentlemanly and politically dangerous in bringing these pious phrases to the test of conduct.

PART III: WAR AND REVOLUTION

We carried [German religious reformer Martin] Luther's [1483–1546] doctrine of Justification by Faith to the insane point of believing that as long as a man says what we have agreed to accept as the right thing it does not matter in the least what he actually does. In fact, we do not clearly see why a man need introduce the subject of morals at all, unless there is something questionable to be whitewashed. The unprejudiced foreigner calls this hypocrisy: that is why we call him prejudiced. But I, who have been a poor man in a poor country, understand the foreigner better.

Now, from the general to the particular. In describing the course of the diplomatic negotiations by which our Foreign Office achieved its design of at last settling accounts with Germany at the most favorable moment from the Militarist point of view, I shall have to exhibit our Secretary of State for Foreign Affairs as behaving almost exactly as we have accused the Kaiser of behaving. Yet I see him throughout as an honest gentleman, "perplexed in the extreme" [as was Othello: *Othello* 5.2] meaning well, revolted at the last moment by the horror of war, clinging to the hope that in some vague way he could persuade everybody to be reasonable if they would only come and talk to him as they did when the big Powers were kept out of the Balkan war [1912–13], but hopelessly destitute of a positive policy of any kind, and therefore unable to resist those who had positive business in hand. And do not for a moment imagine that I think that the conscious Sir Edward Grey was Othello, and the subconscious, Iago. I do think that the Foreign Office, of which Sir Edward is merely the figurehead, was as deliberately bent on a long deferred Militarist war with Germany as the Admiralty was; and that is saying a good deal. If Sir Edward Grey did not know what he wanted, no such perplexity troubled [then First Lord of the Admiralty and subsequently British Prime Minister] Mr Winston Churchill [1874–1965]. He was not an "ist" of any sort, but a straightforward holder of the popular opinion that if you are threatened you should hit out, unless you are afraid to. Had he had the conduct of the affair he might quite possibly have averted the war (and thereby greatly disappointed himself and the British public) by simply frightening the Kaiser. As it was, he had arranged for the co-operation of the French and British fleets; was spoiling for the fight; and must have restrained himself with great difficulty from taking off his coat in public whilst [Prime Minister] Mr [Herbert] Asquith [1852–1928] and Sir Edward Grey were giving the country the assurances which were misunderstood to mean that we were not bound to go to war, and not more likely to do so than usual. But though Sir Edward did not clear up the misunderstanding, I think he went to war with the heavy heart of a Junker Liberal (such centaurs exist) and not with the exultation of a Junker Jingo.

[Shaw goes on to a detailed analysis of the events leading up to the war, exposing political ineptitude and miscalculations by both German and British leaders, all more intent to find reasons to fight than ways of avoiding war. But he concedes that once Germany invaded Belgium and France, Britain had no choice but to respond, though in the cause of democracy, not to fulfil militaristic zeal.]

[Germany's invasion of France and Belgium] left us quite clearly in the position of the responsible policeman of the west. There was nobody else in Europe strong enough to chain "the mad dog." Belgium and Holland, Norway and Sweden, Denmark and Switzerland could hardly have been expected to take that duty on themselves, even if Norway and Sweden had not good reason to be anti-Russian, and the Dutch capitalists were not half convinced that their commercial prosperity would be greater under German than under native rule. It will not be contended that Spain could have done anything; and as to Italy, it was doubtful whether she did not consider herself still a member of the Triple Alliance [of Germany, Austria-Hungary, and Italy, 1882]. It was evidently England or nobody. For England to have refrained from hurling herself into the fray, horse, foot, and artillery, was impossible from every point of view. From the democratic point of view it would have meant an acceptance of the pretension of which Potsdam, by attacking the French Republic, had made itself the champion: that is, the pretension of the Junker class to dispose of the world on Militarist lines at the expense of the lives and limbs of the masses. From the international Socialist point of view, it would have been the acceptance of the extreme nationalist view that the people of other countries are foreigners, and that it does not concern us if they choose to cut one another's throats. Our Militarist Junkers cried "If we let Germany conquer France it will be our turn next." Our romantic Junkers added "and serve us right too: what man will pity us when the hour strikes for us, if we skulk now?" Even the wise, who loathe war, and regard it as such a dishonor and disgrace in itself that all its laurels cannot hide its brand of Cain, had to admit that police duty is necessary and that war must be made on such war as the Germans had made by attacking France in an avowed attempt to substitute a hegemony of cannon for the comity of nations. There was no alternative. Had the Foreign Office been the International Socialist Bureau, had Sir Edward Grey been [French Socialist Jean-Léon] Jaurès [1859–1914], had [British Labour politician] Mr Ramsay MacDonald [1866–1937; Prime Minister 1924, 1929–31, 1931–35] been Prime Minister, had Russia been Germany's ally instead of ours, the result would still have been the same: we must have drawn the sword to save France and smash Potsdam as we smashed and always must smash Philip, Louis, Napoleon, *et hoc genus omne* [and all of this kind; i.e., Philip II of Spain (1527–98), Louis XIV of France (1638–1715), and Napoleon Bonaparte (1769–1821)].

The case for our action is thus as complete as any *casus belli* [occasion of war] is ever likely to be. In fact its double character as both a democratic and military (if not Militarist] case makes it too complete; for it enables our Junkers to claim it entirely for themselves, and to fake it with pseudo-legal justifications which destroy nine-tenths of our credit, the military and legal cases being hardly a tenth of the whole: indeed, they would not by themselves justify the slaughter of a single Pomeranian [in central Europe] grenadier. For instance, take the Militarist view that we must fight Potsdam because if the Kaiser is victorious it will be our turn next! Well: are we not prepared to fight always when our turn comes? Why should not we also depend on our navy, on the extreme improbability of Germany, however triumphant, making two such terrible calls on her people in the same generation as a war involves, on the sympathy of the defeated, and on the support of American and European public opinion when our turn comes, if there is nothing at stake now but the difference between defeat and victory in an otherwise indifferent military campaign? As mere competitors in race of armaments and an Olympic game conducted with ball and cartridge, or as plaintiffs in a technical case of international law... we might as well be beaten or not, for all the harm that will ensue to anyone but ourselves, or even to ourselves apart from our national vanity. It is as the special constables of European life that we are important, and can send our men to the trenches with the assurance that they are fighting in a worthy cause. In short, the Junker case is not worth twopence: the Democratic case, the Socialist one, the International case is worth all it threatens to cost....

Now that we begin to see where we really are, what practical morals can we draw?

First, that our autocratic foreign policy, in which the Secretary for Foreign Affairs is always a Junker and makes war and concludes war without consulting the nation, or confiding in it, or even refraining from deceiving it as to his intentions, leads inevitably to a disastrous combination of war and unpreparedness for war. Wars are planned which require huge expeditionary armies trained and equipped for war. But as such preparation could not be concealed from the public, it is simply deferred until the war is actually declared and begun, at the most frightful risk of such an annihilation of our little peace army as we escaped by the skin of our teeth at Mons and Cambrai [sites of battles fought in August 1914]. The military experts tell us that it takes four months to make an infantry and six to make a cavalry soldier. And our way of getting an army able to fight the German army is to declare war on Germany just as if we had such an army, and then trust to the appalling resultant peril and disaster to drive us into wholesale enlistment, voluntary or (better still from the Junker point of view) compulsory. It seems to me that a nation which tolerates such insensate methods and outrageous risks must shortly perish from sheer lunacy. And it is all pure superstition: the retaining of the methods of Edward the First [1239–1307, King of England 1272–1307] in the reign of George the Fifth [1865–1936, King of the United Kingdom, 1910–36] I therefore suggest that the first lesson of the war is that the Secretary of State for Foreign Affairs be reduced to the level of a simple Prime Minister, or even of a constitutional monarch, powerless to fire a single shot or sign a treaty without the authority of the House of Commons [which never formally voted to go to war against Germany]....

And now as to the question of recruiting. Time is pressing, because it is not enough for the Allies to win: we and not Russia must be the decisive factor in the victory, or Germany will not be fairly beaten, and we shall be only the rescued protégés of Russia instead of the saviors of Western Europe. We must have the best army in Europe; and we shall not get it under existing arrangements. We are passing out of the first phase of the war fever, in which men flock to the colors by instinct, by romantic desire for adventure, by the determination not, as Wagner put it, "to let their lives be governed by fear of the end," by simple destitution through unemployment, by rancor and pugnacity excited by the inventions of the Press, by a sense of duty inculcated in platform orations which would not stand half an hour's discussion, by the incitements and taunts of elderly non-combatants and maidens with a taste for mischief, and by the verses of poets jumping at the cheapest chance in their underpaid profession. The difficulty begins when all the men susceptible to these inducements are enlisted, and we have to draw on the solid, sceptical, sensible residuum who know the value of their lives and services and liberties, and will not give them except on substantial and honorable conditions. These Ironsides know that it is one thing to fight for your country, and quite another to let your wife and children starve to save our rich idlers from a rise in the supertax. They also know that it is one thing to wipe out the Prussian drill sergeant and snob officer as the enemies of manhood and honor, and another to let that sacred mission be made an excuse for subjecting us to exactly the same tyranny in England....

And here is where the Labor Party should come in. The Labor Party's business is to abolish the Militarist soldier, who is only a quaint survivor of the King's footman (himself a still quainter survival of the medieval baron's retainer), and substitute for him a trained combatant with full civil rights, receiving the Trade Union rate of wages proper to a skilled worker at a dangerous trade. It must co-operate with the Trade Unions in fixing this moral minimum wage for the citizen soldier, and in obtaining for him a guarantee that the wage shall continue until he obtains civil employment on standard terms at the conclusion of the war. It must make impossible the scandal of the monstrously rich peer (his riches, the automatic result of ground landlordism, having "no damned nonsense of merit about them" [as former Prime Minister Lord Melbourne said about honors such as the Order of the Garter]) proclaiming the official weekly allowance for the child of the British soldier in the trenches. That allowance is eighteen pence, being less than one third of the standard allowance for an illegitimate child under an affiliation order. And the Labor Party must deprive the German bullet of its present double effect in killing an Englishman in France and simultaneously reducing his widow's subsistence to seven-and-sixpence a week. Until this is done, we are simply provoking Providence to destroy us.

I wish I could say that it is hardly necessary to add that Trade Unionism must be instituted in the Army, so that there shall be accredited secretaries in the field to act as a competent medium of communication between the men on service and the political representatives of their class at the War Office (for I shall propose this representative innovation presently). It will shock our colonels; but I know of no bodies of men for whom repeated and violent shocking is more needed and more likely to prove salutary than the regimental messes of the British army. One rather pleasant shock in store for them is the discovery that an officer and a gentleman, whose sole professional interest is the honor and welfare of his country, and who is bound to the mystical equality of life-and-death duty for all alike, will get on much more easily with a Trade Union secretary than a commercial employer whose aim is simply private profit and who regards every penny added to the wages of his employees as a penny taken off his own income. Howbeit, whether the colonels like it or not—that is, whether they have become accustomed to it or not—it has to come, and its protection from Junker prejudice is another duty of the Labor Party. The Party as a purely political body must demand that the defender of his country shall retain his full civil rights unimpaired; that the unnecessary, mischievous, dishonorable and tyrannical slave code called military law, which at its most savagely stern point produced only [the Duke of] Wellington's complaint that "it is impossible to get a command obeyed in the British army," be carted away to the rubbish heap of exploded superstitions [Wellington, 1769–1852, famously defeated Napoleon at the Battle of Waterloo in 1815]; and that if Englishmen are not to be allowed to serve their country in the field as freely as they do in the numerous civil industries in which neglect and indiscipline are as dangerous as they are in war, their leaders and Parliamentary representatives will not recommend them to serve at all. In wartime these things may not matter: discipline either goes by the board or keeps itself under the pressure of the enemy's cannon; and bullying sergeants and insolent officers have something else to do than to provoke men they dislike into striking them and then reporting them for two years hard labor without trial by jury. In battle such officers are between two fires. But soldiers are not always, or even often, at war; and the dishonor of abdicating dearly-bought rights and liberties is a stain both on war and peace. Now is the time to get rid of that stain. If any officer cannot command men without it, as civilians and police inspectors do, that officer has mistaken his profession and had better come home.

Another matter needs to be dealt with at the same time. There are immense numbers of atheists in this country; and though most of them, like the Kaiser, regard themselves as devout Christians, the best are intellectually honest enough to object to profess beliefs they do not hold, especially in the solemn act of dedicating themselves to death in the service of their country....

...[A]ll these oaths [to God and the King] are obstructive and useless institutions. No recruit will hesitate to pledge his word of honor to fight to the death for his country or for a cause with which he sympathizes; and that is all we require. There is no need to drag in Almighty God and no need to drag in the King. Many an Irishman, many a colonial Republican, many an American volunteer who would fight against the Prussian monarchy shoulder to shoulder with the French

PART III: WAR AND REVOLUTION

Republicans with a will, would rather not pretend to do it out of devotion to the British throne. To vanquish Prussia in this war we need the active aid or the sympathy of every Republican in the world. America, for instance, sympathizes with England, but classes the King with the Kaiser as an obsolete institution....

The Labor Party should also set its face firmly against the abandonment of Red Cross work and finance, or the support of soldiers' families, or the patrolling of the streets, to amateurs who regard the war as a wholesome patriotic exercise, or as the latest amusement in the way of charity bazaars, or as a fountain of self-righteousness. Civil volunteering is needed urgently enough: one of the difficulties of war is that it creates in certain departments a demand so abnormal that no peace establishment can cope with it. But the volunteers should be disciplined and paid: we are not so poor that we need spunge on anyone.... No charity and no amateur anarchy and incompetence should be tolerated.

[Shaw insists throughout Common Sense About the War *that the interests of the working class not be ignored. This included not discharging them from the armed forces until suitable civilian postwar employment was found for them, and that political debate and civil liberties continue during the war, despite the government's wish to suspend them.]*

...[U]nder the first scare of war, we shut our eyes and opened our mouths to every folly. For example, there was a cry for the suspension of all controversy in the face of the national danger. Now the only way to suspend controversial questions during a period of intense activity in the very departments in which the controversy has arisen is to allow them all to be begged. Perhaps I should not object if they were all begged in favor of my own side, as, for instance, the question of Socialism was begged in favor of Socialism when the Government took control of the railways; bought up all the raw sugar; regulated prices; guaranteed the banks; suspended the operation of private contracts; and did all the things it had been declaring utterly and eternally Utopian and impossible when the Socialists advocated them. But it is now proposed to suspend all popular liberties and constitutional safeguards: to muzzle the Press, and actually to have no contests at bye-elections! This is more than a little too much. We have submitted to have our letters, our telegrams, our newspapers censored, our dividends delayed, our trains cut off, our horses and even our houses commandeered, our streets darkened, our restaurants closed, and ourselves shot dead on the public highways when we were slow to realize that some excited person bawling in the distance was a sentry challenging us. But that we are able to be politically gagged and enslaved as well; that the able-bodied soldier in the trenches, who depends on the able-minded civilian at home to guard the liberties of his country and protect him from carelessness or abuse of power by the authorities whom he must blindly and dumbly obey, is to be betrayed the moment his back is turned to his fellow citizens and his face to the foe, is not patriotism: it is the paralysis of mortal funk: it is the worst kind of cowardice in the face of the enemy. Let us hear no more of it, but contest our elections like men, and regain the ancient political prestige of England at home as our expeditionary force has regained it abroad.

[There was no doubt in Shaw's mind that Britain would win the war against Germany: "This war will stop when Germany throws up the sponge, which will happen long before she is utterly exhausted, but not before we ourselves shall be glad of a rest." He therefore turned his thoughts to the terms of peace, which, he argued, should not be vindictive (they were), but should ensure that Germany should be disabled from further aggression. How?]

PART III: WAR AND REVOLUTION

...Well, that is quite simple, if you are Militarist enough to do it. Loading Germany with debt will not do it. Towing her fleet into Portsmouth [a naval port on the south coast of England] or sinking it will not do it. The effective method is far shorter and more practical. What has made Germany formidable in this war? Obviously her overwhelmingly superior numbers. That was how she rushed us back almost to the gates of Paris. The organization, the readiness, the sixteen-inch howitzer helped; but it was the multitudinous *Kanonenfutter* [cannon fodder] that nearly snowed us under. The British soldier at Cambrai and Le Cateau killed and killed until his rifle was too hot to hold and his hand was paralyzed with slayer's cramp; but still they came and came.

Well, there is no obscurity about that problem. Those Germans who took but an instant to kill had taken the travail of a woman for three-quarters of a year to breed, and eighteen years to ripen for the slaughter. All we have to do is to kill, say, 75 per cent of all the women in Germany under sixty. Then we may leave Germany her fleet and her money, and say "Much good may they do you!" Why not, if you are really going in to be what you, never having read "this Neech they talk of," call a Nietzschean Superman [i.e., German philosopher Friedrich Nietzsche's (1844–1900) concept of the Übermensch]? War is not an affair of sentiment. Some of our newspapers complain that the Germans kill the wounded and fire on field hospitals and Red Cross Ambulances. These same newspapers fill their columns with exultant accounts of how our wounded think nothing of modern bullet wounds and hope to be back at the front in a week, which I take to be the most direct incitement to the Germans to kill the wounded that could be devised. It is no use being virtuously indignant: "stone dead hath no fellow" is an English proverb, not a German one. Even the killing of prisoners is an Agincourt tradition [English King Henry V ordered the execution of French prisoners at the Battle of Agincourt in 1415]. Now it is not more cowardly to kill a woman than to kill a wounded man. And there is only one reason why it is a greater crime to kill a woman than a man, and why women have to be spared and protected when men are exposed and sacrificed. That reason is that the destruction of the women is the destruction of the community. Men are comparatively of no account: kill 90% of the German men, and the remaining 10% can repeople her. But kill the women, and *Delenda est Carthago* ["Carthage must be destroyed," as demanded by Roman senator Cato the Elder (234–149 BCE) to eliminate Rome's enemy]. Now this is exactly what our Militarists want to happen in Germany. Therefore the objection to killing women becomes in this case the reason for doing it. Why not? No reply is possible from the Militarist disable-your-enemy point of view. If disablement is your will, there is your way, and the only effectual way....

Nietzsche would certainly have agreed that we must kill the German women if we mean business when we talk of destroying Germany. But he would also have answered my Why not?, which is more than any consistent Militarist can. Indeed, it needs no philosopher to give the answer. The first ordinary anti-Militarist human person you meet will tell you that it would be too horrible; that life would be unbearable if people did such things. And he would be quite right; so please let us hear no more of kicking your enemy when he is down so that he may be unable to rise for a whole century. We may be unable to resist the temptation to loot Germany more or less if we conquer her. We are already actively engaged in piracy against her, stealing her ships and selling them in our prize courts, instead of honestly detaining them until the war is over and keeping a strict account for them. When gentlemen rise in the House of Commons and say that they owe Germans money and do not intend to pay it, one must face the fact that there will be a strong popular demand for plunder. War, after all, is simply a letting loose of organized murder, theft, and piracy on a foe; and I have no doubt the average Englishman will say to me what Falstaff said to Pistol concerning his share in the price of the stolen fan: "Reason, you rogue, reason: do you think I'll endanger my soul gratis?" [Shakespeare, *Merry Wives of Windsor*, 2.2.15]. To which I reply, "If you cannot resist the booty, take it frankly, and know yourself for half patriot, half brigand; but don't talk nonsense about disablement. Cromwell tried it in Ireland. He had better have tried Home Rule. And what Cromwell could not do to Ireland we cannot do to Germany."

Finally we come to the only body of opinion in which there is any hope for civilization: the opinion of the people who are bent, not on gallantry nor revenge nor plunder nor pride nor panic nor glory nor any of the invidiousness of patriotism, but on the problem of how to so redraw the map of Europe and reform its political constitutions that this abominable crime and atrocious nuisance, a European war, shall not easily occur again.... And the new map must be settled, not by conquest, but by consent of the people immediately concerned.

[After reviewing various historical and potential postwar geopolitical configurations in Europe, Shaw advocates what he calls a "Hegemony of Peace," in which England, France, and Germany must play the central role. The three countries, he says, must "solemnly pledge themselves to maintain the internal peace of the west of Europe, and renounce absolutely all alliances and engagements that bind them to join any Power outside the combination in military operations, whether offensive or defensive, against one inside it." Regardless of national alliances, however, the underlying problem from Shaw's point of view concerns the ideological struggle between European Capitalism and Socialism. "Several good things," he says, "may come out of the present war if it leaves anybody alive to enjoy them." And foremost of those would be the triumph of Socialism over Capitalism.]

Socialism has lost its leader on the Continent [Jean-Léon Jaurès, assassinated by a French nationalist on 31 July 1914]; but it is solid and representative on the main point: it loathes war; and it sees clearly that war is always waged by working men who have no quarrel, but on the contrary a supreme common interest. It steadily resists the dangerous export of capital by pressing the need for uncommercial employment of capital at home: the only practicable alternative. It knows that war, on its romantic side, is "the sport of kings"; and it concludes that we had better get rid of kings unless they can kill their tedium with more democratic amusements. It notes the fact that though the newspapers shout at us that these battles on fronts a hundred miles long, where the slain outnumber the total forces engaged in older campaigns, are the greatest battles known in history, such machine-carnages bore us so horribly that we are ashamed of our ingratitude to our soldiers in not being able to feel about them as about comparatively trumpery scraps like Waterloo [Napoleonic Wars, 1815] or even Inkerman [Crimean War, 1854] and Balaclava [Crimean War, 1854]. It never forgets that as long as higher education, culture, foreign travel, knowledge of the world: in short, the qualification for comprehension of foreign affairs and intelligent voting, is confined to one small class, leaving the masses in poverty, narrowness, and ignorance, and being itself artificially cut off at their expense from the salutary pressure of the common burden which alone keeps men unspoilt and sane, so long will that small class be forced to obtain the support of the masses for its wars by flattering proclamations of the national virtues and indignant denunciations of the villainies of the enemy, with, if necessary, a stiffening of deliberate falsehood and a strenuous persecution of any attempt at inconvenient truthtelling....

The state of things would be bad enough if the governing classes really sought the welfare of the governed, and were deceiving them for their own good. But they are doing nothing of the sort. They are using their power secondarily, no doubt, to uphold the country in which they have so powerful and comfortable a position; but primarily their object is to maintain that position by the organized legal robbery of the poor; and to that end they would join hands with the German Junkers as against the working class in Germany and England as readily as Bismarck joined hands with [French President Adolphe] Thiers [1797–1872] to suppress the Commune of Paris [1871]. And even if this were not so, nothing would persuade the working classes that those who sweat them so ruthlessly in commercial enterprise are any more considerate in public affairs, especially when there is any question of war, by which much money can be made for rich people who deal in the things most wanted and most highly paid for in war time: to wit, armaments and money. The direct interest of our military caste in war accounts for a good deal; but at least it involves personal risk and hardship and bereavement to the members of that caste. But the capitalist who has shares in explosives and cannons and soldiers' boots runs no risk and suffers no hardship; whilst as to the investor pure and simple, all that happens to him is that he finds the unearned income obtainable on Government security larger than ever. Victory to the capitalists of Europe means that they can not only impose on the enemy a huge indemnity, but lend him the money to pay it with whilst the working classes produce and pay both principal and interest.

As long as we have that state of things, we shall have wars and secret and mendacious diplomacy. And this is one of many overwhelming reasons for building the State on equality of income, because without it equality of status and general culture is impossible. Democracy without equality is a delusion more dangerous than frank oligarchy and autocracy. And without Democracy there is no hope of peace, no chance of persuading ourselves that the sacredness of civilization will protect it any more than the sacredness of the cathedral of Rheims has protected it, not against the Huns and Vandals, but against educated German gentlemen.

[Shaw concluded his long essay with a seven-point "Recapitulation".]

1 The war should be pushed vigorously, not with a view to a final crushing of the German army between the Anglo-French combination and the Russian millions, but to the establishment of a decisive military superiority by the Anglo-French combination alone. A victory unattainable without Russian aid would be a defeat for Western European Liberalism: Germany would be beaten not by us but by a Militarist autocracy worse than her own....

2 We cannot smash or disable Germany, however completely we may defeat her, because we can do that only by killing her women; and it is trifling to pretend that we are capable of any such villainy. Even to embarrass her financially by looting her would recoil on ourselves, as she is one of our commercial customers and one of our most frequently visited neighbors.... We and France have to live with Germany after the war; and the sooner we make up our mind to do it generously, the better. The word after the fight must be *sans rancune* [without rancor]; for without peace between France, Germany, and England, there can be no peace in the world.

3 War, as a school of character and a nurse of virtue, must be formally shut up and discharged by all the belligerents when this war is over....

4 Neither England nor Germany must claim any moral superiority in the negotiations. Both were engaged for years in a race for armaments. Both indulged and still indulge in literary and oratorical provocation. Both claimed to be "an Imperial race" ruling other races by divine right. Both showed high social and political consideration to parties and individuals who openly said that the war had to come. Both formed al-

liances to reinforce them for that war.... It must be added that nothing can extenuate the enormity of the brute fact that an innocent country [Belgium, invaded by Germany in August 1914] has been horribly devastated because her guilty neighbors [Germany and England] formed two explosive combinations against one another instead of establishing the peace of Europe; but that is an offence against a higher law than any recorded on diplomatic scraps of paper; and when it comes to judgment, the outraged conscience of humanity will not have much patience with the naughty child's plea, "He began it."

5 Militarism must not be treated as a disease peculiar to Prussia. It is rampant in England; and in France it has led to the assassination of her greatest statesman. If the upshot of the war is to be regarded and acted upon simply as a defeat of German Militarism by Anglo-French Militarism, then the war will not only have wrought its own immediate evils of destruction and demoralization, but will extinguish the last hope that we have risen above the "dragons of the prime that tare each other in their slime" [from "In Memoriam," by Alfred Lord Tennyson, 1809–92]. We have all been equally guilty in the past.... In short, Militarism, which is nothing but State Anarchism, has been carried to such a pitch that it has been imitated and countered by a movement of popular Anarchism, and has exploded in a European war because the Commercialist Governments of Europe had no faith in the effective guidance of any modern State by higher considerations than Lord Roberts's "will to conquer," the weight of the Kaiser's mailed fist, and the interests of the Bourses and Stock Exchanges. Unless we are all prepared to fight Militarism at home as well as abroad, the cessation of hostilities will last only until the belligerents have recovered from their exhaustion.

6 It had better be admitted on our side that as to the conduct of the war there is no trustworthy evidence that the Germans have committed any worse or other atrocities than

those which are admitted to be inevitable in war or accepted as part of military usage by the Allies. By "making examples" of towns, and seizing irresponsible citizens as hostages and shooting them for the acts of armed civilians over whom they could exercise no possible control, the Germans have certainly pushed these usages to a point of Terrorism which is hardly distinguishable from the deliberate murder of non-combatants; but as the Allies have not renounced such usages, nor ceased to employ them ruthlessly in their dealings with the hill tribes and fellaheen [peasants] and Arabs with whom they themselves have to deal (to say nothing of the notorious domestic Terrorism of the Russian Government), they cannot claim superior humanity. It is therefore a waste of time for the pot to call the kettle black....

7 To sum up, we must remember that if this war does not make an end of war in the west, our allies of today may be our enemies of tomorrow as they are of yesterday, and our enemies of today our allies of tomorrow as they are of yesterday; so that if we aim merely at a fresh balance of military power, we are as likely as not to negotiate our own destruction. We must use the war to give the *coup de grâce* to medieval diplomacy, medieval autocracy, and anarchic export of capital, and make its conclusion convince the world that Democracy is invincible, and Militarism a rusty sword that breaks in the hand. We must free our soldiers, and give them homes worth fighting for. And we must, as the old phrase goes, discard the filthy rags of our righteousness, and fight like men with everything, even a good name, to win, inspiring and encouraging ourselves with definite noble purpose (abstract nobility butters no parsnips) to face whatever may be the price of proving that war cannot conquer us, and that he who dares not appeal to our conscience has nothing to hope from our terrors.

PART III: WAR AND REVOLUTION

2. From "Cataclysm," October 1917. [*What I Really Wrote About the War*, pp. 271–84]

[*"Democracy is invincible," Shaw had claimed in* Common Sense About the War, *and the overthrow of Russian imperialism in October 1917, "the terrific sweep of the new broom in Moscow," as he put it, illustrated the power of a united people. Ironically, however, the Russian Revolution, as its leaders dealt ruthlessly with political opponents, also demonstrated to Shaw ways in which totalitarian government could achieve political outcomes much more effectively than Democracy, an insight that was to become increasingly central to Shaw's political thinking.*]

The war dragged on; and I sedulously assured everyone who discussed it with me that it would last thirty years; for the war of attrition, as it was called, attrited both sides impartially, the great offensives always petering out just before their consummation, and the momentary successes producing no more decisive result than the tediously protracted failures....

Suddenly came the cataclysm. It was the crash of an epoch. The mountainous dyke within which western Capitalism had been working for centuries cracked and left a gap the whole width of Europe from the Baltic to the Black Sea. Mere writing cannot describe it; it makes metaphor silly. Nobody here had the least notion of its magnitude and significance; nor has it dawned on us yet: our elder statesmen and journalists are still yapping at it like lapdogs at a stampede of elephants. And it began as an incident of the war.

...[I]n *Common Sense About the War* I had said that if the soldiers had any sense they would go home and attend to their own affairs.... With the general reader it had passed as a pious and wellworn commonplace, of no importance because there was no apparent possibility of its being acted on.

In 1917 the Russian soldiers acted on it.

They went home. They combined politically with the peasants (being mostly peasants themselves) in bodies with a name new to western Europe: Soviets. They found elaborately educated middle class idealists like [Vladimir Ilyich] Lenin [1870–1924] and [Leon] Trotsky [1879–1940], and the proletarian men of action like [Nikolai] Markin [1893–1918], to command them; and they set up as their deceased prophet a German Jewish Protestant lawyer's university-trained son, Karl Marx [1818–83], famous as a historian of British Capitalism, and its implacable foe. [Marx's *Das Kapital* was published in 1867.] These leaders and captains, though theorists in economics and novices in administration, were in action realists who understood that the political establishment of their ideas and their faith involved the ruthless extermination or subjection of those who actively opposed them, and the careful education of children in that faith so that all inculcated opposition to them might perish with the existing generation. Their opponents, equally clear on the subject of the extermination, raised a White Army which did what it could in that direction; but young Russia rose up miraculously as a Red Army at Trotsky's summons and smashed them. English and French precedent was followed by killing the Tsar [Nicholas II, 1868–1918], but departed from by sparing him the mockery and long-drawn-out torment of trial, sentence, and formal public execution before a gaping crowd [English King Charles I and French King Louis XVI were publicly tried and executed in 1649 and 1793 respectively]. Instead, the Bolsheviks indulged him with an elaborate and comforting religious service without telling him why, and then, his soul being at peace, shot him at thirty seconds notice and his whole family with him. They did not kill their Archbishop as we killed Laud [executed in 1645 after a long trial]; but they convinced him that it was as much as his life was worth to conspire or preach against them. He forebore, and survived. They "expropriated the expropriators" as a matter of Marxian course. They took the land from the landlords and distributed it among the husbandmen, only to find later on that they must take the cultivation of the land in hand themselves as public work if its full modern possibilities were to be realized. They hanged the remonstrant landlords, and shot the drunken workmen and the corrupt overseers. To all those who were perverted by class prejudices or university education they were merciless, refusing them employment, especially as teachers, and treating them as persons in whose continued existence the country had a negative rather than positive interest. The successful farmer who had acquired three horses or more where his neighbors had only one or none they taught to prefer the general prosperity to his own by taking his three horses from him and systematically excluding him from all share in the direction of the communal farms. When it was found impossible to dispense altogether with private trading the trader was treated as a pariah, and his children denied the communal higher education (the only one available) unless at the age of fourteen they solemnly abandoned and renounced him. They left the churches open for the women to burn candles in as a weakness permissible to their sex, and for the priests to conduct services for those who desired them; but in the schools they taught the children science and told them that the religion of the old Churches was an opiate to reconcile the people to slavery in this world by promises of bliss and revenge in the next, and took care that every child should grow up knowing quite well that many of the statements presented in the Bible and prayerbook as statements of facts are fables like those in ordinary books. In short, from the point of view of the English landed gentry and plutocracy they were a gang of murderers, thieves, and blasphemers whom to destroy as vermin was a most sacred duty, whilst from the proletarian point of view they, doing those things that we ought to have done and leaving undone those things that we ought not to have done, were the sole hope and promise of civilization.

All this followed from the refusal of the Russian soldiers to go on with the war in 1917, and would have been impossible without it. To us it seemed nothing but an infamous backing out of our war by an Ally on whom we had depended to steamroller our enemies on their eastern front. When the steamroller went over our own toes our fury was unbounded. We cared nothing for Marxian ideology: all we knew was that the Russians had stopped fighting and intended to make peace with Germany. We could not stand that at any price. The most intransigeant Socialist and champion of Karl Marx in England, the late Henry Mayers Hyndman [1842–1921, founder of the Social Democratic Federation, 1881], outdid Mr Winston Churchill in his denunciations of Lenin and Bolshevism. The projected treaty of Brest Litovsk [the 1918 peace treaty between Russia and Germany] acted on his Marxist internationalism like a wet sponge on a schoolchild's slate, and gave the Russians one of the many lessons they were receiving at that time on how little international Socialism can depend on its old literary supporters when it comes to business and outrages their patriotism and their ingrained and almost unconscious assumption that our old parliamentary contrivances for shackling monarchs and obstructing all attempts of governments to substitute public for private enterprise are sacred bulwarks of liberty. Our Socialist centre, represented by the Labor Party, was estranged from the Bolsheviks not so much by its own recoil as by the enormous gap between anything it could pretend or hope to do and the terrific sweep of the new broom in Moscow.

The Russians, like most of the agents of great changes, have never quite realized how much they owed to circumstances. If our British army had been demobilized and thrown on the world without a penny or a job, the fate would have been in the fire here too. But British Capitalism knew better than to let anything of the kind happen. It was quite unable to employ our victorious and well fed soldiers after the crash which followed a delusive ecstasy of overcapitalization (called prosperity) in 1921; but it did not wait to be held to ransom by them: it bought them off by doles which were so effective that now, twelve years after the armistice, we have many ablebodied young proletarians who have never done a stroke of industrial work in their lives, and yet have more money in their pockets than their hardworking grandfathers ever enjoyed. If the Tsardom could have afforded similar precautions who can say that Lenin and Trotsky could have saved themselves from Siberia?...

3. From *How to Settle the Irish Question*. London: Constable, 1917. [*The Matter with Ireland*, pp. 153–73.]

[*As part of the United Kingdom, Ireland was directly involved in the First World War against Germany. The Irish independence movement, however, which had been gathering momentum throughout the nineteenth century, was not put on hold. In April 1916 Irish nationalists rebelled, seized the General Post Office building in Dublin, and proclaimed an independent Irish Republic. The rebellion was quickly crushed by British forces, and its leaders were executed. Shaw supported more devolution of political authority to Ireland, but opposed full independence ("separation is out of the question").*]

...My qualification for dealing with the subject is that though I am an Irishman of the Protestant landlord variety, I have not lived in Ireland since I left in 1876, and that though I have since then been occupied almost continually with the problems of modern political science, I have studied them from the point of view of white civilization as a whole, having no constituency to conciliate and no social ambition to further;

for it has been my fortune to secure by my artistic activities a public position infinitely preferable to any that political life or office has to offer. I can, without compromising that position, say things that no party politician dares say, and that even those politicians whose public spirit is above party can hardly say without too much offence to the factions they are striving to reconcile....

[Shaw then reviews the apparently irreconcilable position of the political factions struggling over the future of Ireland before proposing his solution, a "federation of the British Isles."]

Even more important than the setting up of an Irish Parliament is the abolition of the now hopelessly obsolete institution at Westminster that calls itself an imperial Parliament, and is neither imperial nor national nor English nor Scottish nor Irish, neither flesh nor fowl nor good red herring. It was hopelessly beaten by its work in the old days of *laisser-faire*, when it was believed that the secret of government is not to govern. Today, when it has been discovered that the secret of government is to let nothing alone, it has been reduced to absurdity; and the country is being governed partly by the major-generals, and partly by bodies unknown to the Constitution.

There is only one Dublin Castle in Ireland [i.e., the seat of the British government]: there are a dozen in England. When is that wretched country going to insist on enjoying Irish liberty? Sir Horace Plunkett [1854–1932, Chair of the Irish Convention, 1917–18] has not to demand Home Rule for Ireland: he has to offer it to England, to Scotland, and even to Wales, if Wales cares for it. At present the four nations are supposed to be governed by an Anglo-Scottish-Irish-Welsh Parliament, in which the Irish, though representing only one-tenth of the population of the whole and less than a third of the area, has more than a sixth of the membership [105 of 670 seats, or 15.7 percent], holds the balance of power, and occupies so much of the time of the House that its business seems to consist mainly of Irish legislation and the discussion of Irish grievances, though Ireland is in every way a happier and freer country to live in than England.

The Irish members also interfere extensively in English and Scottish business, but are so successful in keeping Ireland out of British arrangements that until very lately Irish clocks did not keep the same time as English ones. Irish laborers and small cultivators live in cottages built for them out of public funds, whilst English navvies and skilled workers in the building trade pay half-a-crown a week for half a bed in a room containing six or eight inmates, and are fortunate if they can find even this accommodation within two miles of their job. Irish farmers buy their land cheaply on English security, whilst Englishmen can hardly obtain even allotments at exorbitant prices. The English laborer is forced into the trenches to fight for Ireland; the Irish laborer pleases himself as to whether he joins the army or not. [The 1916 Military Service Act introduced conscription in Great Britain, but did not apply to Ireland.] Any nation less sheepish than the English would have cut the cable long ago and insisted on having a Parliament of its own for its own affairs.

Therefore Ireland must force English Home Rule on England as a measure of common humanity and good political sense. Scotland will not refuse a Scottish Parliament, and Wales can have a Welsh one if she likes. But Ireland will not let England go quite free: the British military forces are too valuable an asset; and Ireland has too much to gain... by pooling services and pooling rent with the other island. Besides, England, left to herself, would go to the devil politically, and her fate would involve the others. There must, therefore, be a Federal Parliament in addition to the national Parliament; and in this Federal Parliament of the British Isles, Ireland will retain her representation, and probably continue to occupy more than her share of attention.

But she will have a further representation. The Empire (for convenience's sake I use that offensive and inaccurate term) will be held together by a Conference, which will be a new experiment in democracy, forced on us by the fact that the Dominions will not stand the imposition on them of a central body with legislative or coercive powers of any sort. This Conference will be a representative body, and its business will be to consider the affairs of the Empire as a whole, and to recommend necessary simultaneous measures to the Federal Parliaments. It must consist of representative statesmen from all the federations concerned. Some of the British federation's representatives will be Irish statesmen. Ireland will thus have her national Parliament, her representation in the Federal Parliament, and her voices in the Imperial Conference.

The Irishmen who want anything less than this are clearly Separatist; and, I repeat, separation is out of the question, as it would leave England with as strong a hold over Ireland as over Belgium, whilst Ireland would have no hold over England at all.

From the moment the word "Convention" was mentioned, it was clear to those who knew the history of such conventions that the federal solution was inevitable. The British North America Act [1867] was the outcome of the Quebec Convention [1864]. The Australian Commonwealth was the outcome of the Sydney Convention [1883]. When the Irish talk of "Dominion Home Rule" they seldom know very accurately what Dominion Home Rule is, because neither in the Canadian, Australian, or New Zealand federations, nor in the Union of South Africa, is there anything like the ridiculous Home Rule Bill [1886] on which [Irish politician Charles Stewart] Parnell [1846–91] and the Irish Parliamentary Party wasted thirty years [in] ignoble squabbling, only to find, when it came to the point, that Ireland wants national self-government and not a grudged latchkey given with an intimation that the door will be bolted at half-past ten every night. What is meant by "Dominion Home Rule" is, roughly, that Ireland is to be like Canada and Australia and South Africa, and not like Egypt and India. And this means a federation of the British Islands....

This solution sweeps Catholic Sinn Fein and Ulster Sinn Fein into the same dustbin. [Founded in 1900, Sinn Fein (Gaelic for "Ourselves Alone") advocated total independence for Ireland.] The childish parochialism of "We Ourselves" and "We won't have it" becomes ridiculous when Ireland is seen in its relation to the political system of which it forms a part. It is no use pretending that what is good enough for England, for Scotland, for Quebec, for Ontario, for New South Wales is not good enough for Ireland. Ireland sulking in a corner by herself is nothing; Ireland with her finger in every pie will gather more than her fair share of plums.

One result will be that Ireland will cease to be Republican. Being a Republican myself, I think this is a pity; but it is impossible to ignore the steady resistance of the Dominions to the substitution of any stronger link than the Crown for the Britannic Alliance (as the Fabian Society calls the Empire). The explanation is plain enough. The "crowned Republic," which is the hollowest of journalistic phrases in England, is a reality in Australia, in South Africa, and in Canada. There the career is open to male political ambition and female social ambition as completely as in any republic, which is very far from being the case in London. And the control of the King is negligible, whereas that of a President might be formidable. Now, this is precisely the state of things that will be produced in Ireland by Federal Home Rule. We are thus within easy distance of the time when England, seething with Republicanism, will have the Crown firmly held down on her writhing brows by all the other members of the Britannic Alliance, headed vociferously by Ireland.

General [Jan] Smuts [1870–1950, Prime Minister of South Africa 1919–24, 1939–48] has voiced for us the cry of the Empire overseas: No Imperial Federation, and no Republicanism. Let Mr [Eamon] de Valera [1882–1975, Prime Minister (three times) and President (1959–73) of Ireland] take counsel accordingly. It may be the fate of America, with France and Russia, to impose the discrowned republic on Ireland and the other crowned republics as Mr [Woodrow] Wilson [1856–1924, 28th President of the United Sates, 1913–21] has so bluntly threatened to impose it on Germany; but Ireland will certainly not impose it on England, nor even want to when she is restored to normal political health by Federal Home Rule.

Sir Horace Plunkett, then, must draft his Bill to establish Federal Home Rule not only in Ireland, but in England and Scotland as well. It will not be necessary to consult England—nobody ever does consult her about her own business—she will swallow it as she has swallowed Dora [DORA, the 1914 Defence of the Realm Act] and the bureaucratic autocracy of the new departments. Scotland will not object—the days when no Scot leaving his country to make his career ever took a return ticket are passing—Scotland will acquiesce. The danger is not that the scheme will be rejected, but that the new national Parliaments may be weakened, and the Federal Parliament, the London Parliament, unduly exalted by excessive provincialism....

[Sir Horace Plunkett did not take Shaw's advice, nor did the British government. In 1921 the Anglo-Irish Treaty established the independent Irish Free State, partitioned from the six counties of Northern Ireland, which remained part of the United Kingdom. In the meantime, the First World War was drawing to a close, and the attention of the western world was turning toward postwar circumstances.]

4. Monarchy v. Republicanism. An Unpublished Letter to *The Times*, 22 April 1917. [*Agitations*, pp. 211–14]

[*On 21 April 1917 the* Times *published a letter from H.G. Wells in which he suggested that "it would be a thing agreeable to our friends and Allies, the Republican democracies of France, Russia, the United States, and Portugal, to give some clear expression to the great volume of Republican feeling that has always existed in the British community." Wells stopped short of advocating the abolition of the monarchy in the United Kingdom, but did suggest the formation of Republican Societies throughout the country for the purpose of liaising with "our fellow-Republicans abroad." The* Times *predictably responded with an editorial critical of Wells's proposal. Shaw responded with a letter that the* Times *declined to publish. Unsurprisingly, the letter revealed Shaw's opposition to the monarchy, based as it was, he argued, on an "idolatry that can no longer be maintained," but he didn't consider the institution nearly important enough to justify American- or French-style revolutions.*]

I congratulate *The Times* on having the courage to publish Mr Wells's letter. I have tried in vain to find the same courage in much more radical quarters. I am not, however, in the slightest degree convinced by the leading article in which you undertake to demonstrate that clever men can sometimes write very foolishly. What you have proved is that able editors can sometimes handle a difficult situation prudently. The moment has not yet come for *The Times* to convulse the country houses and the clubs by throwing over the monarchy. The monarchy is a popular and convenient institution. The persons who now represent it are perhaps the most blameless it has enjoyed since the reign of Alfred the Great [849–99, King from 871 to his death]. Nobody says a hard word against the [current] King [George V]; and everybody speaks well and kindly of the Heir Apparent [the future Edward VIII, who abdicated shortly after acceding to the throne in 1936]. Only a very small group of people, all resident within a few square miles of Buckingham Palace, have the faintest suspicion of how powerful the monarchy is, or are personally subject to its pleasure and displeasure. The people whom you call the "half-educated" all believe that England is more republican than the republics, and will endorse your article line for line as "what they always say." You are absolutely right in your view that "republican feeling has never been general in those countries." You might have gone further and said that public feeling has never been general in them. There is no more feeling against the monarchy than there was five years ago against voluntary military service. Nevertheless it has been necessary for the Government to take the extremely unpopular and inconvenient step of instituting compulsory service. If we discard the monarchy it is quite likely that the change will be as unpopular as it will be in some ways inconvenient. He who imagines that therefore it will not be taken knows little either of human nature or English history. If Mr Wells stood absolutely alone in England as an individual with a personal taste for a republican constitution and a personal dislike for thrones, his letter, which contains all the essential truths of the immediate situation created by the war, would not shake the throne any the less. His contemporary history is very much to the point. Can you say as much of your courtly academic sketch of our constitutional history?

You say that the King has far less personal power than the President of the United States. I feel quite sure that when the King read that bit of your article on Saturday morning, he winked at the Queen. Whilst London Society is organized by the Court, and whilst politicians' sons want careers, and politicians' wives want to make good matches for their daughters, you may give the Cabinet all the power you boast of its having, and give the people all the votes and all the initiatives and referendums and democratic safeguards that you can devise, leaving the King no ostensible powers at all; and you will yet find it easier to induce a Cabinet minister to tear five million nobodies from their firesides and places of business, and send them to freeze under fire in the trenches, than to cut a single button from the livery of a palace page boy. The Prime Minister [David Lloyd George, 1863–1945, Prime Minister 1916–22] is a powerful person; Lord Northcliffe [1865–1922, proprietor of the *Times* from 1908 to his death] is a powerful person; Sir William Robertson [1860–1933, Chief of the Imperial General Staff, 1916–18] is a powerful person; but I should like to see any of them dare tell the King that he is a clever fool with absurd, half-educated views. Sooner than be suspected of the least coldness to monarchy, they would follow you to the desperate length of saying all that about Mr Wells, who is perhaps in his way a greater power than any of the three.

There is every reason why a President should have more power for four years than [Emperor of Austria and King of Hungary] Franz Josef [1830–1916] had when he was a dangerous dotard and threw the match into the European powder magazine [to begin the First World War]. It is a commonplace of politics that a democratic ruler's word is better than an autocrat's bond, and that an agreement for four years can be made more stringent than an agreement for forty. When you say that the Crown is the keystone of the Empire, and that "It binds the whole of the vast fabric together as no other institution does or can do," our minds go back to George III, the keystone of the Empire that once included the realm of President [Woodrow] Wilson [1856–1924, 28th President of the United States (1913–21)] and to Abraham Lincoln [1809–65, 16th President of the United States (1861–65)], the keystone of the United States which held where the Empire broke. But it is idle to appeal to history in this matter. I could, I think, make a far better case for monarchy than your case, which comes to no more, after all, than that it really doesn't matter, as the King is a nobody. Among the heap of trumped-up special pleadings that are called history I know none thinner than the Liberal case for limited monarchy. It is not half so well supported by facts as the crude statement that republican revolutions have mostly replaced monarchical governments by governments of thieves and assassins. But neither testimonials nor indictments and recriminations will settle the matter. The fundamental case against monarchy is that it rests on a basis of idolatry that can no longer be maintained. When you say, as in effect you do in your criticism of Mr Wells, that a king, far from being any wiser and fuller of divine grace than a President, is really to be bolstered up because he is not even a President but only the puppet of the Cabinet, you not only insult the King's manhood to an extent that for a moment rallies me, an inveterate republican, to his side in pure human revolt and indignation, but give your whole case away and allow Mr Wells a walk-over. When a king cannot even cut off the head of an editor who pleads such an unkingly case for him, it is time to put up the shutters in the palace; sell the crown to the theatrical costumier; and welcome King George as member, elected by an overwhelming majority, for the once royal borough of Windsor, free at last to tell Cabinet ministers and editors what he thinks of them and knows about them [a hypothetical political situation explored by Shaw in his 1929 play *The Apple Cart*], and to speak with Mr Wells in the gate as man to man. The home truths would not then be all on one side, I think.

The immediate case for Republicanism, as far as it can be packed into a nutshell, is that political homogeneity has become a necessity of that international organization which war has forced on the most powerful existing empires. Not one of them has been able to stand alone. Germany has had the advantage of monarchical homogeneity; whilst we and the French have been horribly embarrassed by the heterogeneity of Russian and British monarchy and French and

American republicanism. The revolution in Russia has not only eased the situation prodigiously, but swept away the last hope of the survival of monarchy as a typical modern form of the State. I for one am therefore prepared to part with the throne on terms which will proclaim the most cordial relations with its occupant. I am a regicide, not a homicide. I hope His Majesty will talk it over with Mr Lloyd George; it is obviously not a business for societies and public meetings and public opinion and the like.

5. From "Peace Conference Hints," The League of Nations, 1919. [*What I Really Wrote About the War*, pp. 286–355]

[*After the surrender of Germany and the signing of the Armistice on 11 November 1918, international attention focused on the terms of the peace settlement. The peace conference was held in Paris, and Shaw, "in spite of the obvious fact," he said, "that nobody was paying the slightest attention to my criticisms and proposals," offered his advice in a long essay, "Peace Conference Hints," published as a pamphlet on 12 March 1919, and subsequently as part of* What I Really Wrote About the War *in 1931. Central to Shaw's approach was the need to avoid punitive treatment of Germany, and the establishment of a League of Nations, based on postwar peace principles ("fourteen points") made by United States President Woodrow Wilson in January 1918. The fourteen points included a reduction in armaments, respect for Russia's political self-determination, the creation of an independent Polish state, and the restoration of occupied territories.*]

...The main question, then, to be considered is the practicability of an efficient League of Nations. That it is practicable within certain limits, and that those limits will not disable it as a bar to any renewal of Armageddon in Europe and North America, I hope to demonstrate convincingly....

[*The "certain limits" that Shaw had in mind were far more restrictive than the global, multicultural inclusiveness of the United Nations, the successor to the League of Nations, but they were, Shaw believed, necessary for an effective means of preventing further conflict among western nations, and did not preclude other political and cultural groupings from forming similar organizations of their own.*]

But there must be much more than pledges between the constituents of the League of Nations. They must form a supernational legislature, and set up a supernational tribunal, exactly as the United States had to set up a superstate legislature [i.e., Congress] and a superstate tribunal [i.e., the Supreme Court]. To put it in more intimate terms, they must have, for affairs wider than their national affairs, a common legislature and a common tribunal. Now people cannot have a common legislature and a common court of justice unless they have common ideas of right and wrong, law and justice. They must have a common language, however its dialects may vary from English to French, and from German to Swedish. They may have half a dozen different words for justice, or for wife, or for God, or for honor, or for humanity; but unless the different words mean pretty nearly the same thing, no common legislature or tribunal is possible. Attempts at common action between people who believe in fifty gods and make human sacrifices to them and people who believe in one god or in no god will not work. People to whom women are mere breeding cattle to be bought by the dozen if a man can afford so many will not get on with people to whom women are wives and mothers in the western sense. Nations on whose territory it is an offence punishable by torture and death for a laborer to criticize the Government can have nothing in common politically with nations in which every man has a vote, and may vituperate his rulers with tongue and pen to his heart's content. Nations which cannot inter-

PART III: WAR AND REVOLUTION

marry without a strong sense of miscegenation will hardly arrive at laws or verdicts by the same process of reasoning.

The difficulty, then, in forming a League of Nations is not to get every nation into it, but to keep the incompatible nations out of it. Twelve years ago the most zealous claimant for admission to a League of nations would have been the Tsar of Russia, whose example would immediately have been followed by the Empress of China and possibly the Lama of Thibet. Their admission would have produced either complete paralysis of the League or else such a reduction to absurdity as occurred in the southern States of America after the Civil War, when the American crank was allowed to force heterogeneous white and black legislation and justice on the emancipated slave States. ["Crank" was a term popularly applied to Horace Greeley, 1811–72, unsuccessful candidate in the 1872 Presidential election won by incumbent Ulysses S. Grant, President 1869–72, and 1872–77.]

The moment it is recognized that the League must be founded on a basis of common ideas, common institutions, common level of civilization, and, generally and roughly, a common philosophy of life, it becomes apparent, first, that the materials for a League of which the British Empire and the United States are to be constituents are to be found between the Carpathians and the Rocky Mountains, and not further afield. Its constituents must be either republics or constitutional monarchies in which the monarch has much less personal power than an American President would have if he were elected for life. It must have a well developed Labor movement, Socialist movement, and Science movement. And it would have to be prepared for the formation of other Leagues of Nations in the yellow world, the Indian world, perhaps in the Slav world and the Spanish-Indian world. Human political society is in solution; and it will not crystallize into one solid lump for a long time yet. The possibility of putting and end to war lies not in waiting for one solid lump, but in the first League being so formidable, and, let us hope, so well intentioned, that no foreign leagues would dare attempt such a monstrous and perilous enterprise as a war on it would be.

With the ground of speculation thus cleared, we can see quite plainly where we must begin. Without a League between the United States, Great Britain, France, and Germany there can be no peace in the world, and consequently no League of Nations in the sense now contemplated. Anything short of this would be simply the present offensive and defensive alliance made permanent. By the acceptance of the fourteen points, and the acceptance of an armistice (virtually a surrender) on their basis, these four countries have consented to the League in principle. And it is clear that when the League is once formed and believed to be genuine, Belgium, Holland, Denmark, Norway, and Sweden will join in automatically. Whether Italy, Spain, and Greece would commit themselves at once, or consider the possibility of a separate League with South America, need not be too curiously considered; for they would certainly not hold aloof with any purpose of reviving the wars of religion against the new crystallization of the Protestant North. They would be friendly. Frankly, on the score of an undeniable heterogeneity of temperament, the combination might be more workable without them. The northern combination would be strong enough to begin with; and enough is enough. The danger of biting off more than we can chew is very obvious: superfluous strength would be dearly purchased at the cost of a great increase of friction....

[Shaw's hope that punitive treatment of Germany would be avoided was dashed by the Treaty of Versailles in 1919. The treaty laid full responsibility for the war on Germany and imposed territorial concessions and war reparations that, Shaw later contended, enabled the resurgence of German nationalism under Hitler in the 1930s.

PART III: WAR AND REVOLUTION

The League of Nations was formed in 1920 with Germany as a member, but it failed to prevent increasing military aggression in Europe in the 1930s that led ultimately to the outbreak of the Second World War in 1939. The United States never joined the League of Nations, but became a founding member of the United Nations, the League's successor, in 1946.]

Part IV: Democracy, Communism, Fascism, Capitalism

In the years following the end of the First World War, Shaw, like many of his contemporaries, became increasingly impressed by the new ideologies of Communism and Fascism, embracing the hope that he believed these new ideologies offered as Capitalism in Europe and the United States conspicuously failed to address the massive social problems of unemployment, poverty, and inequality.

1. From "The Dictatorship of the Proletariat," *The Labour Monthly*, October 1921. [*Practical Politics*, pp. 162–78]

[*Written a decade before Shaw visited Russia, this essay applauds the achievements of those who established Communism, however ruthlessly, following the Revolution of 1917, and reflects Shaw's despair with the inability of Democracy to implement political reform in Great Britain.*]

The proletariat is the vast body of persons who have no other means of living except their labor.

A dictatorship is the office of an individual whom the people, made desperate by the absence of government, and unable to govern themselves, have invited or allowed to dictate a political constitution for their country, and control its administration, and who has the necessary will and conscience to use that power from his own point of view, to the complete disfranchisement of every hostile point of view....

As the proletariat is necessarily always in an overwhelming majority in modern industrial States, and cannot be finally and physically coerced except by itself, nothing can stand long between it and such a dictatorship but its own refusal to support it. The proletariat is not oppressed because its oppressors despise it and mistrust it, but because it despises and mistrusts itself. The proletariat is not robbed by persons whom it regards as thieves, but by persons whom it respects and privileges as specially honorable, and whom it would itself rob with the entire approval of its conscience if their positions were reversed. When it falls on itself and slaughters itself in heaps, tearing down its own cities, wrecking its own churches, blowing its own children to fragments, or leaving them to starve in millions, it does so, not because diplomatists and generals have any power in themselves to force it to commit such atrocities, but because it thinks it is behaving heroically and patriotically instead of suicidally. It obeys its rulers, and compels malcontents to submit to them, because its conscience is the same as that of its rulers.

As long as this sympathy exists between the proletariat and its rulers, no extension of the franchise will produce any change, much less that aimed at by the so-called Dictatorship of the Proletariat. On the contrary, adult suffrage will make all changes impossible. Revolutionary changes are usually the work of autocrats. Peter the Great [1672–1725, Tsar of Russia 1682–1721, Emperor 1721–25], personally a frightful blackguard who would have been tortured to death if he had been a peasant or a laborer, was able to make radical changes in the condition of Russia. Cromwell turned the realm of England into a Republican Commonwealth [1649–60] sword in hand after throwing his parliamentary opponents neck and crop into the street, a method copied by Bismarck two centuries later. [Cardinal] Richelieu [1585–1642, First Minister of France 1624–42] reduced the powerful and turbulent feudal barons of old France to the condition of mere court flunkies without consulting the proletariat. A modern democratic electorate would have swept all three out of power and replaced them by men who, even if they had wanted to, would not have dared to suggest any vital change in the established social order....

Accordingly, a real dictatorship of the proletariat cannot be advocated as leading necessarily to better results than the present dictatorship of the Proprietariat. It might easily lead to worse. It would almost certainly do so in certain respects at first. It is advocated because certain changes which Socialists desire to bring about cannot be effected whilst the Proprietors, politically called the Capitalists, are predominant, and could not be maintained unless the Proletariat were permanently predominant. Consequently we have on the one hand the fear that the Proletariat in power would play the devil with the whole business of the country and provoke a reaction into oligarchy or Napoleonism, and, on the other, the belief that Capitalism will wreck civilization, as it has often done before, unless it can be forced to give way to Communism....

It follows that the task of the advocates of a change-over to Socialism, whether they call themselves Labor leaders, Socialists, Communists, Bolsheviks, or what not, is to create a Socialist conscience.... And when this task is accomplished, there is still the very arduous one of devising a new constitution to carry out the new ethic of the new conscience. For there is all the difference in the world between driving an old locomotive and constructing an aeroplane. And there is the same difference between operating the established Capitalist system, and devising, setting up, and administering the political, legal, and industrial machinery proper to Socialism. Until this is done, no admission of Labor leaders, Socialists, Communists, or Bolshevists into Parliament or even into the Cabinet can establish Socialism or abolish Capitalism....

What, exactly, does making a new constitution mean? It means altering the conditions on which men are permitted to live in society. When the alteration reverses the relation between the governing class and the governed, it is a revolution. Its advocates must therefore, if they succeed, undertake the government of the country under the new conditions, or make way for men who will and can. The new rulers will then be faced with a responsibility from which all humane men recoil with intense repugnance and dread. Not only must they, like all rulers, order the killing of their fellow creatures on certain provocations; but they must determine afresh what those provocations are to be. Further, they have to see that in every school a morality shall be inculcated which will reconcile the consciences of their executive officers to the carrying out of such grim orders. That is why reformers cling so desperately to gradual modifications of existing systems rather than face revolutionary changes. It is quite easy to sign a death warrant or order the troops to fire on the mob as part of an old-established routine as to which there is no controversy, and for which the doomster has no personal responsibility. But to take a man and kill him for something a man has never been killed for before: nay, for which he has been honored and idolized before, or to fire on a body of men for exercising rights which have for centuries been regarded as the most sacred guarantees of popular liberty: that is a new departure that calls for iron nerve and fanatical conviction. As a matter of fact it cannot become a permanently established and unquestioned part of public order unless and until the conscience of the people has been so changed that the conduct they formerly admired seems criminal, and the rights they formerly exercised seem monstrous.

There are several points at which Socialism involves this revolutionary change in our constitution; but I need only deal with the fundamental one which would carry all the rest with it. That one is the ruthless extirpation of parasitic idleness. Compulsory labor, with death as the final penalty (as curtly stipulated by St Paul), is the keynote of Socialism. "If a man will not work, neither shall he eat" [Second Epistle of *Paul to the Thesselonians*, 3:10] is now evasively interpreted as "If a man has no money to buy food with, let him starve." But a Socialist State would make a millionaire work without the slightest regard to his money exactly as our late war tribunals made him fight. To clear our minds on this point, we must get down to the common morality of Socialism, which, like all common moralities, must be founded on a religion: that is, on a common belief binding all men together through their instinctive acceptance of the fundamental dogma that we must at all costs not only keep the world going but increase our power and our knowledge in spite of the demonstration (any rationalist can make it) that the game, as far as the individual is concerned, is not worth the candle except for its own sake....

The Socialist morality on the subject is quite simple. It regards the man who evades his debt to the community, which is really his debt to Nature, as a sneak thief to be disfranchised, disowned, disbanded, unfrocked, cashiered, struck off the registers, and, since he cannot, as Shakespeare suggested in the case of Parolles [a comic but unsavory character in *All's Well That Ends Well*], be transported to some island where there were women that had suffered as much shame as he, that he might begin an impudent nation (for Socialists do not desire to begin impudent nations, but to end them) subjected to all the penalties of a criminal and all the disabilities of a bankrupt. Every child in a Socialist State would be taught from its earliest understanding to feel a far deeper horror of a social parasite than anyone can now pretend to feel for the outcasts of the Capitalist system. There would be no concealment of the fact that the parasite inflicts on the community exactly the same injury as the burglar and the pickpocket, and that only in a community where the laws were made by parasites for parasites would any form of parasitism be privileged....

[*Shaw recognizes, however, that the proletariat—especially the Trade Unions—will resist compulsory labor.*]

There is ghastly comedy in the fact that this right to be idle which keeps the proletariat enslaved is cherished by them, not only as a privilege, but actually as a weapon. They call it the right to strike, and do not perceive that it is only a form of the right to commit suicide or to starve on their enemy's doorstep. This folly reaches its climax in the panacea of the general strike, the only sort of strike that could not possibly succeed even temporarily, because just in proportion to its completeness would be the suddenness and ignominy of its collapse. The ideal strike is a lightning strike of the waiters in a fashionable restaurant, hurting nobody but the enemy, and putting him for the moment in a corner from which he will extricate himself by any reasonable sacrifice. A general strike is a general suicide....

[Shaw continues to insist that compulsory labor is the "keynote to Socialism," but concedes that the British parliamentary system will never allow its implementation.]

Such a change as this, however little its full scope may be understood at first, is far too revolutionary to make itself effective by a simple majority of votes in a Parliamentary division under normal circumstances. The civil service would not administer it in good faith; the tribunals would not enforce it; the citizens would not obey it in the present state of the public conscience. The press would strain all its powers of comminatory [threatening] rhetoric to make it infamous. Therefore, if circumstances remain normal, several years of explicit propaganda will be necessary to create even a nuclear social conscience in its favor....

[But, says Shaw, "circumstances may not remain normal," and he takes hope from the 1917 Russian Revolution.]

[Communists] no sooner took the country in hand than they were led by the irresistible logic of facts and of real responsibility to compulsory social service on pain of death as the first condition, not merely of Communism, but of bare survival. They shot men not only for shirking and slacking, but for drinking at their work. Now it is clear that in point of ignorance, incompetence, social myopia, class prejudice, and everything that can disqualify statesmen and wreck their countries, the sort of people who can get returned to Parliament at khaki elections [i.e., elections influenced by war] in the west of Europe and in the United States can hold their own with anybody the Tsardom ever put into power in Russia. Capitalism is much stronger in the west than in Russia, where it was relatively undeveloped: but though it had not reached its climax there and was in its infancy, it has passed its climax here, and is getting unsteady on its feet of clay. It may also ditch its car, and leave the most capable realists to save the situation.

In that case, we may have the Dictatorship of the Proletariat in the sense in which the phrase is being used by the Russian Communist statesmen. To them dictatorship means overriding democracy. For example, though there are elected Soviets [councils] everywhere in Russia, and it sometimes happens that on some vital question the voting is 20 for the Government and 22 against it... the Government does not thereupon say "Your will be done: the voice of the majority is the voice of God." It very promptly dissolves that Soviet, and intimates to its constituents that until they elect a preponderantly Bolshevik Soviet they shall have no Soviet at all. It may even treat the majority as rebels. The British democrat is scandalized by this; and even those who are too cynical or indifferent to be scandalized say "What is the use of having a Soviet at all under such conditions?" But the rulers of Russia reply that the use of it is that they know where they are. They find out from it how public opinion is tending, and what districts are backward and need to be educated. The British democrat, dazed, asks whether it is cricket to exclude the Opposition from the governing bodies. The Russian Statesmen reply that they are fighting a class war, and that during a war an Opposition is the enemy. They are asked further whether they have any right to impose new institutions on their country until they have persuaded a majority of the inhabitants to demand it. They reply that if no political measure had ever been passed until the majority of the inhabitants understood it and demanded it, no political measure would ever have been passed at all. They add that any party, however revolutionary in theory, which refuses in a highminded manner to take any action until it is supported by a constitutional majority, is clearly led by *fainéants* [idlers] (not to say cowards and incapables) who are making their democratic principles an excuse for staying out of trouble....

[Shaw predicts that the class war in England will eventually "come to blows."]

However, the Capitalists may very well take heart for the present. They have on their side the colossal inertia of established institutions; and the souls of the children in the schools are in their hands. They have the *soi-disant* [so-called] brain workers on their side.... Even our university engineers, receiving less than the wage of a common fitter, dread the Communism that would raise their incomes to the level of a common fitter's. This straightforward exposition of mine, which might be dangerous (except that it would be superfluous) if men were politically intelligent and the working classes had not been commercialized to the bone by two centuries of wage slavery, will drop into the sea of Labor politics as a pebble drops into the sea when a boy throws it from the cliff. Labor leaders will still brandish the weapon of the strike: indeed already the Trade Unions, having found the Triple Alliance [an alliance of three major British trade unions] a failure, are organizing alliances of still higher numerical powers, so as to achieve the nearest possible approximation to the general strike and make failure quite certain. Many of them believe that the Triple Alliance might have succeeded if its organizers had dared to fire the gun they had so carefully loaded. A word in favor of compulsory service, or of any compulsion except the compulsion of starvation and the miserable eyes of hungry children, would send any Labor leader back to the bench or down the mine, cashiered and never-to-be-pardoned traitor to freedom.... It may be that the reasons our civilizations always break down and send us back to the fields is that we were never meant to be civilized animals, and that the collapses of empires are not catastrophes but triumphs of sanity, blessed awakenings from fevered dreams. If so, it looks as if we are in for another triumph presently; and then we—or at any rate, the handful of survivors—will enjoy a respite from both Capitalism and Communism until the fever breaks out again. But personally I am no Arcadian; and I should very much like to see Communism tried for a while before we give up civilization as a purely pathological phenomenon. At any rate, it can hardly produce worse results than Capitalism.

2. From *The Intelligent Woman's Guide to Socialism and Capitalism*. London: Constable, 1928.

[*In 1924 Shaw's sister-in-law, Mary Cholmondeley, asked him to explain his views on Socialism. The result was a 470-page book, divided into 84 chapters and an appendix, published in 1928. Shaw took the opportunity to re-affirm some of his beliefs in Socialism—equality of income, equitable division of labor, eradication of poverty, equal rights for women—and does so in what is for him a restrained, nonbelligerent tone. His political alignments, however, are plain to see: "The more Communism, the more civilization"; the "rush of Capitalism towards the abyss" has gathered momentum and so, to save itself from calamity, "Europe has begun to clamor for political disciplinarians [such as Mussolini] to save her."*]

A Closed Question Opens

It would be easy, dear Madam, to refer you to the many books on modern Socialism which have been published since it became a respected constitutional question in this country in the eighteen-eighties. But I strongly advise you not to read a line of them until you and your friends have discussed for yourselves how wealth should be distributed in a respectable civilized country, and arrived at the best conclusion you can.

For Socialism is nothing but an opinion held by some people on that point. Their opinion is not necessarily better than your opinion or anyone else's. How much should you have and how much should your neighbors have? What is your own answer?

As it is not a settled question, you must clear your mind of the fancy with which we all begin as children, that the institutions under which we live, including our legal ways of distributing income and allowing people to own things, are natural, like the weather. They are not. Because they exist everywhere in our little world, we take it for granted that they have always existed and must always exist, and that they are self-acting. That is a dangerous mistake. They are in fact transient makeshifts; and many of them would not be obeyed, even by well-meaning people, if there were not a policeman within call and a prison within reach. They are being changed continually by Parliament, because we are never satisfied with them. Sometimes they are scrapped for new ones; sometimes they are altered; sometimes they are simply done away with as nuisances. The new ones have to be stretched in the law courts to make them fit, or to prevent them fitting too well if the judges happen to dislike them. There is no end to this scrapping and altering and innovating. New laws are made to compel people to do things they never dreamt of doing before (buying insurance stamps, for instance). Old laws are repealed to allow people to do what they used to be punished for doing (marrying their deceased wives' sisters and husbands' brothers, for example). Laws that are not repealed are amended and amended and amended like a child's knickers [breeches] until there is hardly a shred of the first stuff left. At the elections some candidates get votes by promising to make new laws or to get rid of old ones, and others by promising to keep things just as they are. This is impossible. Things will not stay as they are....

That is why you must approach the question as an unsettled one, with your mind as open as you can get it. And it is from my own experience in dealing with such questions that I strongly advise you not to wait for a readymade answer from me or anyone else, but to try first to solve the problem for yourself in your own way. For even if you solve it all wrong, you will become not only intensely interested in it, but much better able to understand and appreciate the right solution when it comes along.

Dividing-Up

Everybody knows now that Socialism is a proposal to divide-up the income of the country in a new way. What you perhaps have not noticed is that the income of the country is being divided-up every day and even every minute at present, and must continue to be divided-up every day as long as there are two people left on earth to divide it. The only possible difference of opinion is not as to whether it shall be divided or not, but as to how much each person should have, and on what conditions he should be allowed to have it....

How Much for Each?

...What should that share be? How much is each of us to have; and why is each of us to have that much and neither more nor less? If the hardworking widow with six children is getting two loaves a week whilst some idle and dissolute young bachelor is wasting enough every day to feed six working families for a month, is that a sensible way of dividing up? Would it not be better to give more to the widow and less to the bachelor? These questions do not settle themselves; they have to be settled by law. If the widow takes one of the bachelor's loaves the police will put her in prison, and send her children to the workhouse. They do that because there is a law that her share is only two loaves. That law can be repealed or altered by parliament if the people desire it and vote accordingly. Most people, when they learn this, think the law ought to be altered. When they read in the papers that an American widow left with one baby boy, and an allowance of one hundred and fifty pounds a week to bring him up on, went to the courts to complain that it was not enough, and had the allowance increased to two hundred, whilst other widows who had worked hard early and late all their lives, and brought up large families, were ending their days in the workhouse, they feel that there is something monstrously unjust and wicked and stupid in such a dividing-up, and that it must be changed. They get it changed a little by taking back some of the rich American widow's share in taxes, and giving it to the poor in old-age pensions and widows' pensions and unemployment doles and "free" elementary education and other things. But if the American widow still has more than a hundred pounds a week for the keep of her baby boy, and a large income for herself besides, whilst the poor widow at the other end of town has only ten shillings a week pension between her and the workhouse, the difference is still so unfair that we hardly notice the change. Everybody wants a fairer division except the people who get the best of it; and as they are only one in ten of the population, and many of them recognize the injustice of their own position, we may take it that there is a general dissatisfaction with the existing daily division of wealth, and a general intention to alter it as soon as possible among those who realize that it can be altered.

But you cannot alter anything unless you know what you want to alter it to. It is no use saying that it is scandalous that Mrs A should have a thousand pounds a day and poor Mrs B only half a crown. If you want the law altered you must be prepared to say how much you think Mrs A should have, and how much Mrs B should have. And that is where the real trouble begins. We are all ready to say that Mrs B ought to have more, and Mrs A less; but when we are asked to say exactly how much more and how much less, some say one thing; others say another; and most of us have nothing to say at all except perhaps that Mrs A ought to be ashamed of herself or that it serves Mrs B right.

People who have never thought about the matter say that the honest way is to let everyone have what she has the money to pay for, just as at present. But that does not get us out of the difficulty. It only sets us asking how the money is to be allotted. Money is only a bit of paper or a bit of metal that gives its owner a lawful claim to so much bread or beer or diamonds or motor-cars or what not. We cannot eat money, nor drink money nor wear money. It is the goods that money can buy that are being divided-up when money is divided-up. Everything is reckoned in money; and when the law gives Mrs B her ten shillings when she is seventy years old and young Master A his three thousand shillings before he is seven minutes old, the law is dividing-up the loaves and the fishes, the clothes and the houses, the motor-cars and perambulators between them as if it were handing out these articles directly instead of handing out the money that buys them.

No Wealth without Work

Before there can be any wealth to divide-up, there must be labor at work. There can be no loaves without farmers and bakers. There are a few little islands thousands of miles away where men and women can lie basking in the sun and live on the cocoa-nuts the monkeys throw down to them. But for us there is no such possibility. Without incessant daily labor we should starve. If anyone is idle someone else must be working for both or there would be nothing for either of them to eat. That was why St Paul said [in Thessalonians 3:10] "If a man will not work neither shall he eat." The burden of labor is imposed on us by Nature, and it has to be divided-up as well as the wealth it produces.

But the two divisions need not correspond to one another. One person can produce much more than enough to feed herself. Otherwise the young children could not be fed; and the old people who are past work would starve. Many a woman with nothing to help her but her two hands has brought up a family on her own earnings, and kept her aged parents into the bargain, besides making rent for a ground landlord as well. And with the help of water power, steam power, electric power, and modern machinery, labor can be so organized that one woman can turn out more than a thousand women could turn out 150 years ago.

This saving labor by harnessing machines to natural forces, like wind and water and the heat latent in coal, produces leisure, which also has to be divided-up. If one person's labor for ten hours can support ten persons for a day, the ten can arrange in several different ways. They can put the ten hours work on one person and let the other nine have all the leisure as well as free rations. Or they can each do one hour's work a day and each have nine hours leisure. Or they can have anything between these extremes. They can also arrange that three of them shall work ten hours a day each, producing enough for thirty people, so that the other seven will not only have nothing to do, but will be able to eat enough for fourteen and to keep thirteen servants to wait on them and keep the three up to their work into the bargain.

Another possible arrangement would be that they should all work much longer every day than was necessary to keep them, on condition that they were not required to work until they were fully grown and well educated, and were allowed to stop working and amuse themselves for the rest of their lives when they were fifty. Scores of different arrangements are possible between out-and-out slavery and an equitable division of labor, leisure, and wealth. Slavery, Serfdom, Feudalism, Capitalism, Socialism, Communism are all at bottom different arrangements of this division. Revolutionary history is the history of the effects of a continual struggle by persons and classes to alter the arrangement in their own favor. But for the moment we had better stick to the question of dividing-up the income the labor produces; for the utmost difference you can make between one person and another in respect of their labor or leisure is as nothing compared to the enormous difference you can make in their incomes by modern methods and machines. You cannot put more than 24 hours into a rich man's day; but you can put 24 million pounds into his pocket without asking him to lift his little finger for it.

Communism

If I have made this clear to you, will you try to make up your mind how you would like to see the income of your country divided-up day by day? Do not run to the Socialists or the Capitalists, or to your favorite newspaper, to make up your mind for you: they will only unsettle and bewilder you when they are not intentionally misleading you. Think it out for yourself. Conceive yourself as a national trustee with the entire income of the country placed in your hands to be distributed so as to produce the greatest social well being for everybody in the country....

Here, then, are some plans that have been tried or proposed.

Let us begin with the simplest: the family plan of the apostles and their followers. Among them everybody threw all that she or he had into a common stock; and each took from it what she or he needed. The obligation to do this was so sacred that when Ananias and Sapphira kept back something for themselves, St Peter struck them dead for "lying to the Holy Ghost" [Acts 5].

This plan, which is Communism in its primitive purity, is practised to this day in small religious communities where the people live together and are all known to one another. But it is not so simple for big populations where the people do not live together and do not know each other. Even in the family we practise it only partially; for though the father gives part of his earnings to the mother, and the children do the same when they are earning anything, and the mother buys food and places it before all of them to partake in common, yet they all keep some of their earnings back for their separate use; so that family life is not pure Communism, but partly Communism and partly separate property. Each member of the family does what Ananias and Sapphira did [i.e., lied to the apostles about money gained from the sale of property, and dropped dead when the lie was exposed (Acts 5:1–12]; but they need not tell lies about it (though they sometimes do) because it is understood between them that the children are to keep back something for pocket money, and the father for beer and tobacco, and the mother for her clothes if there is any left.

Besides, family Communism does not extend to the people next door. Every house has its own separate meals; and the people in the other houses do not contribute to it, and have no right to share it. There are, however, exceptions to this in modern cities. Though each family buys its own beer separately, they all get their water communistically. They pay what they call a water-rate into a common fund to pay for a constant supply to every house; and they all draw as much or as little water as they need.

In the same way they pay for the lighting of the streets, for paving them, for policemen to patrol them, for bridges across the rivers, and for the removal and destruction of dustbin refuse. Nobody thinks of saying "I never go out after dark; I have never called a policeman in my life; I have no business on the other side of the river and never cross the bridge; and therefore I will not help to pay the cost of these things." Everybody knows that town life could not exist without lighting and paving and bridges and police and sanitation, and that a bedridden invalid who never leaves the house, or a blind man whose darkness no street lamp can dispel, is as dependent on these public services for daily supplies of food and for safety and health as any healthy person. And this is as true of the army and navy as of the police force, of a lighthouse as of a street lamp, of a Town Hall as of the Houses of Parliament: they are all paid for out of the common stock made up by our rates and taxes; and they are for the benefit of every body indiscriminately. In short, they are Communistic.

When we pay our rates to keep up this Communism we do not, like the apostles, throw all we have into the common stock [Acts 4:32–33]: we make a contribution according to our means; and our means are judged by the value of the house we live in. But those who pay low contributions have just the same use of the public services as those who pay high ones; and strangers and vagrants who do not pay any contribution at all enjoy them equally. Young and old, prince and pauper, thrifty and wasteful, drunk and sober, tinker, tailor, soldier, sailor, rich man, poor man, beggarman and thief, all have the same use and enjoyment of these communistic conveniences and services which cost so much to keep up. And it works perfectly. Nobody dreams of proposing that people should not be allowed to walk down the street without paying and producing a certificate of character from two respectable householders. Yet the street costs more than any of the places you pay to go into, such as theatres, or any of the places where you have to be introduced, like clubs.

Limits to Communism

Would you ever have supposed from reading the newspapers that Communism, instead of being the wicked invention of Russian revolutionaries and British and American desperadoes, is a highly respectable way of sharing our wealth, sanctioned and practised by the apostles, and an indispensable part of our own daily life and civilization? The more Communism, the more civilization. We could not get on without it, and we are continually extending it. We could give up some of it if we liked. We could put turnpike gates on the roads and make everybody pay for passing along them: indeed we may still see the little toll houses where the old turnpike gates used to be. We could abolish the street lamps, and hire men with torches to light us through the streets at night: are not the extinguishers formerly used by hired linkmen still to be seen on old-fashioned railings? We could even hire policemen and soldiers by the job to protect us, and then disband the police force and the army. But we take good care to do nothing of the sort. In spite of the way people grumble about their rates and taxes they get better value for them than for all the other money they spend. To find a bridge built for us to cross the river without having to think about it or pay anyone for it is such a matter of course to us that some of us come to think, like the children, that bridges are provided by nature, and cost nothing. But if the bridges were allowed to fall down, and we had to find out for ourselves how to cross the river by fording it or swimming it or hiring a boat, we should soon realize what a blessed thing Communism is, and not grudge the few shillings that each of us has to pay the rate collector for the upkeep of the bridge. In fact we might come to think Communism such a splendid thing that everything ought to be communized.

But that would not work. The reason a bridge can be communized is that everyone either uses the bridge or benefits by it. It may be taken as a rule that whatever is used by everybody or benefits everybody can be communized. Roads, bridges, street lighting, and water supply are communized as a matter of course in cities, though in villages and country places people have to buy and carry lanterns on dark nights and get their water from their own wells. There is no reason why bread should not be communized: it would be an inestimable benefit to everybody if there were no such thing in the country as a hungry child, and no housekeeper had to think of the cost of providing bread for the household.

Railways could be communized. You can amuse yourself by thinking of lots of others services that would benefit everyone, and therefore could and should be communized.

Only, you will be stopped when you come to services that are not useful to everyone. We communize water as a matter of course; but what about beer? What would a teetotaller say if he were asked to pay rates or taxes to enable his neighbors to have as much beer as they want for the asking? He would have a double objection: first, that he would be paying for something he does not use; and second, that in his opinion beer, far from being a good thing, causes ill-health, crime, drunkenness, and so forth. He would go to prison rather than pay rates for such a purpose.

The most striking example of this difficulty is the Church. The Church of England is a great communistic institution: its property is held in trust for God; its temples and services are open to everybody; and its bishops sit in Parliament as peers of the realm. Yet, because we are not all agreed as to the doctrines of the Church of England, and many of us think that a communion table with candles on it is too like a Roman Catholic altar, we have been forced to make the Church rate a voluntary one: that is, you may pay it or not as you please. And when the Education Act of 1902 gave some public money to Church schools, many people refused to pay their rates, and allowed their furniture to be sold year after year, sooner than allow a penny of theirs to go to the Church. Thus you see that if you propose to communize something that is not used or at least approved of by everybody, you will be asking for trouble. We all use roads and bridges, and agree that they are useful and necessary things; but we differ about religion and temperance and playgoing, and quarrel fiercely over our differences. That is why we communize roads and bridges without any complaint or refusal to pay rates, but have masses of voters against us at once when we attempt to communize any particular form of public worship, or to deal with beer or spirits as we deal with water, and we should deal with milk if we had sense enough to value the nation's health....

Also there are many things that only a few people understand or use which nevertheless everybody pays for because without them we should have no learning, no books, no pictures, no high civilization. We have public galleries of the best pictures and statues, public libraries of the best books, public observatories in which astronomers watch the stars and mathematicians make abstruse calculations, public laboratories in which scientific men are supposed to add to our knowledge of the universe. These institutions cost a great deal of money to which we all have to contribute. Many of us never enter a gallery or a museum or a library even when we live within easy reach of them; and not one person in ten is interested in astronomy or mathematics or physical science; but we all have a general notion that these things are necessary; and so we do not object to pay for them.

Besides, many of us do not know that we pay for them: we think we get them as kind presents from somebody. In this way a good deal of Communism has been established without our knowing anything about it. This is shown by our way of speaking about communized things as free. Because we can enter the National Gallery or the British Museum or the cathedrals without paying at the doors, some of us seem to think that they grow by the roadside like wild flowers. But they cost a great deal of money from week to week.... We get nothing for nothing; and if we do not pay every time we go into these places, we pay in rates and taxes....

We see then that some of the Communism we practise is imposed on us without our consent: we pay for it without knowing what we are doing. But, in the main, Communism deals with things that are either used by all of us or necessary to all of us, whether we are educated enough to understand the necessity or not.

Now let us get back to the things as to which tastes differ. We have already seen that Church of England services and beer and wine and spirits and intoxicants of all sorts are considered necessary to life by some people, and pernicious and poisonous by others. We are not agreed even about tea and meat. But there are many things that no one sees any harm in; yet everybody does not want them. Ask a woman what little present she would like; and one woman will choose a pet dog, another a gramaphone. A studious girl will ask for a microscope when an active girl will ask for a motor bicycle. Indoor people want books and pictures and pianos: outdoor people want guns and fishing-rods and horses and motor cars. To communize these things would be ridiculously wasteful. If you made enough gramophones and bred enough pet dogs to supply every woman with both, or enough microscopes and motor bicycles to provide one each for every girl, you would have heaps of them left on your hands by the women and girls who did not want them and would not find house room for them. They could not even sell them, because everybody who wanted one would have one already. They would go into the dustbin.

There is only one way out of this difficulty. Instead of giving people things you must give them money and let them buy what they like with it....

That is the use of money: it enables us to get what we want instead of what other people think we want.... Money is the most convenient thing in the world: we could not possibly do without it. We are told that the love of money is the root of all evil; but money itself is one of the most useful contrivances ever invented: it is not its fault that some people are foolish or miserly enough to be fonder of it than of their own souls.

You now see that the great dividing-up of things that has to take place year by year, quarter by quarter, month by month, week by week, day by day, hour by hour, and even minute by minute, though some of it can be done by the ancient simple family communism of the apostles, or by the modern ratepayers' communism of the roads and bridges and street lamps and so forth, must in the main take the form of a dividing-up of money. And as this throws you back again on the old questions: how much is each of us to have? what is my fair share? what is your fair share? and why? Communism has only partly solved the problem for you; so we must have another shot at it.

Seven Ways Proposed

A plan which has often been proposed, and which seems very plausible to the working classes, is to let every person have that part of the wealth of the country which she has herself produced by her work (the feminine pronoun here includes the masculine). Others say let us all get what we deserve; so that the idle and dissolute and weak shall have nothing and perish, and the good and industrious and energetic shall have all and survive. Some believe in "the good old rule, the simple plan, that they shall take who have the power, and they shall keep who can," though they seldom confess it nowadays. Some say let the common people get enough to keep them alive in that state of life to which it has pleased God to call them; and let the gentry take the rest, though that, too, is not now said so openly as it was in the eighteenth century. Some say let us divide ourselves into classes; and let the division be equal in each class though unequal between the classes; so that laborers shall get thirty shillings a week, skilled workers three or four pounds, bishops two thousand five hundred a year, judges five thousand, archbishops fifteen thousand, and their wives what they can get out of them. Others say simply let us go on as we are.

What the Socialists say is that none of these plans will work well, and that the only satisfactory plan is to give everybody an equal share no matter what sort of person she is, or how old she is, or what sort of work she does, or who or what her father was.

If this, or any of the other plans, happens to startle and scandalize you, please do not blame me or throw my book into the fire. I am only telling you the different plans that have been proposed and to some extent actually tried. You are not bound to approve of any of them; and you are quite free to propose a better plan than any of them if you can think one out. But you are not free to dismiss it from your mind as none of your business. It is a question of your food and lodging, and therefore part of your life. If you do not settle it for yourself, the people who are encouraging you to neglect it will settle it for you; and you may depend on it they will take care of their own shares and not of yours, in which case you may find yourself some day without any share at all....

[Shaw then goes on to discuss the various alternatives to Socialism, under the headings of TO EACH WHAT SHE PRODUCES, TO EACH WHAT SHE DESERVES, TO EACH WHAT SHE CAN GRAB, OLIGARCHY, DISTRIBUTION BY CLASS, *and* LAISSER-FAIRE, *which he describes as "the policy of letting things alone, in the practical sense that the Government should never interfere with business or go into business itself," adding that "it has broken down so completely in practice that it is now discredited; but it was all the fashion in politics a hundred years ago, and is still influentially advocated by men of business and their backers who naturally would like to be allowed to make money as they please without regard to the interests of the public." He then moves on to Socialism.]*

How Much Is Enough?

We seem now to have disposed of all the plans except the Socialist one. Before grappling with that, may I call your attention to something that happened in our examination of most of the others. We were trying to find out a sound plan of distributing money; and every time we proposed to distribute it according to personal merit or achievement or dignity or individual quality of any sort the plan reduced itself to absurdity. When we tried to establish a relation between money and work we were beaten: it could not be done. When we tried to establish a relation between money and character we were beaten. When we tried to establish a relation between money and the dignity that gives authority we were beaten. And when we gave it up as a bad job and thought of leaving things as they are we found that they would not stay as they are.

Let us then consider for a moment what any plan must do to be acceptable. And first, as everybody except the Franciscan Friars and the Poor Clares [Roman Catholic orders committed to a vow of poverty] will say that no plan will be acceptable unless it abolishes poverty (and even Franciscan poverty must be voluntary and not compelled) let us study poverty for a moment....

Such poverty as we have today in all our great cities degrades the poor, and infects with its degradation the whole neighborhood in which they live. And whatever can degrade a neighborhood can degrade a country and a continent and finally the whole civilized world, which is only a large neighborhood. Its bad effects cannot be escaped by the rich. When poverty produces outbreaks of virulent infectious disease, as it always does sooner or later, the rich catch the disease and see their children die of it. When it produces crime and violence the rich go in fear of both, and are put to a good deal of expense to protect their persons and property. When it produces bad manners and bad language the children of the rich pick them up no matter how carefully they are secluded; and such seclusion as they get does them more harm than good. If poor and pretty young women find, as they do, that they can make more money by vice than by honest work, they will poison the blood of rich young men who, when they marry, will infect their wives and children, and cause them all sorts of bodily troubles, sometimes ending in disfigurement and blindness and death, and always doing them more or less mischief. The old notion that people can "keep themselves to themselves" and not be touched by what is happening to their neighbors, or even to the people who live a hundred miles off, is a most dangerous mistake. The saying that we are members one of another is not a mere pious formula to be repeated in church without any meaning: it is a literal truth; for though the rich end of the town can avoid living with the poor end, it cannot avoid dying with it when the plague comes. People will be able to keep themselves to themselves as much as they please when they have made an end of poverty; but until then they will not be able to shut out the sights and sounds and smells of poverty from their daily walks, nor to feel sure from day to day that its most violent and fatal evils will not reach them through their strongest police guards.

Besides, as long as poverty remains possible we shall never be sure that it will not overtake ourselves. If we dig a pit for others we may fall into it: if we leave a precipice unfenced our children may fall over it when they are playing. We see the most innocent and respectable families falling into the unfenced pit of poverty every day; and how do we know that it will not be our turn next?...

We must therefore take it as an indispensable condition of a sound distribution of wealth that everyone must have a share sufficient to keep her or him from poverty. This is not altogether new. Ever since the days of Queen Elizabeth [1533–1603; Queen of England 1558–1603] it has been the law of England that nobody must be abandoned to destitution. If anyone, however undeserving, applies for relief to the Guardians of the Poor as a destitute person, the Guardians must feed and clothe and house that person. They may do it reluctantly and unkindly; they may attach to the relief the most unpleasant and degrading conditions they can think of; they may set the pauper to hateful useless work if he is able-bodied, and have him sent to prison if he refuses to do it; the shelter they give him may be that of a horrible general workhouse in which the old and the young, the sound and the diseased, the innocent girl and lad and the hardened prostitute and tramp are herded together promiscuously to contaminate one another; they can attach a social stigma to the relief by taking away the pauper's vote (if he has one), and making him incapable of filling certain public offices or being elected to certain public authorities; they may, in short, drive the deserving and respectable poor to endure any extremity rather than ask for relief; but they must relieve the destitute willy nilly if they do ask for it. To that extent the law of England is at its root a Communistic law. All the harshness and wickedness with which it is carried out are gross mistakes, because instead of saving the country from the degradation of poverty they actually make poverty more degrading than it need be; but still, the principle is there. Queen Elizabeth said that nobody must die of starvation and exposure. We, after the terrible experience we have had of the effects of poverty on the whole nation, rich or poor, must go further and say that nobody must be poor. As we divide-up our wealth day by day the first charge on it must be enough for everybody to be fairly respectable and well-to-do. If they do anything or leave anything undone that gives ground for saying that they do not deserve it, let them be restrained from doing it or compelled to do it in whatever way we restrain or compel evildoers of any other sort; but do not let them, as poor people, make everyone else suffer for their shortcomings....

What We Should Buy First

...Think of the whole country as a big household, and the whole nation as a big family, which is what they really are. What do we see? Half-fed, badly clothed, abominably housed children all over the place; and the money that should go to feed and clothe and house them properly being spent in millions on bottles of scent, pearl necklaces, pet dogs, racing motor cars, January strawberries that taste like corks, and all sorts of extravagances. One sister of the national family has a single pair of leaking boots that keep her sniffing all through the winter, and no handkerchief to wipe her nose with. Another has forty pairs of high-heeled shoes and dozens of handkerchiefs. A little brother is trying to grow up on a penn'orth [a penny's worth] of food a day, and is breaking his mother's heart and wearing out her patience by asking continually for more, whilst a big brother, spending five or six pounds on his dinner at a fashionable hotel, followed by supper at a night club, is in the doctor's hands because he is eating and drinking too much.

Now this is shockingly bad political economy. When thoughtless people are asked to explain it they say "Oh, the woman with the forty shoes and the man drinking at the night club got their money from their father who made a fortune by speculating in rubber; and the girl with the broken boots, and the troublesome boy whose mother has just clouted his head, are only riffraff from the slums." That is true; but it does not alter the fact that the nation that spends money on champagne before it has provided enough milk for its babies, or gives dainty meals to Sealyham terriers and Alsatian wolf-hounds and Pekingese dogs whilst the infant mortality rate shows that its children are dying by thousands from insufficient nourishment, is a badly managed, silly, vain, stupid, ignorant nation, and will go to the bad in the long run no matter how hard it tries to conceal its real condition from itself by counting the pearl necklaces and Pekingese dogs as wealth, and thinking itself three times as rich as before when all the pet dogs have litters of six puppies a couple. The only way in which a nation can make itself wealthy and prosperous is by good housekeeping: that is, by providing for its wants in the order of their importance, and allowing no money to be wasted on whims and luxuries until necessities have been thoroughly served....

It is no excuse for such a state of things that the rich give employment. There is no merit in giving employment: a murderer gives employment to the hangman; and a motorist who runs over a child gives employment to an ambulance porter, a doctor, an undertaker, a clergyman, a mourning-dressmaker, a hearse driver, a gravedigger: in short, to so many worthy people that when he ends by killing himself it seems ungrateful not to erect a statue to him as a public benefactor. The money with which the rich give the wrong sort of employment would give the right sort of employment if it were equally distributed; for then there would be no money offered for motor cars and diamonds until everyone was fed, clothed, and lodged, nor any wages offered to men and women to leave useful employments and become servants to idlers. There would be less ostentation, less idleness, less wastefulness, less uselessness; but there would be more food, more clothing, better houses, more security, more health, more virtue: in a word, more real posterity.

Capitalism

...Both Capitalism and Socialism claim that their object is the attainment of the utmost welfare for mankind. It is in their practical postulates for good government, their commandments if you like to call them so, that they differ. These are, for Capitalism, the upholding of private property in land and capital, the enforcement of private contracts, and no other State interference with industry or business except to keep civil order; and, for Socialism, the equalization of income, which involves the complete substitution of personal for private property and of publicly regulated contract for private contract, with police interference whenever equality is threatened, and complete regulation and control of industry and its products by the State.

Women in the Labor Market

The effect of the system [created by the Industrial Revolution] on women was worse in some respects than on men. As no industrial employer would employ a woman if he could get a man for the same money, women who wished to get any industrial employment could do so only by offering to do it for less than men. This was possible, because even when the man's wage was a starvation wage it was the starvation wage of a family, not of a single person. Out of it the man had to pay for the subsistence of his wife and children, without whom the Capitalist system would soon have come to an end for want of any young workers to replace the old ones. Therefore even when the men's wages were down to the lowest point at which their wives and children could be kept alive, a single woman could take less without being any the worse off than her married neighbors and their children. In this way it became a matter of course that women should be paid less than men; and when any female rebel claimed to be paid as much as a man for the same work ("Equal wages for equal work"), the employer shut her up with two arguments: first, "If you don't take the lower wage there are plenty of others who will," and, second, "If I have to pay a man's wages I will get a man to do the work."...

In this way the labor market is infested with subsidized wives and daughters willing to work for pocket money on which no independent solitary woman or widow can possibly subsist. The effect is to make marriage compulsory as a woman's profession: she has to take anything she can get in the way of a husband rather than face penury as a single woman. Some women get married easily; but others, less attractive or amiable, are driven to every possible trick and stratagem to entrap some man into marriage; and that sort of trickery is not good for a woman's self-respect, and does not lead to happy marriages when the men realize that they have been "made a convenience of."...

In short, Capitalism acts on women as a continual bribe to enter into sex relations for money, whether in or out of marriage; and against this bribe there stands nothing beyond the traditional respectability which Capitalism ruthlessly destroys by poverty, except religion and the inborn sense of honor which has its citadel in the soul and can hold out (sometimes) against all circumstances....

The Runaway Car of Capitalism

...The hopes that we founded on the extension of the franchise, first to working men and finally to women, which means in effect to all adults, have been disappointed as far as controlling Capitalism is concerned, and indeed in most other respects too. The first use the women made of their votes was to hurl Mr MacDonald out of Parliament [Labour Prime Minister Ramsay MacDonald was defeated (in his Leicester constituency) in the general election of 1924] and vote for hanging the Kaiser and making Germany pay for the war, both of them impossibilities which should not have imposed on even a male voter. [Liberal Prime Minister David Lloyd George was re-elected in the 1918 general election on a platform that included revenge against Germany for starting the First World War; the Kaiser was, however, not hanged.] They got the vote mainly by the argument that they were as competent politically as the men; and when they got it they at once used it to prove that they were just as incompetent. The only point they scored at the election was that the defeat of Mr MacDonald by their vote in Leicester showed that they were not, as the silliest of their opponents had alleged, sure to vote for the best-looking man.

What the extension of political power to the whole community (Democracy, as they call it) has produced is a reinforcement of the popular resistance to government and taxation at a moment when nothing but a great extension of government and taxation can hope to control the Gadarene rush of Capitalism towards the abyss. [Some 2,000 maddened Gadarene swine rush to their death over a cliff in Mark 5.] And this has produced a tendency which is the very last that the old Suffragists and Suffragettes dreamt of, or would have advocated if they had dreamt of it: namely, a demand for the abandonment of parliamentary government and the substitution of a dictatorship. In desperation at the failure of Parliament to rescue industry from the profiteers, and currency from the financiers (which means rescuing the livelihood of people from the purely predatory side of Capitalism), Europe has begun to clamor for political disciplinarians to save her. Victorious France with her currency in the gutter, may be said to be advertising for a Napoleon or a political Messiah. Italy has knocked its parliament down and handed the whip to Signor Mussolini [who became absolute ruler of Italy in 1925] to thrash Italian democracy and bureaucracy into some sort of order and efficiency. In Spain the king [Alfonso XIII] and military commander-in-chief have refused to stand any more democratic nonsense, and taken the law into their own hands. In Russia a minority of devoted Marxists maintain by sheer force such government as it is possible in the teeth of an intensely recalcitrant peasantry. In England... our inability to govern ourselves lands us in such a mess that we hand the job over to any person strong enough to undertake it; and then our unwillingness to be governed at all makes us turn against the strong person, the Cromwell or the Mussolini, as an intolerable tyrant, and relapse into the condition of Bunyan's Simple, Sloth, and Presumption [in John Bunyan's 1678 allegory *The Pilgrim's Progress*] the moment his back is turned or his body buried. We clamor for a despotic discipline out of the miseries of our anarchy, and, when we get it, clamor out of the severe regulation of our law and order for what we call liberty. At each blind rush from one extreme to the other we empty the baby out with the bath[water], learning nothing from our experience, and furnishing examples of the abuses of power and the horrors of liberty without ascertaining the limits of either....

3. From the Preface to *The Apple Cart*, 1930. [*The Bodley Head Bernard Shaw*, VI:249–79]

[*Shaw's increasing skepticism about the ability of democratic parliamentary systems to free society from the stranglehold of Capitalism—he advocates reform "that will make a complete revolution in our political machinery and procedure"—is addressed in this extract from the preface to his play* The Apple Cart *and in the accompanying text of a 1929 BBC radio broadcast.*]

...On the subject of Democracy generally I have nothing to say that can take the problem farther than I have already carried it in my *Intelligent Woman's Guide to Socialism and Capitalism*. We have to solve two inseparable main problems: the economic problem of how to produce and distribute our subsistence, and the political problem of how to select our rulers and prevent them from abusing their authority in their own interests or those of their class or religion. Our solution of the economic problem is the Capitalist system, which achieves miracles in production, but fails so ludicrously and disastrously to distribute its products rationally, or to produce in the order of social need, that it is always complaining of being paralysed by its "overproduction" of things of which millions of us stand in desperate want. Our solution of the political problem is Votes for Everybody and Every Authority Elected by Vote, an expedient originally devised to prevent rulers from tyrannizing by the very effectual method of preventing them from doing anything, and thus leaving everything to irresponsible enterprise. But as private enterprise will do nothing that is not profitable to its little self, and the very existence of civilization now depends on the swift and unhampered public execution of enterprises that supersede private enterprise and are not merely profitable but vitally necessary to the whole community, this purely inhibitive check on tyranny has become a stranglehold on genuine democracy. Its painfully evolved machinery of parliament and Party System and Cabinet is so effective in obstruction that we take thirty years by constitutional methods to do thirty minutes work, and shall presently be forced to clear up thirty years arrears in thirty minutes by unconstitutional ones unless we pass a Reform Bill that will make a complete revolution in our political machinery and procedure. When we see parliaments like ours kicked into the gutter by dictators, both in kingdoms and republics, it is foolish to wait until the dictator dies or collapses, and then do nothing but pick the poor old things up and try to scrape the mud off them: the only sane course is to take the step by which the dictatorship could have been anticipated and averted, and construct a political system for rapid positive work instead of slow nugatory work, made to fit into the twentieth century instead of into the sixteenth.

Until we face this task and accomplish it we shall not be able to produce electorates capable of doing anything by their votes except pave the way to their own destruction. An election at present, considered as a means of selecting the best qualified rulers, is so absurd that if the last dozen parliaments had consisted of the candidates who were at the foot of the poll instead of those who were at the head of it there is no reason to suppose that we should have been a step more or less advanced than we are today. In neither case would the electorate have had any real choice of representatives.... As it is, the voters have no real choice of candidates: they have to take what they can get and make the best of it according to their lights, which is often the worst of it by the light of heaven. By chance rather than by judgment they find themselves represented in parliament by a fortunate proportion of reasonably honest and public spirited persons who happen to be also successful public speakers. The rest are in parliament because they can afford it and have a fancy for it or an interest in it.

[Shaw then prints the text of a BBC Radio talk on Democracy that he gave on 14 October 1929.]

...Democracy, as you know it, is seldom more than a long word beginning with a capital letter, which we accept reverently or disparage contemptuously without asking any questions. Now we should never accept anything reverently until we have asked it a great many very searching questions... [and] I am going to ask you to begin our study of Democracy by considering it first as a big balloon, filled with gas or hot air, and sent up so that you shall be kept looking at the sky whilst other people are picking your pockets. When the balloon comes down to earth every five years or so you are invited to get into the basket if you can throw out one of the people who are sitting tightly in it; but as you can afford neither the time nor the money, and there are forty millions of you and hardly room for six hundred in the basket, the balloon goes up again with very much the same lot in it and leaves you where you were before. I think you will admit that the balloon as an image of Democracy corresponds to the parliamentary facts.

Now let us examine a more poetic conception of Democracy. Abraham Lincoln is represented as standing amid the carnage of the battlefield of Gettysburg, and declaring that all that slaughter of Americans by Americans occurred in order that Democracy, defined as government *of* the people *for* the people *by* the people, should not perish from the earth. Let us pick this famous peroration to pieces and see what there really is inside it....

...Number One: Government *of* the people: that, evidently, is necessary: a human community can no more exist without a government than a human being can exist without a co-ordinated control of its breathing and blood circulation. Number Two: Government *for* the people, is most important. Dean [William] Inge [1860–1954, Dean of St Paul's Cathedral] put it perfectly for us [in a prior BBC broadcast] when he called Democracy a form of society which means equal consideration for all. He added that it is a Christian principle, and that, as a Christian, he believes in it. So do I. That is why I insist on equality of income. Equal consideration for a person with a hundred a year and one with a hundred thousand is impossible. But Number Three: Government *by* the people is a different matter. All the monarchs, all the tyrants, all the dictators, all the Diehard Tories are agreed that we must be governed. Democrats like the Dean and myself are agreed that we must be governed with equal consideration for everybody. But we repudiate Number Three on the ground that the people cannot govern. The thing is a physical impossibility. Every citizen cannot be a ruler any more than every boy can be an engine driver or a pirate king. A nation of prime ministers or dictators is as absurd as an army of field marshals. Government by the people is not and never can be a reality: it is only a cry by which demagogues humbug us into voting for them. If you doubt this—if you ask me "Why should not the people make their own laws?" I need only ask you "Why should not the people write their own plays?" They cannot. It is much easier to write a good play than to make a good law. And there are not a hundred men in the world who can write a play good enough to stand daily wear and tear as long as a law must....

Democracy, then, cannot be government by the people: it can only be government by consent of the governed. Unfortunately, when democratic statesmen propose to govern us by our own consent they find that we don't want to be governed at all, and that we regard rates and taxes and rents and death duties as intolerable burdens. What we want to know is how little government we can get along with without being murdered in our beds. That question cannot be answered until we have explained what we mean by getting along. Savages manage to get along. Unruly Arabs and Tartars get along. The only rule in the matter is that the civilized way of getting along is the way of corporate action, not individual action; and corporate action involves more government than individual action.

Thus government, which used to be a comparatively simple affair, today has to manage an enormous development of Socialism and Communism. Our industrial and social life is set in a huge communistic framework of public roadways, streets, bridges, water supplies, power supplies, lighting, tramways, schools, dockyards, and public aids and conveniences, employing a prodigious army of police, inspectors, teachers, and officials of all grades in hundreds of departments. We have found by bitter experience that it is impossible to trust factories, workshops, and mines to private management. Only by stern laws enforced by constant inspection have we stopped the monstrous waste of human life and welfare it cost when it was left uncontrolled by the Government. During the war our attempt to leave the munitioning of the army to private enterprise led us to the verge of defeat and caused an appalling slaughter of our soldiers. When the Government took the work out of private hands and had it done in national factories it was at once successful. The private firms were still allowed to do what little they could; but they had to be taught to do it economically, and to keep their accounts properly, by Government officials. Our big capitalist enterprises now run to the Government for help as a lamb runs to its mother. They cannot even make an extension of the Tube railway in London without Government aid. Unassisted private capitalism is breaking down or getting left behind in all directions. If all our Socialism and Communism and the drastic taxation of unearned incomes which finances it were to stop, our private enterprises would drop like shot stags, and we should all be dead in a month. When [Conservative politician and Prime Minister] Mr [Stanley] Baldwin [1867–1947] tried to win the last election [1929] by declaring that Socialism had been a failure whenever and wherever it had been tried, Socialism went over him like a steam roller and handed his office to a Socialist Prime Minister [Ramsay MacDonald]. Nothing could save us in the war but a great extension of Socialism; and now it is clear enough that only still greater extensions of it can repair the ravages of the war and keep pace with the growing requirements of civilization.

What we have to ask ourselves, then, is not whether we will have Socialism and Communism or not, but whether Democracy can keep pace with the developments of both that are being forced on us by the growth of national and international corporate action.

Now corporate action is impossible without a governing body. It may be the central Government: it may be a municipal corporation, a county council, a district council, or a parish council. It may be the board of directors of a joint stock company, or of a trust made by combining several joint stock companies. Such boards, elected by the votes of the shareholders, are little States within the State, and very powerful ones, too, some of them. If they have not laws and kings, they have by-laws and chairmen. And you and I, the consumers of their services, are more at the mercy of the boards that organize them than we are at the mercy of parliament. Several active politicians who began as Liberals and are now Socialists have said to me that they were converted by seeing that the nation had to choose, not between government control of industry and control by separate individuals kept in order by their competition for our custom, but between governmental control and control by gigantic trusts wielding great power without responsibility, and having no object but to make as much money out of us as possible. Our Government is at this moment having much more trouble with the private corporations on whom we are dependent for our coals and our cotton goods than with France or the United States of America. We are in the hands of our corporate bodies, public or private, for the satisfaction of our everyday needs. Their powers are life and death powers. I need not labor the point: we all know it....

Now let us get down to our problem. We cannot govern ourselves; yet if we entrust the immense powers and revenues which are necessary in an effective modern Government to an absolute monarch or dictator, he goes more or less mad unless he is a quite extraordinary and therefore very seldom obtainable person. Besides, modern government is not a one-man job: it is too big for that. If we resort to a committee or parliament of superior persons, they will set an oligarchy and abuse their power for their own benefit. Our dilemma is that men in the lump cannot govern themselves; and yet, as William Morris put it, no man is good enough to be another man's master. We need to be governed, and yet to control our governors. But the best governors will not accept any control except that of their own consciences; and, as we who are governed are also apt to abuse any power of control we have, our ignorance, our passions, our private and immediate interests are constantly in conflict with the knowledge, the wisdom, and the public spirit and regard for the future of our best qualified governors.

Still, if we cannot control our governors, can we not at least choose them and change them if they do not suit?

...We have votes. I have used mine a few times to see what it is like. Well, it is like this. When the election approaches, two or three person of whom I know nothing write to me soliciting my vote and enclosing a list of meetings, an election address, and a polling card. One of the addresses reads like an article in The Morning Post [a Conservative newspaper], and has a Union Jack on it. Another is like The Daily News or Manchester Guardian [Liberal newspapers]. Both might have been compiled from the editorial waste paper baskets of a hundred years ago. A third address, more up-to-date and much better phrased, convinces me that the sender has had it written for him at the headquarters of the Labor Party. A fourth, the most hopelessly out of date of them all, contains scraps of the early English translations of the Communist Manifesto of 1848. I have no guarantee that any of these documents were written by the candidates. They convey nothing whatever to me as to their character or political capacity. The half-tone photographic portraits which adorn the front pages do not even tell me their ages, having been taken twenty years ago. If I go to one of the meetings I find a schoolroom packed with people who find an election meeting cheaper and funnier than a theatre. On the platform sit one or two poor men who have worked hard to keep party politics alive in the constituency. They ought to be the candidates; but they have no more chance of such eminence than they have of possessing a Rolls-Royce car. They move votes of confidence in the candidate, though as the candidate is a stranger to them and to everybody else present nobody can possibly feel any such confidence. They lead the applause for him; they prompt him when questions are asked; and when he is completely floored they jump up and cry "Let me answer that, Mr Chairman!" and then pretend that he has answered it. The old shibboleths are droned over; and nothing has any sense or reality in it except the vituperation of the opposition party, which is received with shouts of relief by the audience. Yet it is nothing but an exhibition of bad manners. If I vote for one of these candidates and he or she is elected, I am supposed to be enjoying a democratic control of the government—to be exercising government *of* myself, *for* myself, *by* myself. Do you wonder that the Dean [Inge] cannot believe such nonsense? If I believed it I should not be fit to vote at all. If this is Democracy, who can blame Signor Mussolini for describing it as a putrefying corpse?

The candidates may ask me what more they can do for me but present themselves and answer any questions I may put to them. I quite admit that they can do nothing; but that does not mend matters. What I should like is a real test of their capacity. Shortly before the war a doctor in San Francisco discovered that if a drop of a candidate's blood can be obtained on a piece of blotting paper it is possible to discover within half an hour what is wrong with him physically. What I am waiting for is the discovery of a process by which on delivery of a drop of his blood or a lock of his hair we can ascertain what is right with him mentally. We could then have a graded series of panels of capable persons for all employments, public or private, and not allow any person, however popular, to undertake the employment of governing us unless he or she were on the appropriate panel. At the lower end of the scale there would be a panel of persons qualified to take part in a parish meeting; at the higher end a panel of persons qualified to act as Secretaries of State for Foreign Affairs or Finance Ministers. At present not more than two per thousand of the population would be available for the highest panel.... My choice of candidates would be perhaps more restricted than at present; but I do not desire liberty to choose windbags and nincompoops to represent me in parliament; and my power to choose between one qualified candidate and another would give me as much control as is either possible or desirable. The voting and counting would be done by machinery: I should connect my telephone with the proper office; touch a button; and the machinery would do the rest.

Pending such a completion of the American doctor's discovery, how are we to go on? Well, as best we can, with the sort of government that our present system produces. Several reforms are possible without any new discovery. Our present parliament is obsolete: it can no more do the work of a modern State than Julius Caesar's galley could do the work of an Atlantic liner. We need in these islands two or three additional federal legislatures, working on our municipal committee system instead of our parliamentary party system. We need a central authority to co-ordinate the federal work. Our obsolete little internal frontiers must be obliterated, and our units of local government enlarged to dimensions compatible with the recent prodigious advances in facility of communications and co-operation. Commonwealth affairs and supernational activities through the League of Nations or otherwise will have to be provided for, and Cabinet function to be transformed. All the pseudo-democratic obstructive functions of our political machinery must be ruthlessly scrapped, and the general problem of government approached from a positive viewpoint at which mere anarchic national sovereignty as distinguished from self-government will have no meaning.

I must conclude by warning you that when everything has been done that can be done, civilization will still be dependent on the consciences of the governors and the governed. Our natural dispositions may be good; but we have been badly brought up, and are full of anti-social personal ambitions and prejudices and snobberies. Had we not better teach our children to be better citizens than ourselves? We are not doing that at present. The Russians are. That is my last word. Think it over.

PART IV: DEMOCRACY, COMMUNISM, FASCISM, CAPITALISM

4. Fascism. *Daily Telegraph*, 25 February 1931. [Gibbs, Shaw: *Interviews and Recollections*, pp. 354–55]

[Shaw succinctly explains why he believes that unless government by Democracy can be radically reformed, government by Fascism and other forms of totalitarianism is inevitable.]

The third Reich (the Hitlerites' name for their proposed State) owes its existence and its vogue solely to the futility of liberal parliamentarism on the English model. What we need now is positive and efficient State control and enterprise and initiative everywhere. What we get is resistance to the State, obstruction and endless talk about liberty—200 years out of date.

Hence we are being swept into the dustbin by Steel Helmets, Fascists, Dictators, military councils, and anything else that represents a disgusted reaction against our obsolescence and uselessness. The remedy is to reform our political institutions and set to work on social problems with new and effective political machinery so as to outbid the Third Reich in efficiency and rapidity of social change.

If we do this, the Steel Helmets will melt in the sun. If not, no eloquence about democracy, no protest in the name of liberty will help us in the least. We shall simply be kicked out of the way; and serve us right.

5. "The Only Hope of the World," *The New Leader* (London), 7 August 1931. [*Platform and Pulpit*, pp. 218–26]

[In the years following his embrace of the Russian Revolution in 1917, Shaw followed Russian politics carefully, welcoming what he saw as a necessary and exemplary response to Capitalism. But it wasn't until 1931, close to his seventy-fifth birthday, that Shaw vis-

ited Russia with the purpose of seeing for himself what "this great communistic experiment" had achieved: "here at last is a country which has established Socialism... and turned its back on Capitalism." Shaw gave an account of what he saw and learned in Russia in a lecture to the Labour Party Summer School in Digswell Park (just outside London) in August 1931.]

When I gave my usual undertaking to fill up one of your mornings here I did not know what I should talk about. Afterwards an opportunity arose from my visit to Russia. Now, everybody who can possibly do so should go to Russia. That does not mean that a very large proportion will be able to go, because it is not a specially cheap undertaking. But I have been preaching Socialism all my political life and here at last is a country which has established Socialism, made it the basis of its political system, definitely thrown over private property, and turned its back on Capitalism—a country which has succeeded in conducting industry successfully, and in achieving a political constitution. It is, therefore, almost a duty for people in those Capitalist countries who have been preaching Socialism in the wilderness to go over and find out exactly how the thing is being done and how it came about. It is full of surprises, and when I give you a rough and chatty description of what it is, I do so with a consciousness that, if the Soviet leaders were present here, they would regard me as one of the most monstrous paradoxes, to say nothing of liars, that ever existed.

For instance, the first thing I discovered with great satisfaction is that the Socialism which has established itself is Fabian Socialism. [Laughter.] You see, you laugh, but I am perfectly serious. What is more, [Joseph] Stalin [1879–1953; dictator of Russia 1928–53] and Trotsky would laugh, because they regard a Fabian as a harmless person who is not a revolutionary. The Fabians have turned out to be perfectly right, and the system which has established itself is a Fabian system. I didn't say that to them, by the way. That was one of the things which I observed. The other thing which I did say quite freely to his [Stalin's] intense and great amusement is that it is a definitely religious system. Russia is a religious country. They could not imagine that we were serious when we said that the Third International is a Church, distinctly and unmistakably, but it is perfectly true. But I say it is Fabian Socialism, and its inspiration is a religious one all through. And here I am speaking the exact and careful truth.

There is so much to be said that I can only take odd bits and scraps to illustrate. It is amazing the rate at which things have changed. The fact that they are making a success of it is not so enormously creditable to them in comparison to us as it may seem. I don't want to grudge them credit, but you must remember that they are working under conditions which are almost ideal. They are working the machines with oil in their bearings, while we are working our machines with sand in the bearings, and the friction is enormous. That friction does not exist in Russia. Here you have private proprietors and a proletariat which lives by selling its labor. The principle of the whole thing here is that the capitalist's business is to get as much as he can out of the proletariat and to give the people as little as possible in return, and the principle of the proletariat is to get as much as possible, and to give as little as it can.

I remember going through a big electrical factory in Moscow. I was keeping my eyes open for the things I wanted to see, things they never thought of showing me. (I may say at once that all this rubbish of people who say you will only see what they want to show you is just rubbish.) I don't want to go to Russia to see what remains of poverty and ignorance from the Capitalist system. I can see that within twenty minutes of my own door in London. I want to see the best that can be done. While I was in this factory a young man, with an air of conscious virtue, was presented to me. He had an Order of some sort pinned to his coat, and he was the young man who had set the pace in that factory in the carrying out of the Five Year Plan [established by Stalin in 1928]. He had done more than any other, and I said to him, "Young man, if you were in England, and you set up about double the pace of your fellow workers, you would not be a popular character, you would be called a 'slogger'—at least, that was the old fashioned word, I don't know what it may be now—and you would run the risk of a brick being dropped on your head in a dark lane. If you are going on in this way, my friend, you stay in Russia."...

There are things which perhaps will surprise some of you in Russia. They may seem a little too Fabian for you. In Russia you pay rent for the place you live in. The Russians are not people who are strong on what you might call privacy, and if you want to understand how Russians live you must understand that. They never seem to live less than five in a room and have no particular objection to ten in a room, provided there are beds enough. This may seem a little uncomfortable to some of us. I personally can't sleep if there are other people in the room, but they can't sleep unless there are other people in the room....

With reference to rent, the difference here is that you pay it to the man who, for all you know, may go and blow it at Monte Carlo. But in Russia it is paid to a local Soviet and employed for public purposes, of which you get the benefit. Nevertheless, you have to pay for your accommodation.

If all the rents of London were paid to the London County Council there would be no rates [property taxes], and not only would this be very pleasant but there would be a good deal to spend on amusements and amenities. But in London this is Bolshevism, Socialism, Communism, everything frightful and horrible. In other words, people in London are fools and the people of Moscow are sensible people. Which reminds me of a rather interesting point.

It is exceedingly difficult for Russians to believe that we are as stupid as we really are.... But I said our people are not intelligent. That is the very first thing you have to upset. And I could see that Stalin was incredulous that people could be so foolish as not to see the points in the Communist system. You must remember this. An English statesman believes himself to be morally and intellectually superior and superior in education to the Russian statesman. He is totally deceived in this. Morally, he is really abysmally inferior. As for intellectually, what he has got at Eton and Oxford... [original ellipses] well, you know the sort of stuff. In Russia they are not only in the enormously morally superior position of Communism, but they are intellectually superior. They begin by reading Marx, and the danger of that is that it produces an intellectual snobbery. When you have read Marx you know so much more that it makes you believe you know everything, and you are rather apt to despise the man you are dealing with....

There are certain contrasts which strike one....

When [for example] Lady Astor [traveling with Shaw] spoke to Stalin about the children, Stalin turned round with an expression extremely eloquent, and he said, "In England you beat children." And I don't think anything more clearly expresses the enormous difference between England and Russia. In Russia it is a crime to beat children. And children actually summon their parents in the police court for doing it.

Of course there is no capital punishment. Capital punishment is absolutely abolished, and you can do a murder on very reasonable terms; four years, for instance, is about what they give a murderer. Possibly for a very bad one indeed it might be five. But although there is no capital punishment, there is shooting for political offences. If a man begins to sabotage, if he begins speculating, if he tries to take advantage of the system in any way to enrich himself, then the man disappears. After a few days his relatives are told he might like them to send him some food, and after a few more days he either comes back, or his relatives are informed that he does not require any more food, and a few days more they are definitely informed that he has been shot. On all these points they are entirely ruthless.

The speculator here is the man you admire. You send him to represent you in Parliament, you send him to the House of Peers [Lords]. Some years ago speculation began, and just as after the war certain misguided people here began to hoard German notes, so they began to hoard currency in Russia, and commerce was almost paralyzed by the fact that money disappeared. It was dealt with very simply. They searched about a thousand people whom they had reason to suspect, and then they shot two of them in every one of the principal centres of population, and almost the next day money flowed back.

Recalling the reports one has seen that the intelligentsia were less well looked after than the proletariat, that their needs were only provided after those of the proletariat, I was interested to meet authors who looked more prosperous than many I have seen here, authors who never even attempted to borrow money from me. And I said to them, "But you are the intelligentsia." They replied, "We are not the intelligentsia, we are the intellectual proletariat."

And the reason why we can't do anything in this country for the public is that we have a parliamentary system which is the pride and wonder of the capitalist world, and which has reached such a pitch of tremendous efficiency that it takes thirty years to do half-an-hour's work, no matter how urgently necessary. In Russia half-an-hour's work has to be done in half-an-hour, and no mistake about it. There is no Parliament and no nonsense of that sort. There are bodies which do discuss policy, but when a job has to be done it is always by a dictator. That is, someone is made to do it on his own responsibility. If he goes wrong, he crashes. He knows while he is there he must deliver the goods, and if he doesn't, he must make way for somebody who can. No man can turn round, having made a mess of a job, and say, "I am democratically elected and there is nothing to be done about it." There is no danger of Stalin choosing a man who is the eldest son of a duke, or because he met him at dinner last week.

That motive has gone. You can't discover any other motive. They cannot enrich themselves, they cannot keep themselves in their position except by delivering the goods. And, as a result, there is no fear of class selection as we have it here. And that, of course, is a complete reversal of our system. What we call democracy, instead of creating responsibility, absolutely destroys it, and the only people who do anything are those who have the corrupt motive of making themselves rich. And when we get Socialism here, we shall have to introduce that system from beginning to end.

I want to say one word about Lady Astor. She said they could not do without God, and they must come back to religion. There is no need for them to come back to it. They are full of it. The Greek Church and the Russian Church were hopeless Churches. People here are horrified when they hear that one of the great cathedrals has been turned into an anti-theological museum, but I assure I went through that museum, and I wished I could get Martin Luther [German religious reformer, 1483–1546] back from the dead. Or a group of Christians from Belfast. The whole thing is an attack on priestcraft. The priests took and took, and the people got nothing out of it.

But the point is that the whole institution is necessarily religious. It is not saying to the people, "You will have enough to eat and a shorter working day," but the people who are managing it are filled with a purely spiritual impulse. An irreligious man is a man looking after himself, looking after his own stomach, seeing that he has a pleasant house to live in, a man who does not feel that his fate is bound up in the fate of the community around him. A man who is religious is a man who is bored with himself and wants to make the world better, who is looking forward to a future better than the past, working for something greater and larger than himself. That is the essence of religion, to be working for things outside yourself, and it is not sacrifice. You are living far more abundantly because of it....

Part V: America

Just as Shaw's lack of direct experience of Russia (until his 1931 visit) did not deter him from commenting on (almost invariably in a positive way) Russian society and politics, so a similar lack of direct experience of America (until his first visit in 1933) was no barrier to his expressing equally outspoken (though largely negative) opinions on America. Shaw credited an American, Henry George, with introducing him to political science, and Shaw had many American friends. Shaw also made a great deal of money from royalties from productions of his plays in the United States. But personal friendships and significant income did not deter Shaw from fierce criticism of American values, especially as they were reflected in the nation's capitalist ethos.

1. "Look, You Boob! A Little Talk on America." London: Friends of the Soviet Union, 1931. [*Platform and Pulpit*, pp. 226–34]

[*On 11 October 1931 a shortwave radio broadcast commissioned from Shaw by CBS was heard throughout the United States. Shaw's scorn for American Capitalism is evident throughout the talk, as is his unqualified admiration of Russian Communism.*]

Hello, America! Hello, all my friends in America! Hello, all you dear old boobs who have been telling one another for a month past that I have gone dotty about Russia! Well, if the latest news from your side is true, you can hardly be saying that now. Russia has the laugh on us. She has us fooled, beaten, shamed, shown up, outpointed, and all but knocked out. We have lectured her from the heights of our moral superiority, and now we are calling on the mountains to hide our blushes in her presence. We have rebuked her ungodliness, and now the sun shines on Russia as a country with which God is well pleased, whilst His wrath is heavy on us and we don't know where to turn for comfort or approval. We have prided ourselves on our mastery in big business and on its solid foundations in a knowledge of human nature; and now we are bankrupt: your President [Herbert Hoover, 1874–1964; 31st US President, 1929–33], who became famous by feeding the starving millions of war-devastated Europe, cannot feed his own people in time of peace; the despairing cries of our financiers here have resounded throughout the world and created a run on the Bank of England and broken it; our budget shows a deficit of 850 million dollars: yours shows a deficit of 4,500 millions; our businessmen cannot find employment for three millions of our workers and yours have had to turn twice as many into the streets; our statesmen on both sides can do nothing but break the heads of starving men or buy them off with doles and appeals to charity; our agriculture is ruined and our industries collapsing under the weight of their own productiveness because we have not found out how to distribute our wealth as well as produce it. And in the face of all this business incompetence, political helplessness, and financial insolvency, Russia flaunts her budget surplus of 750 millions, her people employed to the last man and woman, her scientific agriculture doubling and trebling her harvests, her roaring and multiplying factories, her efficient rulers, her atmosphere of such hope and security for the poorest as have never before been seen in a civilized country on earth.

Naturally, the contempt of the Russians for us is enormous. "You fools," they are saying to us, "why can you not do as we are doing? You cannot employ nor feed your people: well, send them to us, and if they are worth their salt we will employ and feed them. You cannot even protect your citizens against common theft and murder, or keep your armed gangsters and racketeers from flourishing their pistols in your streets at noonday: well, send them to us and you will have no more trouble with them: people who will not make good as citizens in Russia do not trouble anyone long." And what can we say in reply but "Who would have thought it?" Pretty feeble that, eh? Too true to be pleasant, isn't it?

Well, let me give you a word or two of consolation. After all, some of the most wonderful things the Russians are doing were suggested fifty years ago by Americans, many of whom have been sent to jail for their pains. I am not an American, but I am the next worst thing—an Irishman. When I was a young man I was got hold of by an American named Henry George, who opened my eyes so surprisingly that I felt I must follow up his notions. So I tried a German Jew named Karl Marx, who opened my eyes still wider, leaving it quite plain to me that our capitalist system, though we could foozle along with it for a time at the cost of frightful unhappiness and degrading poverty for nine-tenths of the population, was bound to end in the bankruptcy of civilization. Fourteen years later a Russian named Ulyanov, better known to you as Lenin, followed my example and read Marx.

In 1914 our Imperialists involved us in a war. You tried to keep out of that war, but you were forced in. Thanks to you, that war, instead of doing what the Imperialists meant it to do, abolished three empires, changed Europe from a royal continent to a republican one, and transformed the only European power that was bigger than the United States into a federation of Communist republics. That was not quite what you expected, was it? Your boys were not sent to the slaughter cheering for Karl Marx and echoing his slogan, "Proletarians of all lands, unite." However, that is what happened. This wonderful new power in the world, the USSR, is what you got for your Liberty Loan and the blood of your young men. It was not what you intended to get, but it seems that it was what God intended you to get. Anyhow, you got it, and now you must make the best of it. I know it is hard, because you and poor old England are in the bankruptcy court, where France has already had to compound with her creditors for ten cents in the dollar, whilst the USSR, your baby, is soaring on the upgrade. That looks a little, doesn't it, as if the Russians were managing their affairs better than we?

However, you do not bear all the responsibility for establishing Communism in Russia. You share it with—me, now speaking to you, Bernard Shaw. In 1914, as some of you may remember, I declared [in page 126] that if the soldiers on both sides had any commonsense they would come home and attend to their business instead of senselessly slaughtering one another because their officers ordered them to. Some of you were very angry with me for taking a commonsense view of the war, which is an affair of glory and patriotism and has nothing to do with commonsense. Well, the British soldiers had no commonsense and went on slaughtering. The French soldiers had no commonsense and kept blazing away. The

PART V: AMERICA

German and Austrian soldiers were just as foolish. The Italian soldiers joined up, and presently the American soldiers rushed in and were the silliest of the lot.

But in 1917 an astonishing thing happened. The Russian soldiers took my advice. They said, "We have had enough of this," and came straight home. They formed bodies of workmen and soldiers called Soviets; and they raised the cry of "All power to the Soviets." The government of the Tsar, which was as rotten as it was abominably tyrannical, collapsed like a house of cards; but the Soviets could do nothing without leaders and a plan of social reconstruction. That was the opportunity for Lenin and his friends, who had followed my example and educated themselves politically by reading Marx. They had the courage to jump at it. They took command of the Soviets, and established the Union of Soviet Socialist Republics exactly as [George] Washington [1732–99; first US President, 1789–97] and [Thomas] Jefferson [1743–1826; third US President, 1891–09] and [Alexander] Hamilton [1757–1804] and [Benjamin] Franklin [1706–90] and Tom Paine [1737–1809, author of *The Rights of Man*, 1791–92] had established the United States of America 141 years before. If you have any doubt about the similarity of the two cases let me suggest an amusing Sunday game: one of your Sunday papers might hunt up the material for it. Make a collection of the articles in the royalist newspapers and political pamphlets, American as well as British, issued during the last quarter of the eighteenth century. Strike out the dates, the name of the country, and the names of its leaders. The game is for your friends to fill up the blanks. What country is this, you will ask, which has broken every social bond and given itself over to anarchy and infamy at the bidding of a gang of atheists, drunkards, libertines, thieves, and assassins? Your friends will guess wrong. When the right answer is America they will guess Russia. When the right name is Washington they will cry Trotsky. They will declare that the puzzles are too easy to be worth solving: that Jefferson is Lenin, that Franklin is Litvinoff, that Paine is Lunacharski, that Hamilton is Stalin. When you tell them the truth they will probably never speak to you again, but you will have given them a valuable moral lesson, which ought to be the object of all Sunday games.

Today there is a statue of Washington in London, and tomorrow there will no doubt be a statue of Lenin in New York, with the inscription, "Blessed are ye when men shall revile you and say all manner of evil against you." By the way, you might finish the game by looking at the newspaper you yourself are in the habit of reading; and if, as is possible, you find that it is pumping into your household day by day the same scurrilous venom that your grandfather used to have to swallow about the founders of the United States of America, you might write to the editor to hint that you would prefer something a little more up-to-date, and that if he cannot give you some reasonably believable and cleanmouthed news about the most interesting political experiment in the world, you will have to take in a saner paper, or, if you cannot find one, to read the Bible instead.

And now perhaps you would like to know what was my reaction to Russia when I visited it. Americans always want to know my reaction to the latest thing in scareheads. Well, my first impression was that Russia is full of Americans. My second was that every intelligent Russian has been in America and didn't like it because he had no freedom there. This was only an illusion produced by the fact that all the Russians who thought they could speak English really spoke American. But the same can be said of all European countries now. To get to and from Russia I traveled through France, Belgium, Germany, and Poland. In each of these countries I was received with some sort of official welcome. But in every case the official or deputation advancing to receive me was shoved aside by an enthusiastic American, beaming with hospitality, and shouting genially, "Mr Shaw: welcome to France (or Poland or Russia or Germany, as the case might be): I am an American." That is what makes you so popular all over the world: you make yourself at home everywhere; and you always have the first word. It is such a pleasant surprise for me when I think I am giving my hand coldly and formally to a native king, or a president, or a secretary of state, or an archbishop, or a chairman of the local Academy of Literature, to find that I am being embraced by one of dear old Uncle Jonathan's nephews, who has been only two hours longer in the country than myself. ["Uncle Jonathan," or "Brother Jonathan," was an early personification of America.] Mind, I am not complaining; I like it. But I don't think the kings and presidents and secretaries and chairmen do; so I just thought I'd mention it. You don't mind, do you?

And now let me give you a few traveling tips in case you should join the American rush to visit Russia and see for yourself whether it is all real. If you are a skilled workman, especially in machine industry, and are of suitable age and good character (they are very particular about character in Russia) you will not have much difficulty: they will be only too glad to have you; proletarians of all lands are welcome if they can pull their weight in the Russian boat. Even if you cannot work, and are only a useless lady or gentleman with lots of money, they will graciously allow you to spend as much of it as you like in Russia, and will make you quite comfortable. Only if you are stingy, and spend less than ten roubles a day, they will make you pay the difference before you leave; so there is no use trying to save on that minimum. They will not treat you with the smallest deference, for these Russians do not stand in awe even of an American lady. In fact, I must break it to you that their feeling towards you will be a mixture of pity for you as a refugee from the horrors of American Capitalism, with a colossal intellectual contempt for your political imbecility in not having established Communism in your own unhappy country. But they will be quite friendly and helpful, just as they would be to a lost and starving monkey; and if you are nice to them they will take you to their bosoms and tell you the stories of their lives on the smallest provocation. They are so free from all your worries and anxieties about your affairs and your children and your rents and rates and taxes that they can afford to be kind to you; and they are so proud of their Communistic institutions that they are only too anxious to show them to you.

But you must be careful. You must not count on human nature being the same in Russia as in America. My friend General [Charles G.] Dawes, your ambassador here [ambassador to the United Kingdom, 1929–32, and former US Vice President, 1925–29], was talking to me the other day about human nature: how you can't change it no matter how you change your institutions. Now, before you go to Russia you had better study human nature scientifically. The easiest way to do that is to send to the nearest glazier's for a piece of putty. Putty is exactly like human nature. You cannot change it, no matter what you do. You cannot eat it, nor grow apples in it, nor mend clothes with it. But you can twist it and pat it and model it into any shape you like; and when you have shaped it, it will set so hard that you would suppose that it could never take any other shape on earth. Now, the Russian putty is just like the American putty, except perhaps that the American putty is softer in the head and sets harder. Well, the Soviet Government has shaped the Russian putty very carefully into a shape different from the American, and it has set hard and produced quite a different sort of animal. The noses are much the same, and the chins and ears and eyes not so very different, but the inside doesn't work in the American way. In particular, the conscience is startlingly different, so that the achievements which are an American's pride and glory seem to the Russians to be infamous crimes.

PART V: AMERICA

For instance, the first thing that would occur to a real hundred per cent American in Russia is that with its huge natural wealth it must be a splendid country to make money in. Even without touching the natural resources a good deal might be made by speculating in the difference between the value of the half-dollar rouble in Moscow and the six-cent rouble in Berlin. Wages are low and profits high; so why let all the profits be wasted on the Government when a capable man can organize business for himself, and put the profit in his own pocket? What is the use of wasting good money on the public? As a deceased American financier [William H. Vanderbilt, 1821–85] once said at a public enquiry, "Damn the public!" Men make money by looking after themselves, not by looking after the public.

If you take that line in Russia you will soon get rich. But when this fact comes under the notice of the income tax authorities, they will ask the Gay Pay Oo [OGPU], the celebrated secret police which acts as an Inquisition, to inquire into your methods. An agent will tap you on the shoulder and conduct you to the offices of the famous force. There you will be invited to explain your commercial proceedings and your views on life in general. You will be allowed to vindicate your American business principles and your belief in individualism and self-help to the full hundred per cent. You will not be reproached, nor bullied, nor argued with, nor inconvenienced in any way. All that will happen to you is that when you have made yourself quite clear, you will suddenly find yourself in the next world, if there be a next world. If not, you will simply have ceased to exist, and your relatives will be politely informed that they need have no anxiety about you, as you are not coming home any more.

Now, do not for a moment think that this is a punishment, or that it has anything to do with the criminal law. All it means is that the Russian putty has been shaped to believe that idiots are better dead. Idiot, as you know, is a Greek word which means a person who can see no farther than himself. Your views will satisfy the Russians that you are an idiot, and in mercy to yourself and society they will just liquidate you, as they call it, without causing you a moment's unpleasantness.

In this they are merely carrying out a proposal made by me many years ago. I urged that every person who owes his life to civilized society, and who has enjoyed since his childhood all its very costly protections and advantages, should appear at reasonable intervals before a properly qualified jury to justify his existence, which should be summarily and painlessly terminated if he fails to justify it, and is either a positive nuisance or more trouble than he is worth. Nothing less will make people really responsible citizens, and a great part of the secret of the success of Russian Communism is that every Russian knows that unless he makes his life a paying proposition for his countrymen he will probably lose it.

I am proud to have been the first to advocate this most necessary reform [in page 175 1921]. A well-kept garden must be weeded. So you must be careful.

To console you, let me assure you that if you lose your temper in Russia you need not fear the sort of savagery with which we treat our criminals. If you happen to kill somebody in an honest and natural way you will not be hanged nor roasted in the electric chair, for capital punishment is abolished in Russia. You will probably get off with four or five years of quite mild restraint. They are very lenient to their criminals.

All this will perhaps feel a little strange at first, but once you get the idea of Communism you will understand the Soviet point of view, and find yourself wondering how it would work in Chicago or Pittsburgh or Detroit. It grows on you amazingly after a day or two.

However, you must not expect a paradise. Russia is too big a place for any government to get rid, in fourteen years, of the frightful mass of poverty, ignorance, and dirt left by the Tsardom. Russia is eight million square miles big, which is more than four millions bigger than the United States. The population is nearly 160 millions, seventeen millions more than you have. I am afraid there is still a good deal of the poverty, ignorance, and dirt we know so well at home. But there is hope everywhere in Russia because these evils are retreating there before the spread of Communism as steadily as they are advancing upon us before the last desperate struggle of our bankrupt Capitalism to stave off its inevitable doom by reducing wages, multiplying tariffs, and rallying all the latent savagery and greed in the world to its support in predatory warfare masquerading as patriotism.

But you will not go to Russia to smell out the evils you can see without leaving your own doorstep. Some of you will go because in the great financial storm that has burst on us your own ship is sinking, and the Russian ship is the only big one that is not rolling heavily and tapping out SOS on its wireless. But most of you will go, I hope, with stout hearts, knowing that what is the matter with us is not natural poverty, but sheer stupid mismanagement and lazy abandonment of public interests to private selfishness and vulgar ambition. You will have heard that the Russians have put a stop to this, and you will want to see how they have done it. For what the Russians can do, you can do. You may think you can't, but you can. At present you are like an old prisoner in the Bastille, sawing the bars of his little window with a watchspring so intently that he does not notice that the door has long been wide open.

Perhaps you will all go on sawing in America until you are dead, but I expect your sons will be wiser than you, and will not let themselves be outrun in the great race of civilization by any Russian that ever set foot to the ground.

And so goodbye until next time, and good luck to you!

2. From *The Political Madhouse in America and Nearer Home*. London: Constable 1933.

[*Shaw's next major address (or "harangue," as Shaw himself aptly called it) to the American people was from the stage of the Metropolitan Opera House in New York on 11 April 1933, near the conclusion of his first visit to America. At the invitation of the American Academy of Political Science, Shaw spoke on the topic of "The Future of Political Science in America." There was an audience of 3,500 in the Opera House, and the speech was also broadcast on the NBC radio network. The range of topics covered by Shaw is captured on the title page of the first publication (unauthorized) of the speech by a Hollywood publisher, Ellis O. Jones, shortly after it was given: "Complete Text of the Great British Satirist's New York Address Treating of Bankers, 100% Americans, Orators, Constitutions, Private Czars, Dictators, Hollywood, Mormon Polygamy, Politicians, Newspapers, Stock Brokers, Lunatics, War Debts, Russian Communism, Racketeering, and Many Other Live Topics." At the core of the speech, however, was Shaw's firm view that "the capitalist system has broken down; and [America's] most pressing job is to find a better one." The speech was published in England with the title* The Political Madhouse in America and Nearer Home *(1933) with a conciliatory "Explanation" in which Shaw applies his criticism of America equally to the English.*]

An Explanation

By republishing in England a harangue addressed specifically to Americans in America I lay myself open to an accusation of wantonly holding up my sensitive American friends to British ridicule and contempt, not for their own good, which was my excuse in New York, but solely to gratify our British conceit of moral superiority and the vicious pleasure taken by the meanest of us in the defamation of persons not born in England (mostly in slums).

PART V: AMERICA

I am guiltless of any such incivility. It is to rebuke nationalist *Schadenfreude* [pleasure derived from another's misfortune] that I have consented to supply a British counterpart to the edition of my address now circulating in the United States. It would be the silliest hypocrisy to keep up the pleasantry of implying, as I did at the Metropolitan Opera House in New York on the 11th of last April, that the follies and futilities I ascribed to our American cousins are peculiar to their Continent. To please my American audience I made fun of the Hundredpercent American; but the truth is that the Hpc American is a harmless and well-meaning child compared to the Hpc Englishman, Frenchman, German Nazi, or Japanese. The most complete and colossal example of the Hpc American I can recollect was the late William Jennings Bryan [1860–1925], Bi-Metallist [supporter of a mix of gold and silver to set monetary standards], Fundamentalist, and Hot Air Volcano. Shut him off from the rest of the world and measure him by an American scale and it is easy for me or any other critic to make him appear futile as a statesman, absurd as a thinker, and gaseous as an orator. But place him against the sinister figures of the leading British and Continental Hpcs of his generation and it becomes at once apparent that civilization would be much safer in the hands of a batch of Bryans than in theirs. Bryan never said "My country, right or wrong," though he may have sung "My country, 'tis of thee." He never declared that the manifest divine destiny of the entire human race is to be governed by rich young Americans trained in the public [i.e., private] schools and universities of the United States. He never came back from a Geneva International Conference and said that of course the United States came first with him, nor sat at a Peace Conference declaring that the absolute security for the country in which he happened to be born comes before every other consideration, such absolute security being attainable only by the extermination of everybody except his compatriots, and incidentally of his God (if he believed in one). If he was infatuated about silver he was at least faithful to it, and never won a general election by rallying the nation to its defence immediately before announcing that he was going to save the nation by repudiating it. He did not proclaim the sacredness of ethnographical frontiers, and then, after sacrificing millions of lives to re-establish them, use his victory to establish military frontiers more pregnant with future wars than those he had sworn to redress. In short, Bryan might well pass for an angel of light in contrast with the nationalistic patriots of the old world, with their hands against every man and every man's hands against them (except at Peace Conferences where all the said hands slipped surreptitiously into one another's pockets), their reproaches to honest Pacifists for being the friends of every country but their own, and their pride in the alternative of being the enemies of every country but their own. If I have said, as indeed I have, that the Hpc American is an idiot, he may well smile as he wrings my hand cordially for the hundredth time and replies with a smile "At least, dear friend, you do not call me a scoundrel as well."

The main points of my harangue obviously apply to England as urgently as to the United States. As I write, a folly called The World Economic Conference [12 June–27 July 1933] is collapsing in London in an ignominy of failure and futility even greater than that of all the other Conferences by which our Parliament men try to stave off imminent disasters by another bout of talking round them.... Nothing could differentiate the Conference from a conspiracy of brigands but a common aspiration to the utmost possible production and cheapening of the necessities and luxuries of a decent life. But the delegates with one voice declared that the only thing that can save the world is a general rise in prices and the destruction by natural calamity or deliberate sabotage of the existing supply of food for lack of which thirty millions of unemployed are perishing by inches. After that it is a mere anticlimax to mention that though sane finance depends on an unsleeping sense that credit is only an opinion, and that men can neither eat it, drink it, nor build houses with it, all the delegates believed that credit is a nourishing and succulent diet, and that as a man with food, drink, and bricks and mortar to the value of a thousand pounds has credit for that sum with the banker, he has in effect a thousand pounds in goods plus a thousand pounds credit, and is therefore "worth" two thousand pounds. "Credit schemes" on this basis are enjoying quite a vogue at present. Straitened nations ask, not for goods, but for credits.

I have not time to complete the analysis of the dust storm of delusions which constituted the mental equipment of the delegates. The Russian delegate was the only one who proceeded on mentionable assumptions; and he confessed that his reason was giving way under the strain of having to argue with a World Conference of incurable lunatics. He was saved by his sense of humor; but his sense of humor could not save the world situation. The lunatics have gone home to their respective national asylums; but they are still in charge there; and if our affairs are not taken out of their hands we shall go to smash. For their greatest lunacy of all is that none of them can see the smallest reason why any human being should be allowed to live unless in addition to supporting himself he can produce a privately appropriable profit for the shareholder or a rent for the landlord. Why, they argue, should anyone organize the work of property-less men merely to produce their own food? Rather let them perish, or, if they show signs of muttering "Thou shalt starve ere I starve," let the tax collector collect some crumbs for them from the owners' tables. At such point youths of spirit become car bandits and racketeers and kidnappers. What else do our crazy conference-mongers expect? It is easy to say "If you cannot produce a profit get off the earth: you have no right to live." Proletarians are so blind to this point of view that in the final issue they reply "Que messieurs les assassins commencent" ["Let the gentlemen assassins begin"].

I therefore conciliate my American friends by inviting my English ones to apply everything I say of the Americans in this book to themselves with the assurance that they deserve it no less, and that their day of judgment may be no further off, if so far.

The Political Madhouse

...When you came to examine the American Constitution, you found that it was not really a Constitution but only a Charter of Anarchism. It was not an instrument of government; it was a guarantee to the whole American nation that it should never be governed at all. And that is exactly what the Americans want.

The ordinary man—we have to face it: it is every bit as true of the ordinary Englishman as of the ordinary American—is an Anarchist. He wants to do as he likes. He may want his neighbor to be governed, but he himself doesn't want to be governed. He is mortally afraid of government officials and policemen. He loathes tax collectors. He shrinks from giving anybody any official power whatever. This Anarchism has been at work in the world since the beginnings of civilization; and its supreme achievement up to date is the American Constitution.

It is a formidable instrument, explicit in black and white. In England we have the British Constitution; but nobody knows what it is: it is not written down anywhere; and you can no more amend it than you can amend the east wind. But in the United States you have a real tangible readable document. I can nail you down to every one of its sentences.

And what does it amount to? A great protest against the tyranny of law and order. A final manifesto from the centuries of revolutionary Anarchism in which the struggle went on against government as such, against government by feudal barons, by autocratic Kings, by the Pope and his cardinals, by the parliaments which have gradually ousted all these authorities, each of them in turn being used to disable the others in the glorified cause of what people called Liberty, until, having destroyed the king, the barons, the Church, and finally all effective parliamentary governing power, you found yourselves hopelessly under the thumbs of your private racketeers, from the humble gunman to the great financial magnate, each playing for his own hand without status, without national authority or responsibility, without legal restraint and without any sense of public government. You had perfected a Constitution of negatives to defend liberty, liberty, liberty—life, liberty, and the pursuit of happiness—against the only checks on anarchy that could secure them, and fortified it by a Supreme Court which dealt out nothing but prohibitions, and a political party machinery of legislatures and senates, which was so wonderfully devised that when you sent in one body of men to govern the country, you sent in another body of men along with them to prevent their doing it. In your dread of dictators you established a state of society in which every ward boss is a dictator, every financier a dictator, every private employer a dictator, all with the livelihood of the workers at their mercy, and no public responsibility.

And to symbolize this state of things, this defeat of all government, you have set up in New York Harbour, a monstrous idol which you call Liberty. The only thing that remains to complete that monument is to put on its pedestal the inscription written by Dante on the gate of Hell "All hope abandon, ye who enter here."

Still, I must not reproach you; for you might remind me that you took your Anarchism straight from England, parliament, party system, second chamber and all, and that we are just as incapable as you of doing anything as a nation except talk, talk, talk endlessly. But I do reproach you for a special American propaganda of Anarchism which is having most serious effects throughout the world. Formerly you were not able to affect public morals and public feeling much on the other side of the Atlantic. But now you have an instrument called the cinematograph and a centre called Hollywood, which has brought public and private morals under your influence everywhere....

But now let us get back to the American Constitution. People are beginning to find out that Constitution. The Hundredpercent American is being succeeded by a more highly developed American. He is more muscular and less adipose [fat] than the Hundredpercent American. He has the same imposing presence, the same eloquence, the same vitality, the same dignity, the same enthusiasm. But his dignity is not pompous; and his enthusiasm is attached to definite measures and not to selections from the poetry and rhetoric of the day before yesterday.

I hope Mr Franklin Roosevelt [1882–1945, elected 32nd US President in 1933] is a sample of that new American. I think my friend Mr Randolph Hearst [1863–1951, newspaper magnate] anticipated him years ago. At all events I mention these two gentlemen not only because they illustrate what I mean, but because the main symptom of the change is that they are both very violently against the Constitution. President Roosevelt is appealing to you at the present time to get rid of your confounded Constitution, and give him power to govern the country. He hopes that if you do he will be able to govern it. But he knows he must fail as long as Congress is there to prevent him.

You have tried constitutional presidents before, ladies and gentlemen. You have tried again and again. You tried Mr Hoover. Mr Hoover has shown himself a capable and practical man in certain transactions, connected with feeding people during the [1914–18] war. On that ground you elected him. You wanted a practical man. You were in a practical mood.

PART V: AMERICA

You found him of no use whatever as President. He ceased to be a practical man. Congress would not let him be a practical man. The Constitution was not practical. Everything ended in talk, talk, talk. Then, during his term of office, you had a bad slump. Your political, social and industrial system registered signs of a first-rate earthquake somewhere; and when the Constitution made it impossible for Mr Hoover to save you, you revenged yourself on him by throwing him out. I suppose I must not say you kicked him out, but you certainly sent him to the foot of the poll with extraordinary violence. And then you turned to Mr Roosevelt. Why?

Because, as the practical mood in which you elected Mr Hoover was a disappointment, you reacted into a sentimental mood. Just then Mr Roosevelt, by a happy chance, got photographed with a baby. The baby was a success: Mr Roosevelt went to the White House in its arms. I don't know whether the baby is still there; but I know that you hope a great deal from Mr Franklin Roosevelt. Well, you will get nothing from him if he has to act constitutionally through the usual routine of Congress. His four years will inevitably end in as great a disappointment as Mr Hoover's....

...You, ladies and gentlemen, have just parted with sums of money that are quite considerable during the present crisis. What to do? To hear me talk. You did not know what I was going to say. You guessed that I should not hand you the usual visitor's bouquets. But you love talk because there is something public about it. There is a promise of public action in it. And I, having watched this through my long life, have begun to see that it is also a force which may turn into volcanic political genius if it gets mixed with brains and knowledge.

If only it can get a positive Constitution, if it can find sound intellectual bearings, if it can devise... a frame of reference within which its brains can work, possibly America may save human society yet by solving the great political problems which have baffled and destroyed all previous attempts at permanent civilization. I have hopes, because America has got this irrepressible social instinct, this wonderful surging thing inside itself, that you do not find in the same reckless profusion elsewhere. Will that carry you through? Has America the entrails to do the job? If I were in England I should use a shorter word; but in America I am told I must be careful.

[Shaw then uses Brigham Young (1801–77) as an American example of determined and courageous leadership in a political cause (i.e., the survival of the Latter Day Saints by rapid population expansion). Young, says Shaw, "became immortal in history as an American Moses by leading his people through the wilderness into an unpromised land where they founded a great city on polygamy."]

...nothing that I shall say tonight is more significant than that illustration of American capacity for political action, in view of the necessity to the United States of a new Constitution. I really do entertain a hope—I think I am the only person in the world who entertains it so far—perhaps after my preaching tonight some of you may consider it—that you Americans, in spite of your follies in the past, in spite of your obsolete Uncle Jonathan, in spite of your ridiculous Hundredpercent American, may yet take the lead in political thought and action, and help to save the soul of the world.

I admit that your existing situation is not a very promising one. Your proletariat is unemployed. That means the breakdown of your capitalist system, because, as any political scientist will tell you, the whole justification of the system of privately appropriated capital and land on which you have been working, is its guarantee, elaborately reasoned out on paper by the capitalist economists, that although one result of it must be the creation of a small but enormously rich propertied class which is also an idle class, living at the expense of the propertyless masses who are getting only a bare living, nevertheless that bare living is always secured for them. There must always be employment available; and they will always be able to obtain a subsistence wage for their labor.

When the promise is broken (and never for one moment has it been kept right up to the hilt), when your unemployed are not only the old negligible five per cent of that trade, two per cent of this trade, eight per cent of that trade, two per cent of the other trade, but millions of unemployed, then the capitalist system has broken down; and your most pressing job is to find a better one.

Passing from your starving proletariat, what about your farmers? Your farmers are bankrupt; and they are in armed revolt. Even the newspapers tell you this if you read them carefully, although in all civilized countries at present newspapers exist for the purpose of concealing the truth from the public in such matters.

What about your employers? When I was a young man, the employer in America was master of the industrial situation. He employed the proletariat on his own account and for his own profit. He employed the land of the landlord and paid him a rent for it. He employed the capital of the capitalists and paid them interest for it. What remained was his own. Thus he had the whole business of the country in his hands, and was undisputed cock of the walk in all industrial republics. And any man who could read and write and cipher, and had a reasonable share of business ability, could start as an employer with a little capital either saved by himself or borrowed from his family or his friends.

All that is gone. The ordinary employer of today belongs to the proletariat. He is an employed manager, living on a salary with perhaps a percentage to encourage him to work for others as hard as he formerly worked for himself. Scientific discovery has revealed new methods of producing wealth which require enormous plants costing prodigious amounts of capital. The old-fashioned employer was a very considerable person when he could command a capital of five thousand dollars. Today the dollars needed to start big enterprises are counted in hundreds of millions; and the ordinary employer is utterly unable to find such sums or to prevent the big enterprises swallowing up the little ones. He has, therefore, fallen helplessly into the power of a class of men whose business it is to find millions, the financiers. They are the present masters of the situation. Your country is run by them. Just now they are running it into the ditch; but you still let them run it.

To impress on you how extraordinarily dangerous is the condition of a country which lets itself be governed by private financiers, may I show you the sort of person a private financier is? He is the very contrary of a statesman. The financier is always thinking about what a single individual with money can do at a favorable moment if it pleases him. But the statesman has to consider what millions of individuals, with or without money, can be forced by law to do every day whether they like it or not. That is how the financier's mind forms fixed habits which make him incapable of the point of view of the statesman, who has to remember at every legislative step "Here is something that everybody, rich or poor, will have to do simultaneously if I make this law."...

What happens when you make your financiers statesmen? Their first duty is to find out how much taxation you can bear. For that they must find out how much wealth there is in your hands to tax. They order a clerk to calculate the entire wealth of the United States. The clerk immediately finds out from the income tax returns what is the total income of the country, multiplies it by twenty, and hands in the product as the wealth available for immediate taxation in the United States. Not having a statesman's mind he forgets that if all the people with incomes are driven by law to sell them simultaneously, the Stock Exchange will become a market in which there are all sellers and no buyers, and the value of their securities will be just exactly zero.

That is to say, financiers live in a world of illusion. They count on something which they call the capital of the country which has no existence. Every five dollars they count as a hundred dollars; and that means that every financier, every banker, every stockbroker, is 95 per cent a lunatic. And it is in the hands of these lunatics that you leave the fate of your country!

You also give them a certain hidden power, greater than any public political power, which exists in all large and rich commercial communities. That power is the power latent in banking. How does it arise? Very simply. In a village people can keep their spare money, if they have any, in an old stocking, or bury it in the back garden; but in towns men of business have to handle large sums which they want to have kept safely for them and paid out to their order as and when they need it. They began by leaving their money with the goldsmiths, who were quite willing to keep it for them and let them have it when they had payments to make. You see, the goldsmiths discovered, not by the exercising of any skill on their part, but simply by experiencing what happened, that if they had a large number of people leaving money with them and never drawing it all out—keeping a balance as we call it—they would have a lot of other people's money to play with all the time.... [W]hen the goldsmiths became bankers they found that an astonishing proportion of the money lodged with them remained permanently in their hands, enabling them to enter on the most lucrative of all businesses: the business of money-lending with other people's money.

They ran only one risk, and that was that if all their customers were seized with panic and made a simultaneous rush to draw out their money, the money would not be there; and the bank would break, just as the Bank of England broke the other day because there was a run on gold. But this occurs so seldom that the risk is negligible; and as the Bank of England is still able to pay twelve or thirteen shillings in the pound, its bankruptcy is politely called going off the gold standard.

But now you see that this natural discovery made by the goldsmiths and exploited by them as bankers, sets up automatically in large civilizations like yours a money power so irresistible that it becomes a political and industrial power, not to say a religious power, of the most formidable magnitude. Any nation that leaves this power in the hands of irresponsible private men to use simply for their own enrichment, is either politically ignorant or politically mad to the utmost possible degree.

You applaud; but this is exactly what you are doing. The smallest smattering of political science will tell you that the first thing you must do to get out of your present mess is to nationalize your banks. Well, why not nationalize them instead of merely applauding me?...

...But do not blame the financiers. They are quite honest and patriotic. They do it in their own business, and it works; and they think if it is done in everybody's business it must work. That is why you must breed statesmen who will supersede the financier and put him back in his proper private place.

Let me take a capital instance. We had a war in Europe. You lent Europe about five milliards [five thousand million] of dollars, on England's security. What value did you get for that? You got the destruction of three European Empires, and the substitution of American republicanism for monarchical rule as the typical national rule in Europe. Most European Kings are now exiles and outcasts. The rest are what you call constitutional monarchs, which means that they are not monarchs at all, and consequently have a fairly pleasant and popular time of it. I suggest that this was pretty fair value for your money. But you got something more remarkable than that, that will be yet more important in the future: you achieved the salvation of Russia. I gather from your applause that at last I have met some Americans who know that they saved Russia.

Russia, when the tsardom fell, tried your form of government. It set up what it calls a bourgeois republic. The country was in the most desperate need of reconstruction; but the bourgeois republic could do nothing but talk, just like Congress. It collapsed helplessly when the Bolsheviks took the situation in hand and imposed a real positive government on the distracted and starving country. That government had a terrible job to face. There was Russia with her population of one hundred and sixty million ignorant and half savage peasants, knowing nothing about modern industrial development, not knowing how to handle machinery. There had been a little industrialism before the war; but it was all in the hands of Englishmen, of Belgians, of Italians, and of Germans. Yet when the new Russian rulers, having to rescue this enormous population from famine, savagery, ignorance, dirt and slavery, could do so only by establishing the machinery of modern industry in Russia at all costs, and did not know how to do it, did they turn for instruction to their old exploiters, the English, the Belgians, the Italians, and the Germans? No. By some sort of inspiration, they turned to America; and America saved them. They were guided by the advice and instruction of your American efficiency engineers. The American efficiency engineers did not flatter them. They came and looked, and said "Your condition is appalling: you are making a disastrous mess of your attempts at modern machine industry. It seems utterly impossible that you should ever get out of that mess. We can tell you what to do; but whether your untrained peasants can do it is another matter." And they told them. I know the American who took to Moscow the very remarkable report in which the information was given. That gentleman passed through London on his way, and submitted the report to some English experts. The

English experts made some valuable suggestions; but they said "Do you suppose the Russians will tolerate such an exposure of their inefficiency as this? Go and hand in your report, and they will hand you back across the frontier the next day. They will suppress that report; and nobody will ever hear of it again."

Well, your fellow countrymen, representing an able American firm, said "That will not matter to us. The Russians have paid for a report; we shall give it to them; and they can do what they like with it. They can suppress it as an English or American government would; but at any rate they will get what they paid for and get it good."

The English experts were mistaken. Within forty-eight hours of the handing in of the report in Moscow, the Russians had ten thousand printed copies of it in circulation; and their loudspeakers all over the country were shouting out the lessons of the report and telling the Russian workmen that all waste and breakages and blundering must stop, and that they must learn how to operate and care for their own machines. American workmen were invited to Russia to teach factory work, and American managers to teach factory management; and now, as you know, Russia has pulled through, even though her American teachers said that it was hardly conceivable that she could under the circumstances. You see, the Russian producers were free from the frightful friction of competition that wastes so much in our countries, where every manager is fighting for profit against every other manager, and every factory divided against itself by class conflict. The Russians pulled through because they all pulled together; and the result is that they are now one of the biggest industrial powers in the world, thanks to America.

Some of you may say candidly "This is very gratifying in a way; but did we quite intend to do it?" Well, perhaps not; but may not the blind political instinct which I have given you credit for have carried you on in spite of yourselves to do the right thing? At all events you helped to establish Communism in Russia; and it is now very important to you that Communism should continue in Russia; for have you considered, ladies and gentlemen, what your condition would be if Russia, with all its new resources, were forced back into imperialist capitalism?...

...I ask the mischievously foolish short-sighted gentlemen who write in the American newspapers denouncing Russia, telling every sort of silly lie about Russia, pretending that Russian Communism is bankrupt and the people starving, what they think they are doing? Do they want the tsardom back again? Tsar or no Tsar, do they want to start a Russian capitalist régime to compete with our capitalists for our markets? Do they want to dig up the White Bear from his Communist grave and resuscitate him with all his claws sharpened tenfold?...

Fortunately, Providence, having a kindly eye on America, has made Russia a Communist State; and as long as it remains so you have nothing to fear from it. Your only anxiety ought to be as to what is going to happen in China; and I sincerely hope for your sake that China will settle its scattered affairs by developing its present nucleus of Communism over its entire territory, so that China and Russia will be Communist powers. Then every American can sit under his vine and under his fig tree, and none shall make him afraid. If you cannot appreciate American Communism, at least learn to appreciate the benefit to America of having other countries Communistic. Think of the United States with not only Japan capitalist, but Russia capitalist and China capitalist! You may well shudder....

And now, what are you going to do about [all this]? Do you not feel, as I turn these questions inside out for you, that you need an Academy of Political Science very badly? And it must be an American Academy and not a second-hand European one....

I strenuously advise you, when you come to back up this Academy of Political Science and to take your own part in its work of making a new Constitution, to make it an American Constitution from beginning to end. Don't bother about Karl Marx. Karl Marx was a mighty prophet; but almost all the administrative mistakes the Communists have made in Russia they have made for the sake of Marxist orthodoxy, whilst their success has been established under the leadership of Stalin, who is distinguished by the fact that he is a nationalist in Russia. Stalin says, in effect, "I will establish Communism in Russia, and thereby set an example to Communists everywhere. If they do not choose to follow it, that is their lookout and not mine: Russia is large enough for me; and I will work for the salvation of Russia and leave the other countries to save their own souls."

He is quite right. He has been successful along that line; and I suggest to you that you in America should trust to that volcanic political instinct which I have divined in you and work out the whole thing for yourselves, from the American facts, with American thought, on American lines, until you finally turn the futile Hundredpercent American into a man who is not only one hundred per cent an American but one hundred per cent a statesman....

Part VI: The Dictators

Shaw's support of authoritarian ideologies and governments extended—to different degrees—to support of their leaders. As far as Shaw was concerned, Stalin remained above criticism. Stalin is the only European dictator of the 1930s who is not mocked in Shaw's 1938 play Geneva. Both Mussolini and Hitler—as well as Spanish dictator Francisco Franco—are treated satirically in Geneva, but in Shaw's nondramatic writing it is Hitler who comes in for the sharpest criticism. While Shaw initially praised Hitler for his achievements in leading Germany to renewed national pride and economic recovery from the punitive measures imposed on the country after its defeat in the First World War, Hitler's "Judophobia"—"not a part of Fascism but an incomprehensible excrescence on it," said Shaw—destroyed Shaw's support for Hitler personally and the Nazis generally.

1. "Halt, Hitler!," *Sunday Dispatch*, 4 June 1933. [Gibbs, *Interviews and Recollections*, pp. 355–57]

[Shaw expressed his opinions on Hitler in an interview with American journalist Hayden Church published in the British newspaper the Sunday Dispatch *on 4 June 1933.]*

CHURCH: Well, Mr Shaw, have you returned a Nazi? You came back from Italy to stand up for Mussolini. You came back from Russia to stand up for Stalin. Have you come back from everywhere to stand up for Hitler? [Shaw had recently returned from a world cruise.]

SHAW: The Nazi movement is in many respects one which has my warm sympathy; in fact, I might fairly claim that Herr Hitler has repudiated Karl Marx to enlist under the banner of Bernard Shaw. You can therefore imagine my dismay when at the most critical moment Herr Hitler and the Nazis went mad on the Jewish question.

Herr Hitler has received powers with which only the sanest of statesmen could be trusted; and his first use of them has been to reincarnate Torquemada [Spanish Inquisitor-General, 1420–98], who believed that he was saving the world by not only burning live Jews but digging up and burning dead ones.

CHURCH: Why not have it out with him on paper? If anyone can argue Hitler down, you can.

SHAW: It is idle to argue against this sort of insanity. Judophobia is as pathological as hydrophobia. A statesman infected with it may go on from persecuting Jews to persecuting Jesuits, Freemasons, witches, Laplanders, and perhaps finally Prussians, against whom our handful of British Jewbaiters express a peculiar animus.

The Ku-Klux outrages on Negroes and Catholics in America are a well-known variety of delirium tremens; but no

PART VI: THE DICTATORS

Kleagle [a senior officer of the KKK] has yet been made President of the United States.

The Nazis are suffering from an epidemic of a very malignant disease; and the result is that the British police had to protect Dr Rosenberg [a leading Nazi exponent of racial purity, 1893–1946] when he came to London, expecting, apparently, to be received with open arms by a friendly England, from being treated as mad dogs are treated.

CHURCH: Well, if you won't argue with Hitler, why not psycho-analyse him? Where did he get this anti-Jewish complex? What has it to do with Fascism? Mussolini does not persecute Jews. Why should Hitler?

SHAW: Quite true. Judophobia is not a part of Fascism but an incomprehensible excrescence on it.

CHURCH: But where does the persecution of the Jews come in?

SHAW: Dr Rosenberg replies that the Jew is a profiteer.

CHURCH: There is nothing peculiar to the Jews in that, is there?

SHAW: Nothing whatever, except that the Jew often understands the game better and is cleverer at playing it than the sort of flaxen-haired chump who feels flattered when he is described as Nordic.

There is nothing in Dr Rosenberg's excuse. It is true that as the Nazis are professed Socialists they are pledged to put an end to profiteering. But if there is any lesson that the Socialists have had to learn of late, both from my urgent precepts and from the bitter experience of the Soviets with the Kulaks [entrepreneurial Russian peasants purged by Stalin], it is that a Socialist Government must not expropriate the private employer until it is ready to take his place and do his work.

A silly gaffe like the expulsion of Einstein [whose German citizenship was revoked in 1933], recalling the French Revolution's "the Republic has no need of chemists" when Lavoisier was guillotined [French scientist, executed in 1794], does not matter. Einstein is as great a man out of Germany as in it; and though the colossal laugh which sounded throughout the civilised world at his expulsion was altogether at the expense of the Nazis, still they can pick Einstein's brains as easily when he is beyond the frontier as they can pocket the material property he has had to leave behind him.

But when they ruin their ordinary private employers and put them out of productive action without immediately taking over and carrying on their businesses, they reduce production and presently find the country faced with famine.

CHURCH: As Lenin did in Russia before he saw his mistake and had to undo it.

SHAW: Precisely. Even on the ridiculous assumption that the Jews are the only profiteers in Germany, their persecution and expropriation can only transfer their profiteering businesses to the German profiteers, who are just as greedy for profit.

Now if the Nazis are prepared to injure Germany in this useless and cruel way for the sake of destroying the Jew *qua* Jew, it is evident that they are not acting as Fascists or as Socialists, but simply running amuck in the indulgence of a pure phobia: that is, acting like madmen. By doing so they are throwing away all the sympathy they were entitled to from European public opinion.

CHURCH: Had they any?

SHAW: Most certainly they had. As Fascists they had the sympathy of Italy. As Socialists, using Bolshevist dictatorial tactics, they had the sympathy of Russia, in spite of the rivalry of Fascism and Communism.

And elsewhere they had the sympathy of the vast mass of public opinion which has turned angrily away from the delays, the evasions, the windy impotence and anarchist negations of our pseudo-democratic parliamentary system. All this sympathy has been turned into angry ill-will in a single day by an explosion of senseless Judophobia.

PART VI: THE DICTATORS

2. From the Preface to *On the Rocks*, 1933–34. [*The Bodley Head Bernard Shaw*, VI:574–628]

[Well aware of "the slaughter of millions of quite innocent persons" as a means of gaining and maintaining political power – historically and contemporaneously (e.g., in Stalinist Russia) – Shaw unapologetically defended the strategy in the preface to On the Rocks *(first performed in 1933), predicting that political extermination will one day become a "humane science."]*

Extermination

In this play a reference is made by the Chief of Police to the political necessity of killing people: a necessity so distressing to the statesmen and so terrifying to the common citizen that nobody except myself (as far as I know) has ventured to examine it directly on its own merits, although every Government is obliged to practise it on a scale varying from the execution of a single murderer to the slaughter of millions of quite innocent persons. Whilst assenting to these proceedings, and even acclaiming and celebrating them, we dare not tell ourselves what we are doing or why we are doing it; and so we call it justice or capital punishment or our duty to king and country or any other convenient verbal whitewash for what we instinctively recoil from as a dirty job. These childish evasions are revolting. We must strip off the whitewash and find out what is really beneath it. Extermination must be put on a scientific basis if it is ever to be carried out humanely and apologetically as well as thoroughly.

Killing as a Political Function

That killing is a necessity is beyond question. Unless rabbits and deer and rats are killed, or "kept down" as we put it, mankind must perish; and that section of mankind which lives in the country and is directly and personally engaged in the struggle with Nature for a living has no sentimental doubts that they must be killed. As to tigers and poisonous snakes, their incompatibility with human civilization is unquestioned. This does not excuse the use of cruel steel traps, agonizing poisons, or packs of hounds as methods of extermination. Killing can be cruelly or kindly done; and the deliberate choice of cruel ways, and their organization as popular pleasures, is sinful; but the sin is in the cruelty and the enjoyment of it, not in the killing.

The Sacredness of Human Life

In law we draw a line between the killing of human animals and non-human ones, setting the latter apart as brutes. This was founded on a general belief that humans have immortal souls and brutes none. Nowadays more and more people are refusing to make this distinction. They may believe in The Life Everlasting and The Life to Come; but they make no distinction between Man and Brute, because some of them believe that brutes have souls, whilst others refuse to believe that the physical materializations and personifications of The Life Everlasting are themselves everlasting. In either case the mystic distinction between Man and Brute vanishes; and the murderer pleading that though the rabbit should be killed for being mischievous he himself should be spared because he has an immortal soul and a rabbit has none is as hopelessly out of date as a gentleman duellist pleading his clergy [i.e., seeking a lesser sentence for a first offence]. When the necessity for killing a dangerous human being arises, as it still does daily, the only distinction we make between a man and a snared rabbit is that we very quaintly provide the man with a minister of religion to explain to him that we are not killing him at all, but only expediting his transfer to an eternity of bliss.

Here somebody is sure to interject that there is the alternative of teaching him better manners; but I am not here dealing with such cases: the real necessity arises only in dealing with untameable persons who are constitutionally unable to restrain their violent or acquisitive impulses, and have no compunction about sacrificing others to their immediate convenience. To punish such persons is ridiculous: we might as reasonably punish a tile for flying off a roof in a storm and knocking a clergyman on the head. But to kill them is quite reasonable and very necessary.

Present Exterminations

All this so far is mere elementary criminology, already dealt with very fully by me in my *Essay on Prisons* [in *Doctors' Delusions, Crude Criminology and Sham Education* (1931)], which I recommend to those readers who may feel impelled to ramble away at this point into the prosings about Deterrence beloved by our Prison commissioners and judges. It disposes of the dogma of the unconditional sacredness of human life, or any other incarnation of life; but it covers only a corner of the field opened up by modern powers of extermination. In Germany it is suggested that the Nordic race should exterminate the Latin race. As both these lingual stocks are hopelessly interbred by this time, such a sacrifice to ethnological sciolism is not practicable; but its discussion familiarizes the idea and clears the way for practicable suggestions. The extermination of whole races and classes has not only been advocated but actually attempted. The extirpation of the Jew as such figured for a few mad moments in the program of the Nazi party in Germany. The extermination of the peasant is in active progress in Russia, where the extermination of the class of ladies and gentlemen of so-called independent means has already been accomplished; and an attempt to exterminate the old Conservative professional class and the kulak or prosperous farmer class has been checked only by the discovery that they cannot as yet be done without. Outside Russia the extermination of Communists is widely advocated; and there is a movement in the British Empire and the United

States for the extermination of Fascists. In India the impulse of Moslems and Hindus to exterminate one another is complicated by the impulse of the British Empire to exterminate both when they happen to be militant Nationalists....

Leading Case of Jesus Christ

I dislike cruelty, even cruelty to other people, and should therefore like to see all cruel people exterminated. But I should recoil with horror from a proposal to punish them. Let me illustrate my attitude by a very famous, indeed far too famous, example of the popular conception of criminal law as a means of delivering up victims to the normal popular lust for cruelty which has been mortified by the restraint imposed on it by civilization. Take the case of the extermination of Jesus Christ. No doubt there was a strong case for it. Jesus was from the point of view of the High Priest a heretic and an impostor. From the point of view of the merchants he was a rioter and a Communist. From the Roman Imperialist point of view he was a traitor. From the commonsense point of view he was a dangerous madman. From the snobbish point of view, always a very influential one, he was a penniless vagrant. From the police point of view he was an obstructor of thoroughfares, a beggar, an associate of prostitutes, an apologist of sinners, and a disparager of judges; and his daily companions were tramps whom he had seduced into vagabondage from their regular trades. From the point of view of the pious he was a Sabbath breaker, a denier of the efficacy of circumcision and the advocate of a strange rite of baptism, a gluttonous man and a winebibber. He was abhorrent to the medical profession as an unqualified practitioner who healed people by quackery and charged nothing for the treatment. He was not anti-Christ: nobody had heard of such a power of darkness then; but he was startlingly anti-Moses. He was against the priests, against the judiciary, against the military, against the city (he declared that it was impossible for a rich man to enter the kingdom of heaven), against all the interests, classes, principalities and powers, inviting everybody to abandon all these and follow him. By every argument, legal, political, religious, customary, and polite, he was the most complete enemy of the society of his time ever brought to the bar. He was guilty on every count of the indictment, and on many more that his accusers had not the wit to frame. If he was innocent then the whole world was guilty. To acquit him was to throw over civilization and all its institutions. History has borne out the case against him; for no State has ever constituted itself on his principles or made it possible to live according to his commandments: those States who have taken his name have taken it as an alias to enable them to persecute his followers more plausibly.

It is not surprising that under these circumstances, and in the absence of any defence, the Jerusalem community and the Roman government decided to exterminate Jesus. They had just as much right to do so as to exterminate the two thieves who perished with him. But there was neither right nor reason in torturing him. He was entitled to the painless death of Socrates [by drinking poison]. We may charitably suppose that if the death could have been arranged privately between [Pontius] Pilate [the Roman governor of Judea who ordered the execution of Jesus] and Caiaphas [Jewish high priest] Jesus would have been dispatched as quickly and suddenly as John the Baptist [who was beheaded]. But the mob wanted the horrible fun of seeing somebody crucified: an abominably cruel method of execution. Pilate only made matters worse by trying to appease them by having Jesus flogged. The soldiers, too, had to have their bit of sport, to crown him with thorns and, when they buffeted him, challenge him ironically to guess which of them had struck the blow.

"Crosstianity"

All this was cruelty for its own sake, for the pleasure of it. And the fun did not stop there. Such was and is the attraction of these atrocities that the spectacle of them has been reproduced in pictures and waxworks and exhibited in churches ever since as an aid to piety. The chief instrument of torture is the subject of special Adoration. Little models of it in gold and ivory are worn as personal ornaments; and big reproductions in wood and marble are set up in sacred places and on graves. Contrasting the case with that of Socrates, one is forced to the conclusion that if Jesus had been humanely exterminated his memory would have lost ninetynine percent of its attraction for posterity. Those who were specially susceptible to his morbid attraction were not satisfied with symbolic crosses which hurt nobody. They soon got busy with "acts of faith" which consisted of great public shows at which Jews and Protestants or Catholics, and anyone else who could be caught out on a point of doctrine, were burnt alive. Cruelty is so infectious that the very compassion it rouses is infuriated to take revenge by still viler cruelties.

The tragedy of this—or, if you will, the comedy—is that it was his clearness of vision on this very point that set Jesus so high above his persecutors. He taught that two blacks do not make a white; that evil should not be countered by worse evil but by good; that revenge and punishment only duplicate wrong; that we should conceive God, not as an irascible and vindictive tyrant but as an affectionate father. No doubt many private amiabilities have been inspired by this teaching; but politically it has received no more quarter than Pilate gave it. To all Governments it has remained paradoxical and impracticable. A typical acknowledgement of it was the hanging of a crucifix above the seat of the judge who was sentencing evildoers to be broken on the wheel.

PART VI: THE DICTATORS

Christianity and the Sixth Commandment ["Thou Shalt Not Kill"]

Now it is not enough to satirize this. We must explain why it occurred. It is not enough to protest that evildoers must not be paid in their own coin by treating them as cruelly as they have treated others. We still have to stop the mischief they do. What is to be done with them? It is easy to suggest that they should be reformed by gentleness and shamed by non-resistance. By all means, if they respond to that treatment. But if gentleness fails to reform them and non-resistance encourages them to further aggression, what then? A month spent in a Tolstoyan community [i.e., a work by Russian novelist Leo Tolstoy, 1828–1910] will convince anybody of the soundness of the nearest police inspector's belief that every normal human group contains not only a percentage of saints but also a percentage of irreclaimable scoundrels and good-for-noughts who will wreck any community unless they are expensively restrained or cheaply exterminated. Our Mosaic system of vindictive punishment, politely called "retributory" by Prison Commissioners, disposes of them temporarily; but it wastes the lives of honest citizens in guarding them; sets a horrible example of cruelty and malicious injury; costs a good deal of money that might be better spent; and, after all, sooner or later lets the scoundrel loose again to recommence his depredations. It would be much more sensible and less cruel to treat him as we treat mad dogs or adders, without malice or cruelty, and without reference to catalogues of particular crimes. The notion that persons should be safe from extermination as long as they do not commit wilful murder, or levy war against the Crown, or kidnap, or throw vitriol, is not only to limit social responsibility unnecessarily, and to privilege the large range of intolerable misconduct that lies outside them, but to divert attention from the essential justification for extermination, which is always incorrigible social incompatibility and nothing else.

The Russian Experiment

The only country which has yet awakened to this extension of social responsibility is Russia. When the Soviet Government undertook to change over from Capitalism to Communism it found itself without any instruments for the maintenance of order except a list of crimes and punishments administered through a ritual of criminal law. And in the list of crimes the very worst offences against Communist society had no place: on the contrary they were highly honored and rewarded. As our English doggerel runs, the courts could punish a man for stealing the goose from off the common, but not the man who stole the common from the goose. The idler, that common enemy of mankind who robs everybody all the time, though he is so carefully protected from having his own pocket picked, incurred no penalty, and had actually passed the most severe laws against any interference with his idling. It was the business of the Soviet to make all business public business and all persons public servants; but the view of the ordinary Russian citizen was that a post in public service was an exceptional stroke of good luck for the holder because it was a sinecure carrying with it the privilege of treating the public insolently and extorting bribes from it. For example, when the Russian railways were communized, some of the local stationmasters interpreted the change as meaning that they might now be as lazy and careless as they pleased, whereas in fact it was of life-or-death importance that they should redouble their activity and strain every nerve to make the service efficient. The unfortunate Commissar who was Minister of Transport found himself obliged to put a pistol in his pocket and with his own hand shoot stationmasters who had thrown his telegrams into the dustbin instead of attending to them, so that he might the more impressively ask the rest of the staff whether they yet grasped the fact that orders are meant to be executed.

PART VI: THE DICTATORS

Inadequacy of Penal Codes

Now being Minister of Transport, or Minister of any other public service, is a whole time job: it cannot be permanently combined with that of amateur executioner, carrying with it the reputation in all the capitalist papers of the west of being a ferocious and coldblooded murderer. And no conceivable extension of the criminal code nor of the service disciplines, with their lists of specific offences and specific penalties, could have provided for instant exemplary exterminations of this kind, any more than for the growing urgency of how to dispose of people who would not or could not fit themselves into the new order of things by conforming to its new morality. It would have been easy to specify certain offences and certain penalties in the old fashion: as, for instance, if you hoard money you will be shot; if you speculate in the difference in purchasing power of the rouble in Moscow and Berlin you will be shot; if you buy at the Co-operative to sell at the private trader's shop you will be shot; if you take bribes you will be shot; if you exploit labor you will be shot; and it will be useless to plead that you have been brought up to regard these as normal business activities, and that the whole of respectable society outside Russia agrees with you. But the most elaborate code of this sort would still have left unspecified a hundred ways in which wreckers of Communism could have side-tracked it without ever having to face the essential questions: are you pulling your weight in the social boat? Are you giving more trouble than you are worth? Have you earned the privilege of living in a civilized community? That is why the Russians were forced to set up an Inquisition or Star Chamber, called at first the Cheka and now the Gay Pay Oo (Ogpu), to go into these questions and "liquidate" persons who could not answer them satisfactorily. The security against the abuse of this power of life and death was that the Cheka had no interest in liquidating anybody who could be made publicly useful, all its interests being in the opposite direction.

Limited Liability in Morals

Such a novelty is extremely terrifying to us, who are still working on a system of limited liability in morals. Our "free" British citizens can ascertain exactly what they may do and what they may not do if they are to keep out of the hands of the police. Our financiers know that they must not forge share certificates nor overstate their assets in the balance sheets they send to their shareholders. But provided they observe a few conditions of this kind they are free to enter upon a series of quite legitimate but not the less nefarious operations. For example, making a corner in wheat or copper or any other cornerable commodity and forcing up prices so as to make enormous private fortunes for themselves, or making mischief between nations through the Press to stimulate the private trade in armaments. Such limited liability no longer exists in Russia, and is not likely to exist in the future in any highly civilized state. It may be quite impossible to convict a forestaller or regrator [illegal commodity trader] under a criminal code of having taken a single illegal step, but quite easy to convince any reasonable body of judges that he is what the people call "a wrong one." In Russia such a conviction would lead to his disappearance and the receipt by his family of a letter to say that they need not wait up for him, as he would not return home any more. [Shaw here adds a footnote: "Note, however, that a sentence of extermination should never be so certain as to make it worth the delinquent's while to avoid arrest by murdering his or her pursuers."] In our country he would enjoy his gains in high honor and personal security, and thank his stars that he lived in a free country and not in Communist Russia....

Sooner or later this situation will have to be thoroughly studied and thought out to its logical conclusion in all civilized countries. The lists of crimes and penalties will obsolesce like the doctors' lists of diseases and medicines; and it will become possible to be a judge without ceasing to be a Christian. And extermination, my present subject, will become a humane science instead of the miserable mixture of piracy, cruelty, vengeance, race conceit, and superstition it now is....

3. From the Preface to *The Millionairess*, 1935. [*The Bodley Head Bernard Shaw*, VI:849–81]

[*For the 1936 publication of* The Millionairess (*which also contained* The Simpleton of the Unexpected Isles *and* The Six of Calais) *Shaw wrote a "Preface on Bosses" (dated 28 August 1935), which contains one of Shaw's most forceful denunciations of Democracy. Universal adult suffrage in Great Britain was, he says, "a colossal disappointment and disillusion." By way of contrast, Mussolini proved himself "a true organ of democracy" (never mind "a couple of murders"). There was less praise, however, for Hitler, whose anti-Semitism was "incompatible with civilization."*]

...Neither Mussolini nor Hitler could have achieved their present personal supremacy when I was born in the middle of the nineteenth century, because the prevailing mentality of that deluded time was still hopefully parliamentary. Democracy was a dream, an ideal. Everything would be well when all men had votes. Everything would be better than well when all women had votes. There was a great fear of public opinion because it was a dumb phantom which every statesman could identify with his own conscience and dread as the Nemesis of unscrupulous ambition. That was the golden age of democracy: the phantom was a real and beneficent force. Many delusions are. In those days even our Conservative rulers agreed that we were a liberty loving people: that, for instance, Englishman would never tolerate compulsory military service as the slaves of foreign despots did. [The 1916 Military Service Act legislated conscription in the United Kingdom.]

It was part of the democratic dream that Parliament was an instrument for carrying out the wishes of the voters, absurdly called its constituents. And as, in the nineteenth century, it was still believed that British individual liberty forbad Parliament to do anything that it could possibly leave to private enterprise, Parliament was able to keep up its reputation by simply maintaining an effective police force and enforcing private contracts. Even Factory Acts and laws against adulteration and sweating were jealously resisted as interferences with the liberty of free Britons. If there was anything wrong, the remedy was an extension of the franchise. Like Hamlet, we lived on the chameleon's dish "air, promise crammed" [*Hamlet* 3.2].

But you cannot create a mentality out of promises without having to face occasional demands for their materialization. The Treasury Bench [seating reserved in the House of Commons for senior members of government] was up for auction at every election, the bidding being in promises. The political parties, finding it much less troublesome to give the people votes than to carry out reforms, at last established adult suffrage.

The result was a colossal disappointment and disillusion. The phantom of Democracy, alias Public Opinion, which, acting as an artificial political conscience, had restrained [William Ewart] Gladstone [Liberal Prime Minister four times between 1868 and 1894] and [Benjamin] Disraeli [Conservative Prime Minister 1868 and 1874–80], vanished. The later parliamentary leaders soon learnt from experience that they might with perfect immunity tell the nation one thing on Tuesday and the opposite on Friday without anyone noticing the discrepancy. The donkey had overtaken the carrots at last; and instead of eating them he allowed them to be snatched away from him by any confidence trickster who told him to look up into the sky.

The diplomatists immediately indulged themselves with a prodigiously expensive war [World War I, 1914–18], after which the capitalist system, which had undertaken to find employment for everybody at subsistence wages, and which, though it had never fulfilled that undertaking, had at least found employment for enough of them to leave the rest too few to be dangerous, defaulted in respect of unprecedented millions of unemployed, who had to be bought off by doles [i.e., unemployment benefits] administered with a meanness and cruelty which revived all the infamies of the Poor Law of a century ago (the days of Oliver Twist) and could not be administered in any kinder way without weakening the willingness of its recipients to prefer even the poorliest paid job to its humiliations.

The only way of escape was for the government to organize the labor of the unemployed for the supply of their own needs. But Parliament not only could not do this, but could and did prevent its being done. In vain did the voters use their votes to place a Labor Government, with a Cabinet of Socialists, on the Treasury Bench. [The first British Labour government, with Ramsay MacDonald as Prime Minister, served for nine months in 1924, and again from 1929 to 1935.] Parliament took these men, who had been intransigent Socialists and revolutionists all their lives, and reduced them to a condition of political helplessness in which they were indistinguishable except by name from the most reactionary members of the House of Lords or the military clubs. A Socialist Prime Minister, after trying for years to get the parliamentary car into gear for a move forward, and finding that though it would work easily and smoothly in neutral the only gear that would engage was the reverse gear (popularly called "the axe" because it could do nothing but cut down wages), first formed what he called a national government by a coalition of all parties, and then, having proved by this experiment that it did not make the smallest difference whether members of the Cabinet were the reddest of Bolsheviks or the bluest of Tories, made things easier by handing over his premiership to a colleague who, being a Conservative, and popular and sensible into the bargain, could steal a horse where a Socialist dare not look over a hedge. [Labour were defeated by the Conservative Party in the 1924 General Election. Stanley Baldwin became Prime Minister.] The voters rejected him at the next election [in 1929]; but he retained his membership of the Cabinet precisely as if he had been triumphantly returned. Bismarck could have done no more.

These events, helped by the terrific moral shock of war, and the subsequent exposure of the patriotic lying by which the workers of Europe had been provoked to slaughter one another, made an end of the nineteenth century democratic mentality. Parliament fell into contempt; ballot papers were less esteemed than toilet papers; the men from the trenches had no patience with the liberties that had not saved them from being driven like sheep to the shambles.

Of this change our parliamentarians and journalists had no suspicion. Creatures of habit, they went on as if nothing had occurred since Queen Victoria's death [1901] except a couple of extensions of the franchise and an epochmaking revolution in Russia which they both pooh-poohed as a transient outburst of hooliganism fomented by a few bloodthirsty scoundrels, exactly as the American revolution and the French revolution had been pooh-poohed when they, too, were contemporary.

Here was clearly a big opportunity for a man psychologist enough to grasp the situation and bold enough to act on it. Such a man was Mussolini. He had become known as a journalist by championing the demobilized soldiers, who, after suffering all the horrors of war, had returned to find that the men who had been kept at home in the factories comfortably earning good wages, had seized those factories according to the Syndicalist doctrine of "workers' control," and were wrecking them in their helpless ignorance of business. As one indignant master-Fascist said to me, "They were listening to speeches round red flags and leaving the cows unmilked."

The demobilized fell on the Syndicalists with sticks and stones. Some, more merciful, only dosed them with castor oil. They carried Mussolini to Rome with a rush [in October 1922, when he became Prime Minister]. This gave him the chance of making an irreparable mistake and spending the next fifteen years in prison [i.e., in the Italian parliamentary system]. It seemed just the occasion for a grand appeal for liberty, for democracy, for a parliament in which the people were supreme: in short, for nineteenth century resurrection pie. Mussolini did not make that mistake. With inspired precision he denounced liberty as a putrefying corpse. He declared that what people needed was not liberty but discipline, the sterner the better. He said that he would not tolerate Oppositions: he called for action and silence. The people, instead of being shocked like good Liberals, rose to him. He was able to organize a special constabulary who wore black shirts and applied the necessary coercion.

Such improvised bodies attracted young men of military tastes and old soldiers, inevitably including a percentage of ruffians and sadists. The fringe of undesirables soon committed outrages and a couple of murders, whereupon all the Liberal newspapers in Europe shrieked with horror as if nothing else was happening in Italy. Mussolini refused to be turned aside from his work like a parliamentary man to discuss "incidents." All he said was "I take the responsibility for everything that has happened." When the Italian Liberals joined in the shrieking he seized the shriekers and transported them to the Lipari Isles [north of Sicily]. Parliament, openly flouted, chastised, and humiliated, could do nothing. The people were delighted; for that was just how they wanted to see Parliament treated. The doctrinaires of liberty fled to France and England, preferring them to Lipari, and wrote eloquent letters to the papers demanding whether every vestige of freedom, freedom of speech, freedom of the press, freedom of Parliament, was to be trampled under the heel of a ruthless dictator merely because the Italian trains were running punctually and travellers in Italy could depend on their luggage not being stolen without actually sitting on it. The English editors gave them plenty of space, and wrote sympathetic articles paraphrasing John Stuart Mill's *Essay on Liberty* [1859]. Mussolini, now Il Duce [from 1925], never even looked round: he was busy sweeping up the elected municipalities, and replacing them with efficient commissioners of his own choice, who had to do their job or get out. The editors had finally to accord him a sort of Pragmatic Sanction by an admission that his plan worked better than the old plan; but they were still blind to the fact staring them in the face that Il Duce, knowing what the people wanted and giving it to them, was responding to the real democratic urge whilst the cold tealeaves of the nineteenth century were making them sick. It was evident that Mussolini was master of Italy as far as such mastership is possible; but what was not evident to Englishmen who had their necks twisted the other way from their childhood was that even when he deliberately spat in the face of the League of Nations at Corfu [rejecting offers by the League to negotiate an end to Italy's occupation of Corfu], and defiantly asked the Powers whether they had anything to say about it, he was delighting his own people by the spectacle of a great Italian bullying the world, and getting away with it triumphantly. Parliaments are supposed to have their fingers always on the people's pulse and to respond to its slightest throb. Mussolini proved that parliaments have not the slightest notion of how the people are feeling, and that he being a

PART VI: THE DICTATORS

good psychologist and a man of the people himself to boot, was a true organ of democracy.

I, being a bit of a psychologist myself, also understood the situation, and was immediately denounced by the refugees and their champions as an anti-democrat, a hero worshipper of tyrants, and all the rest of it.

Hitler's case was different; but he had only one quality in common with Il Duce: he knew what the victorious Allies [in 1918] would fight for and what they would only bluster about. They had already been forced to recognize that their demands for plunder had gone far beyond Germany's utmost resources. But there remained the clauses of the Versailles treaty [1919] by which Germany was to be kept in a condition of permanent, decisive, and humiliating military inferiority to the other Powers, and especially to France. Hitler was political psychologist enough to know that the time had arrived when it would be quite impossible for the Allies to begin the war over again to enforce these clauses. He saw his opportunity and took it. He violated the clauses, and declared that he was going to go on violating them until a fully re-armed Germany was on equal terms with the victors. He did not soften his defiance by any word of argument or diplomacy. He knew that his attitude was safe and sure of success; and he took care to make it as defiant as that of Ajax challenging the lightning [in Homer's *Iliad*]. The Powers had either to renew the war or tear up the impossible clauses with a good grace. But they could not grasp the situation, and went on nagging pitifully about the wickedness of breaking a treaty. Hitler said that if they mentioned the subject again Germany would withdraw from the League of Nations [which Germany did in 1933] and cut the Powers dead. He bullied and snubbed as the man who understands a situation can always bully and snub the nincompoops who are only whining about it. He at once became a popular idol, and had the regular executive forces so completely devoted to him that he was able to disband the brownshirted constabulary he had organized on a Mussolini model. He met the conventional democratic challenge by plebiscites of ninety per cent in his favor. The myopia of the Powers had put him in a position so far stronger than Mussolini's that he was able to kill seventy-seven of his most dangerous opponents at a blow and then justify himself completely before an assembly fully as representative as the British Parliament, the climax being his appointment [in 1934] as absolute dictator in Germany for life, a stretch of Caesarism [i.e., Julius Caesar, Roman Emperor assassinated in 44 BCE] no nineteenth century Hohenzollern [a dynasty of the German Empire] would have dreamt of demanding.

Hitler was able to go further than Mussolini because he had a defeated, plundered, humiliated nation to rescue and restore, whereas Mussolini had only an irritated but victorious one. [Italy joined Great Britain and other allies against Germany in 1915.] He carried out a persecution of the Jews which went to the scandalous length of outlawing, plundering, and exiling Albert Einstein, a much greater man than any politician, but great in such a manner that he was quite above the heads of the masses and therefore so utterly powerless economically and militarily that he depended for his very existence on the culture and conscience of the rulers of the earth. Hitler's throwing Einstein to the Antisemite wolves was an appalling breach of cultural faith. [Einstein, 1879–1955, fled Germany in 1932 and settled in the United States.]... [and] to set the police on him because he was a Jew could be justified only on the ground that the Jews are the natural enemies of the rest of the human race, and that as a state of perpetual war necessarily exists between them any Gentile has the same reason for killing any Jew at sight as the Roman soldier had for killing [Greek mathematician] Archimedes [at the siege of Syracuse, c. 212 BCE].

Now no doubt Jews are most obnoxious creatures. Any competent historian or psychoanalyst can bring a mass of

PART VI: THE DICTATORS

incontrovertible evidence to prove that it would have been better for the world if the Jews had never existed. But I, as an Irishman, can, with patriotic relish, demonstrate the same of the English. Also of the Irish. If Herr Hitler would only consult the French and British newspapers and magazines of the latter half of 1914, he would learn that the Germans are a race of savage idolaters, murderers, liars, and fiends whose assumption of the human form is thinner than that of the wolf in *Little Red Riding Hood*.

We all live in glass houses. Is it wise to throw stones at the Jews? Is it wise to throw stones at all?

Herr Hitler is not only an Antisemite, but a believer in the possibility and desirability of a pure bred German race. I should like to ask him why....

Now Herr Hitler is not a stupid German. I therefore urge upon him that his Antisemitism and national exclusiveness must be pathological: a craze, a complex, a bee in his bonnet, a hole in his armor, a hitch in his statesmanship, one of those lesions which sometimes proves fatal. As it has no logical connection with Fascism or National Socialism, and has no effect on them except to bring them into disrepute, I doubt whether it can survive its momentary usefulness as an excuse for plundering raids and *coups d'états* against inconvenient Liberals or Marxists. A persecution is always a man hunt; and man hunting is not only a very horrible sport but socially a dangerous one, as it revives a primitive instinct incompatible with civilization: indeed, civilization rests fundamentally on the compact that it shall be dropped.

And here comes the risk we run when we allow a dominant individual to become a despot....

...Uncommon people, promoted on their merits, are by no means exempt from megalomania. [William] Morris's simple and profound saying that "no man is good enough to be another man's master" holds good unless both master and man regard themselves as equally the fellow servants of God in

States where God still reigns, or, in States where God is dead, as the subjects and agents of a political constitution applying humane principles which neither of them may violate. In that case autocrats are no longer autocrats. Failing any such religious or political creed all autocrats go more or less mad. That is a plain fact of political pathology....

Now the remedy lies, not in the extermination of all dominators and deciders, but on the contrary in their multiplication to what may be called their natural minority limit, which will destroy their present scarcity value. But we must also eliminate the mass of ignorance, weakness, and timidity which force them to treat fools according to their folly. Armies, fanatical sects and mobs, and the blackshirts complained of today by their black and blue victims, have consisted hitherto mostly of people who should not exist in a civilized society. Titus Oates [1649–1705, English anti-Catholic conspirator] and Lord George Gordon [1751–93, Protestant agitator and instigator of anti-Catholic riots in London in 1780] owed their vogue to the London mob. There should not have been any London mob. The soldiers of [the Duke of] Marlborough [1650–1722, victor in major battles against the Spanish in the early eighteenth century] and Wellington were never-do-wells, mental defectives, and laborers with the minds and habits of serfs. Military geniuses could hunt with such products more easily than with a pack of hounds. Our public school and university education equips armies of this kind with appropriate staffs of officers. When both are extinct we shall be able to breathe more freely....

...I say cheerfully to the dominators, "By all means dominate: it is up to us to so order our institutions that you shall not oppress us, nor bequeath any of your precedence to your commonplace children." For when ambition and greed and mere brainless energy have been disabled, the way will be clear for inspiration and aspiration to save us from the fat-headed stagnation of the accursed Victorian snobbery which is bringing us to the verge of ruin.

4. From "The Unavoidable Subject," 1940. [*Platform and Pulpit*, pp. 286–92]

[*Shaw's deep distaste for Hitler's anti-Semitism was expressed in a talk commissioned by the BBC in 1940. From the BBC's point of view, however, the distaste was ambiguously placed in the context of those aspects of Hitler's political career that Shaw admired, and if the BBC was expecting a patriotic clarion call they were sorely disappointed. One comment alone—"Mr Hitler did not begin this war; we did"—was enough to get the talk banned, which it was. (See Conolly pp. 106–14.) Lost to BBC's listeners, then, was Shaw's condemnation of the "pernicious nonsense" of Hitler's racism, in the face of which "there is nothing for it but for the sane men to muster their own physical forces and go for him." We are fighting Hitler, Shaw concluded, "not for his virtues, but for his persecutions and dominations."*]

...we must not give ourselves moral airs as a peace-loving people because we have been deliberately careless [in not adequately preparing for war]. Mr Hitler did not begin this war; we did. It is silly to revile him as a treacherous wolf pouncing on a nation of innocent lambs. We are not innocent lambs; we are the most formidable of all the great European Powers, claiming command of the sea, which is nothing more or less than the power to blockade and starve to death any of our rivals. Having that terrible power we are under the most sacred obligation to use it to defend, not ourselves alone, but common humanity....

...I have no patience with the journalists and the tub thumpers who are breaking our spirits by snivelling about our being the victims of a foul and treacherous aggression.

We are the challengers and the champion fighters for humanity.

The British people, the real British people, feel this instinctively. But they are puzzled by the intellectuals and the politicians and journalists. They want to know exactly why we hit Mr Hitler on the nose, when he had his hands in his pockets—and in some of his neighbors' pockets as well. And they are told officially what fine fellows we are, and that we are sure to win because God is on our side....

What makes it so puzzling is that nine-tenths of what Mr Hitler says is true. Nine-tenths of what [British Nazi] Sir Oswald Mosley [1896–1980] says is true. Quite often nine-tenths of what our parliamentary favorites say to please us is emotional brag, bunk, and nonsense. If we start hotheadedly contradicting everything Mr Hitler and Sir Oswald say, we shall presently find ourselves contradicting ourselves very ridiculously, and getting the worst of the argument. We must sift out the tenth point for which we are fighting, and nail the enemy to that.

Let us come down to brass tacks. What am I, a superannuated non-combatant, encouraging young men to fight against? It is not German national socialism: I was a National Socialist before Mr Hitler was born. I hope we shall emulate and surpass his great achievement in that direction. I have no prejudices against him personally; much that he has written and spoken echoes what I myself have written and spoken. He has adopted even my diet [vegetarianism]. I am interested in him as one of the curiosities of political history; and I fully appreciate his physical and moral courage, his diplomatic sagacity, and his triumphant rescue of his country from the yoke the Allies imposed on it in 1918 [i.e., the punitive Treaty of Versailles]. I am quite aware of the fact that his mind is a twentieth-century mind, and that of our governing class is mentally in the reign of Edward the Third [1327–77], six centuries out of date. In short, I can pay him a dozen compliments which I could not honestly pay to any of our present rulers.

My quarrel with him is a very plain one. I happen to be what he calls a Nordic. In stature, in color, in length of head, I am the perfect blond beast whom Mr Hitler classes as the salt of the earth, divinely destined to rule over all lesser breeds. Trace me back as far as you can; and you will not find a Jew in my ancestry. Well, I have a friend who is a Jew. His name is Albert Einstein; and he is a far greater human prodigy than Mr Hitler and myself rolled into one. The nobility of his character has made his genius an unmixed benefit to his fellow creatures. Yet Adolf Hitler would compel me, the Nordic Bernard Shaw, to insult Albert Einstein; to claim moral superiority to him and unlimited power over him; to rob him, drive him out of his house, exile him, be punished if I allow a relative of mine to marry a relative of his; and finally to kill him as part of a general duty to exterminate his race. Adolf has actually done these things to Albert, bar the killing, as he carelessly exiled him first and thus made the killing impossible. Since then he has extended the list of reprobates from Semites to Celts and from Poles to Slavs; in short, to all who are not what he calls Nordics and Nazis. If he conquers these Islands he will certainly add my countrymen, the Irish, to his list, as several authorities have maintained that the Irish are the lost tribes of Israel.

Now, this is not the sort of thing that sane men can afford to argue with. It is on the face of it pernicious nonsense; and the moment any ruler starts imposing it on his nation or any other nation by physical force there is nothing for it but for the sane men to muster their own physical forces and go for him. We ought to have declared war on Germany the moment Mr Hitler's police stole Einstein's violin. When the work of the police force consists not of *suppressing* robbery with violence but actually *committing* it, that force becomes a recruiting ground for the most infernal blackguards, of whom every country has its natural-born share. Unless such agents are disciplined and controlled, their heads are turned by the authority they possess as a State police; and they resort to physical torture as the easiest way to do their work and amuse themselves at the same time. How is that discipline and control to be maintained? Not by an autocrat, because, as Napoleon said when he heard about Nelson and Trafalgar, an autocrat cannot be everywhere. When his police get out of hand and give his prisons and concentration camps a bad name, he has to back them up because he cannot do without them, and thus he becomes their slave instead of their master....

Remember that the really dangerous Fifth Column consists of the people who believe that Fascism is a better system of government than ours, and that what we call our democracy is a sham. They are not altogether wrong; but the remedy is for us to adopt all the good points of Fascism or Communism or any other Ism, not to allow Mr Hitler and his Chosen Race to impose it on us by his demoralized police. We are fighting him, not for his virtues, but for his persecutions and dominations, which have no logical connection whatever with Fascism and which I hope we will not put up with from Mr Hitler or anyone else. He is as sure that God is on his side as Lord Halifax [1881–1959, Foreign Secretary 1938–40] is that God is on ours. If so, then we shall have to fight God as well as Mr Hitler. But as most of us believe that God made both Mr Hitler and Lord Halifax, we must reasonably believe that God will see fair. And the rest is up to us.

Part VII: Last Thoughts

By the end of the Second World War Shaw was nearly ninety. He had been actively engaged in political debate for 60 years. He had spoken and written voluminously about political issues during that time, and his views had altered in fundamental ways. But he had more to say, still insisting that Democracy (which he now termed "haphazard Mobocracy") had failed to produce the kind of strong political leaders (such as Stalin and Hitler) required for radical reform. In these final political testaments Shaw continues to demonstrate an undiminished ability to enlighten, provoke, challenge, and, perhaps, shock, his readers on a range of political and social topics, including women's suffrage, parliamentary democracy, genetics, distribution of national wealth, and capital punishment.

1. From *Everybody's Political What's What?* London: Constable, 1944

[Not quite as magisterial in scope as The Intelligent Woman's Guide to Socialism and Capitalism, *Shaw's last major work on politics still covered (in 380 pages and 44 chapters) an impressive range of political topics. Its aim, Shaw said, was essentially what he had been attempting throughout his life: "to get as much information as we can and act on it to the best of our fallible judgment."]*

The British Party System

...Since we must give authority to those who are capable of it if we are to save civilization, our pseudo-democratic tradition of government by committees and their majorities brings us up sharply against the fact that majority rule is unnatural because capable rulers are always a minority, though, given fair play, Nature produces enough of them to give the ruled their choice. It also destroys responsibility. A minister of State who accepts and undertakes a public duty on the understanding that if he fails he will be impeached and possibly shot, or at least discharged and discredited, is a responsible minister. But a minister who has only to do what he can persuade a majority in Parliament or in committees to agree to has no responsibility; and neither has anyone else, because majorities cannot be shot except by their own consent, nor can they be demoted, as they have no rank.

One of the best descriptions of this no-thoroughfare is to be found in the autobiography of Adolf Hitler entitled *Mein Kampf*. When he began his work of organizing National Socialism in Germany in 1919 at the age of 30 he found himself a member of a committee of six nobodies with hardly a spare shilling in their collective treasury. Being entirely irresponsible they could do nothing but talk to one another. Adolf's six years training as a soldier had taught him that bodies of men cannot be made effectively active without authority combined with responsibility, neither of which is possible under majority government: a fact we conceal from ourselves by the simple and familiar expedient of calling it responsible government instead of irresponsible government. The Führer was not imposed on by this sort of humbug: hard experience and his ability to learn from experience had taught him better. When he was made chairman of a committee he stayed away from the committee meetings and acted while the rest talked. When he became head of the movement on his personal merits (or demerits if you dislike him) and had to appoint a staff, he gave his officers military authority and held them militarily responsible for their use of it. When he had risen in fourteen years by this method from being an obscure last recruit to a little knot of six persons to being the official leader of sixty millions, and Chancellor for life of the German realm, he kept up his vocal propaganda by occasionally making speeches through the microphone to the sixty millions from the Reichstag; but the Reichstag did not govern: the authority and responsibility were the Führer's; and in his hands and on his head were real authority and responsibility. After five years of this the sixty millions still adored him and made him Commander-in-Chief of their fighting forces.

Let us take this living contemporary instance as the extreme to which authority and responsibility can be pushed in practice. The opposite extreme is represented by the British Parliament in peace time, when authority, responsibility, and activity are reduced to the minimum, and a fortnight's work takes about thirty years unless a war forces Parliament to abandon the Party System, and make a desperate effort to do thirty years work in a fortnight. Our problem is to find the eligible degree between these two extremes.

We must reject the Hitler plan because, though it works successfully in the army, it gives one man more authority and responsibility than one man can bear. If he is weak he is corrupted by his power: if he is strong he is demented by it, and, like Alexander, Hitler, and Napoleon, tries to add the world to his dominions, thus becoming at worst a scourge and tyrant and at best an explorer and adventurer like Julius Caesar or William the Conqueror. The more conquests and adventures and social experiments he undertakes the more he has to delegate and distribute his authority for lack of time to be everywhere and attend to everything. His subgovernors get corrupted or demented in their degree; and finally the system, becoming intolerable, provokes a revolution or a *laisser-faire* reaction towards anarchy, whether the supreme boss is Cromwell, Louis XIV, the Kaiser, or Herr Hitler. The brooms sweep clean when they are new; but when they are spoiled or worn-out the place becomes an Augean stable. [One of the seven labors of Hercules in Greek mythology was to clean out the stables of King Augeas.]

What safeguards are available against these contingencies? Obviously to begin with, election and re-election of rulers for sufficiently short periods to keep them conscious of their dependence on the submissive approval of their subjects. Take the case of the President of the United States of America. Although his office was brought into existence by a successful revolution against the tyranny of the British Government personified by King George III, he was, on Hitlerian principles, given more absolute authority than King George ever possessed. No defeat in committee or Congress can remove him. But his authority lasts only four years. Byron's description of George III as "a poor blind mad and despised old king" can never apply to him. [The quotation is closer to Shelley's line in his *Sonnet: England in 1819*: "An old, mad, blind, despised and dying king."] If any Act of his is unconstitutional there is an appeal against it to the Supreme Court. In certain matters he has to obtain the consent of at least two thirds of the Senate, which must for instance approve his choice of the secretaries who form his council. The separate States of the Union have Governors who are similarly authorized and restricted, similarly responsible and parliament-ridden, trusted and mistrusted, free in respect of religion, sex and color, and limited by age and nationality, place and length of residence. Altogether a queer jumble of precautions against tyranny with measures to provide the security of law and order.

In future we shall have to put more brains into our Constitution making. We must throw our idolization of Parliament and our slogans about British and American liberty and Britons never being slaves into the dustbin. Yet we shall discover that what we need is not only to reform our old parliament but to establish several new ones. Political decisions must not be the whims or phobias of men demented by absolute authority like those of [Roman Emperor] Nero [forced by the army to commit suicide in 68 CE] or Tsar Paul [of Russia, assassinated in 1801] (to say nothing of later examples) with no remedy short of their assassination by their bodyguards or courtiers. Such decisions must be made in council with competent assessors in the light of the best advice and widest information available. We shall need regional councils, vocational councils, industrial councils, co-operative consumers' councils, financial councils, educational councils, planning and co-ordinating councils, councils for supernational affairs, all in constant session, as well as parliamentary congresses (at not too frequent intervals) to ventilate national grievances and contribute any political suggestions Mr Everyman may be capable of. This is what it has come to in ultra-democratic Russia under the inexorable necessities of human nature and circumstances.

The Russian system is not really a revolutionary departure from our own. We are governed more by trade unions, professional associations of doctors and lawyers, the judicial bench, the committees of the Privy Council, the bureaucracy, and by Boards of all sorts than by the Houses of Parliament. The Treasury wields the Power of the Purse far more constantly and potently than the House of Commons; and the Foreign Office declares war and sends us helplessly to the trenches without consulting Parliament, which is simply told next day as in the Four Years War [1914–18], or an hour too late in the present war, what has been irrevocably done over its head and behind its back. The abdication of King Edward VIII [in 1936] was arranged and consummated without a word to the House of Commons or its constituencies. The Prison Commissioners shut the public out of their prisons and can make them much more cruel than concentration camps, as Dartmoor is [opened as a high security prison in 1805], at their pleasure.

A change from our system to the Russian system would be no change at all as far as the multiplicity of governing bodies is concerned. Such bodies cannot be abolished: they are necessary and should be controlled and co-ordinated in the interests of the general welfare, and staffed from panels of competent and responsible persons. At present they are a jumble of casual growths, often unpopular because some of them are out-of-date, led by Party politicians, and operated by petty tyrants, ignorant halfwits, or incurable stick-in-the-muds who are virtually irremovable. But they need not be. In Russia the governing bodies are purged and the slackers "liquidated" (the word covers shooting in grave cases) pretty promptly when they are found out. What the Russians can do we can do....

Democracy: The Next Step

Democracy means the organization of society for the benefit and at the expense of everybody indiscriminately and not for the benefit of a privileged class.

A nearly desperate difficulty in the way of its realization is the delusion that the method of securing it is to give votes to everybody, which is the one certain method of defeating it. Adult suffrage kills it dead. Highminded and well informed people desire it; but they are in a negligible minority at the polling stations. Mr Everybody, as [French philosopher François] Voltaire [1694–1778] called him—and we must now include Mrs Everybody and Miss Everybody—far from desiring the great development of public organization and governmental activity which democracy involves, has a dread of being governed at all, intense dislike of being taxed, and a strong objection to being dictated to by a Government official even when the alternative is to be enslaved and plundered by people like himself without responsibility or authority. His mind, when it is capable of ranging beyond his personal, family, and business affairs, is full of the romance of war and chivalry, and his imagination with hero worship of his favorite platform orator or of famous military and naval commanders who have slaughtered the greatest number of foreigners. He is for any negative law that stands between him and the power of the State: for Magna Carta, Habeas Corpus, Trial by Jury, freedom of his own speech and his own newspaper and the public meetings of his own Party, which he reluctantly extends to other people provided they share his views and preferences; but a hint of any positive legislation sends him rushing to the polling station in his irresistible numbers to vote against it. Only by humbugging him to the top of his bent can he be governed at all. It has therefore always been necessary to humbug him more or less; but to the extent to which he has been able to make Parliament really representative of him his enfranchisement has made democracy impossible. With all his prejudices and superstitions and romantic illusions he knows himself too well to vote for himself. All the same he would resent having his vote taken from him. It remains to be seen how far the handful of real democrats can humbug him into voting for his own emancipation....

I do not see any way out of this difficulty as long as our democrats persist in assuming that Mr Everyman is omniscient as well as ubiquitous, and refuse to reconsider the suffrage in the light of facts and commonsense. How much control of the Government does Mr Everyman need to protect himself against tyranny? How much is he capable of exercising without ruining himself and wrecking civilization? Are these questions really unanswerable? I think not.

I grant that Mr E must be empowered to choose his rulers, were it only to save him from being ruled unbearably well. But how much choice should he have? May he choose a golden calf, as he did in the Sinai desert, or a cat as he did in Egypt, or a tribal idol as the sect called Jehovah's Witnesses now do, or Titus Oates, or Lord George Gordon, or Horatio Bottomley [populist British politician and convicted financial fraudster, 1860–1933], to say nothing of idols now living? Surely not: we might as well let an Infant School loose among the poisons in a druggist's shop, or unbar the cages of all the animals in the Zoo. There is quite enough choice among qualified people to give Mr E all the control that is good for him.

This is so obvious that when democracy began with parliaments we guarded them by a property qualification which secured at least some elementary education for our legislators; but they abused their power so disastrously in their class interest that it was discarded in favor of no qualification at all, which was to jump out of the frying pan into the fire which is consuming us at present.

It is a matter of simple natural history that humans vary widely in political competence. They vary not only from individual to individual but from age to age in the same individual. In the face of this flat fact it is silly to go on pretending that the voice of the people is the voice of God. When Voltaire said that Mr Everybody was wiser than Mr Anybody he had never seen adult suffrage at work. It takes all sorts to make a world; and to maintain civilization some of these sorts have to be killed like mad dogs whilst others have to be put in the command of the State. Until the differences are classified we cannot have a scientific suffrage; and without a scientific suffrage every attempt at democracy will defeat itself as it has always done....

Knowing Our Places

Many years ago I began investigating classification by asking H.M. Stanley [1841–1904], the journalist who explored Africa in search of [British missionary David] Livingstone [1813–73], what proportion of his men he found capable of leadership when he had to leave them in charge of his expedition for a while. He replied instantly and positively "Five per cent." I pressed him as to whether this was an offhand guess or an exact figure. Taking it as such for want of a better estimate we may postulate that out of our population of forty millions two million persons are capable of some degree of government.

Immediately the question arises "What degree?" Stanley found that one in twenty could be left in charge of his African command. But if that job had needed a Julius Caesar he certainly would not have had his choice of one man in every twenty, or even one man in a thousand, but one man in the whole known world, which is another way of saying that he would have had no choice at all. Pope Julius II [1443–1513, Pope 1503–13] could have found plenty of painters to decorate the Sistine Chapel, but only one Michael Angelo. Our first King James [1566–1625; King of England, 1603–25] had dozens of playwrights at his disposal but only one Shakespeare; and after Shakespeare's death his degree became extinct. James II [1633–1701; King of England, 1685–88] could not have found a Shakespeare for love or money.

Between these supreme cases in which a single superman occurs once in fifteen human lifetimes or so and Stanley's everyday five-percenters lie many vocations and many degrees of ability in them. I dare not claim to be the best playwright in the English language; but I believe myself to be one of the best ten, and may therefore perhaps be classed as one of the best hundred.

Outside his natural vocation the greatest genius may be simply feeble minded. In the theatre I am a highly efficient person: in an astronomic observatory I should be sacked at the end of the first week, or else set to dust and polish the telescopes, which I should do worse than any good housemaid. Now the success of any business depends on its operators being vocationally the right persons in their natural places; for a College of Music cannot be successfully conducted by a tone deaf staff nor an Academy of Painting by a color blind one, as some experiments in that direction have proved. Quite the biggest and most difficult business in the world is the organization and administration of a modern democratic State, which must find a remunerative use for every citizen and never put him off with a dole. Managed by the right persons in the wrong places, or the wrong persons in the right places, it will get into a disastrous mess and have to be rescued forcibly by some Napoleonic adventurer foolish enough to be ambitious yet able enough, as Mussolini put it, to clean up the Augean stable.

And here we must make another distinction. Sixty years ago, walking one Sunday in Hyde Park, where any social reformer or religious apostle may collect a crowd by simply stopping and addressing the empty air, I came upon a certain Captain Wilson, now, I fear, forgotten, who was preaching a gospel he called Comprehensionism, and urging his listeners to become Comprehensionists. But a world of Comprehenders might and probably would be a world of duffers. Comprehension is quite distinct from executive faculty. The men of action, skilled and ready in practice, are seldom comprehensive thinkers. The world is full of active solicitors who have no sense of law, doctors for whom biology might as well not exist, priests without a ray of religion, journalists thoughtlessly repeating stock phrases in customary colloctations, boards of directors who do nothing but what was done last time, skilled workmen who know little more about their jobs than the machines they are handling, as well as Chancellors of the Exchequer who, convinced that the more a country exports the richer it is, hold that the ideal height of prosperity for a nation is to produce nothing for its own consumption and everything for foreign trade. I think it was [Viscount] Palmerston [1784–1865], our greatest Secretary for Foreign Affairs [and Prime Minister, 1855–58], who said, "If you wish to be thoroughly misinformed about a country, consult a man who has lived there for thirty years and speaks the language like a native."

Utopians must not conclude that nobody should be allowed to practise any trade or profession which he or she does not thoroughly understand. They might as well hold that a baby should not be put to its mother's breast until it is completely instructed in food metabolism. A great part of our business has to be done by people who do not understand what they are doing, but can do it without understanding it. They may or may not be doing it in the best way; but it has to be done somehow; and the worst way is better than no way at all. For example, parents at present have to see to it that their families are fed. Accordingly some most affectionate mothers feed their infants on gin and red herrings, and their husbands on butchers' meat and fermented or distilled drinks in the full persuasion that without these they could not keep up their strength. They should be taught better in the elementary schools. But meanwhile children and husbands must be fed somehow. Red herrings and gin, beef and beer, may be worse than cereals, vegetable, and soft drinks; but they are better than nothing.

Instruction, however, is limited by the capacity to digest it. Also by the time at the learner's disposal, and the necessity for choosing the most profitable subjects to employ it on. The most gifted genius cannot study everything. I am a competent playwright; but nothing would make a competent mathematician of me. I can manipulate a calculating machine, and I daresay I could be taught to use a table of logarithms just as I use a ready reckoner. But my time is better employed in writing plays and books. Everything else I must leave undone or get somebody else to do it for me, or, if I do it myself, do it by rule of thumb, using the method without pretending to understand it. In literature and drama, I am a celebrity: in an aeroplane factory I should be a mental defective. When I contemplate what I know and have done (not that I ever do) I have a high opinion of myself. When I contemplate what I don't know and cannot do (which I am often forced to do) I feel as a worm might if it knew how big the world is....

Democracy will have to reckon not only with differences of vocation but with degrees of ability within the vocation. When child welfare came to be systematically studied, it was soon found that the author of the popular song "They say there is no other can take the place of mother" knew very little about mothers and children. On the other hand when William Morris said that whoever may be the best people to be in charge of the nation's children there can be no doubt that the parents are the very worst, he was overstating his case. It is always necessary to overstate a case startlingly to make people sit up and listen to it, and to frighten them into acting on it. I do this myself habitually and deliberately....

It is assumed that anyone can conduct a business just as it is assumed that anyone can choose the right Prime Minister. The result is that very few of our businesses are managed by persons who understand them comprehensively; and Prime Ministers capable of a comprehensive policy are very rare birds indeed. Mr Everyman may try his hand at either job and do his damndest in both.

But there is a special democratic requirement in the case of the Everyman family which makes any attempt to restrict their political activities rouse fierce opposition. When the law becomes an instrument of oppression, as laws often do, especially before they have been amended in the light of experience of their working, it is the Everymans who know where the shoe pinches. For them there must be congresses in which they can squeal their complaints, agitate for their pet remedies, move resolutions and votes of confidence or the reverse, draft private bills and call on the Government to adopt and enact them, and criticize the Government to their utmost with impunity. And as such congresses must be attended by the rulers, who could not possibly conduct the business of the country if they had to listen to Mr E and Mrs E and Miss E "ventilating their grievances" for longer or oftener than a few weeks every two years, a day-to-day ventilation and agitation must be effected by the newspapers and pamphlets, which should have the same privileges as the congresses. Thus what we call freedom of congress, freedom of speech, freedom of agitation, freedom of the press are democratic necessities. As they should be as representative of the Everymans as it is possible to make them, congresses should be picked up haphazard like a jury or by some other method that makes party selection impossible. The legislators and rulers should, on the contrary, be as unrepresentative as possible, short of being inhuman.

The Everyman Congress will give us everything desirable that Parliament gives us at present. In depriving it of powers that Parliament does not really possess and never has nor can possess, we shall lose nothing. The supremacy of our Cabinet is as complete as that of the Russian Politbureau or Sovnarkom (or whatever they call their Cabinets of political and industrial thinkers and statesmen in these days of changing names). But the chief mischief is that as Parliament can give this power to whom it pleases without any scientific tests of political capacity to guide it, we get Cabinets and even Prime Ministers who are windbags and do-nothings, religious bigots, rich plutocrats as such, resolute

Conservatives and reactionaries, dangerous undesirables, illiterate anti-intellectuals, and ludicrous misfits of all sorts. The problem remains, how to limit Mr Everyman's choice to the politically competent, classified and graded according to their degrees of such competence. This we cannot do until we know who the competent people are. We must therefore begin by somehow making registers of persons mentally capable of functioning efficiently as parish councillors, district and county councillors, city aldermen, or Secretaries of State for home affairs, treasury finance, foreign affairs and so on. Such registers had better be called panels, as we are now all familiar with panel doctors and can easily go on to panel Prime Ministers.

But this again we cannot do without anthropometric measurements and tests. Our present method of testing fitness for legislative work is by majority of votes in localities varying so widely in population and character that no common measure of competence can be obtained that way. For the highest positions we have selection by the Prime Minister recommending a suitable person to the King. But as neither the Prime Minister nor the King can know all the eligible people in the community their choice is limited to their circle of acquaintance, which is much smaller than the number of available qualified persons. It is obviously not applicable to the permanent public services, which have to be recruited in many thousands from masses of people utterly unknown in Downing Street or Buckingham Palace. For them after a long trial of jobbery at the top and the press gang at the bottom, we have been driven to the Chinese system of literary examination, supplemented by medical tests and personal interviews. Of late, intelligence tests of a simple kind have come into fashion; but they are extensions of the examination system and leave it undisturbed.

Have we really any alternative to the examination system now that we are up against the democratic necessity for a census of political capacity and a hierarchy of panels founded on it?...

Political Summary

Unless the people can choose their leaders and rulers, and can revoke their choice at intervals long enough to test their measures by results, the government will be a tyranny exercised in the interests of whatever classes or castes or mobs or cliques have this choice. And until popular choice is constitutionally guided and limited, political ignorance and idolatry will produce not only Hitleresque dictatorships but stampedes led by liars or lunatics like Titus Oates and Lord George Gordon. The choice should therefore be limited to panels of persons who have passed such tests as we can devise of their wisdom, comprehension, knowledge, and energy. For legislative purposes adult suffrage is out of the question, as only a small percentage of any population has either the requisite faculty or knowledge; but for ventilation of grievances, questioning of ministers and criticism of Cabinets, suggestion of remedies and new methods, moving of resolutions and votes of confidence or the reverse, and generally for keeping the government in touch with the people, a representative popular parliament of men and women in equal numbers is necessary.

Such a Parliament alone may properly be called a House of Commons. It should not have any power to legislate, because legislative capacity is not common. Nature provides only a percentage of persons uncommon enough to be able to devise, revise, or add to the Ten Commandments and administer them. But unless these persons are chosen and removable by the common people, the people, not feeling that they are being governed by their own consent, will become seditious. Fortunately Nature always provides for real needs excessively and even extravagantly. When the chances are a thousand to one against a fish's egg surviving the perils of the sea, Nature provides a million eggs to balance the odds. And when one Prime Minister, one First Consul, or one President with a dozen Secretaries of State, is needed to govern a country, Nature, if not thwarted by avoidable poverty and ignorance, provides a hundred. The percentage of capable legislators in a fullfed and fully educated population is thus sufficient to give the electors a choice of rulers; and a choice is all that is needed to give them as much control of their government as is good for them. To achieve this in practice the capable must be ascertained, tested, and empanelled in their various degrees, making government in this respect a profession like any other profession. The empanelled legislator or administrator will be on the footing of the ordained clergyman, the enrolled lawyer, the registered doctor, and the university graduate. The unempanelled agitator can still have his fling in the Commons. There may even be ways of evading the tests, such as honorary degrees or qualifications conferred on "*bona fide* practitioners" whose competence has been established in the course of events; but such irregular qualifications and evasions should be conferred and allowed by tested rulers only. The tests should be revised at intervals short enough to keep them up to date, and regarded as provisional and changeable, not as sacred and infallible.

The British Party System should be scrapped ruthlessly. It was invented two and a half centuries ago to nullify the House of Commons by obliging the King to select his ministers from the Party commanding a majority in it, and to dissolve Parliament and inflict a costly election on its members whenever that Party is defeated on a division; so that members never vote on the merits of a measure but always on the question of whether the reigning Party is to remain in office, both sides risking the loss of their seats and incurring heavy expense and trouble if they unseat the Government....

2. From the Preface to *Geneva*, 1945. [*The Bodley Head Bernard Shaw*, VII:13–43]

[*First produced in 1938, on the eve of the Second World War, Geneva underwent several revisions as events overtook the topicality of the play. In a preface written in 1945, Shaw once more reflected on the failures of Democracy. Even after the election of a Labour government in 1945, in which "the Utopians carried the day triumphantly," it turned out that "the New World proved the same as the old one."*]

Civilization's Will To Live Always Defeated by Democracy

...[The] insane prescription for perfect democracy of course makes democracy impossible and the adventures of Cromwell, Napoleon, Hitler, and the innumerable conquistadores and upstart presidents of South American history inevitable. There never has been and never will be a government which is both plebiscitary and democratic, because the plebs do not want to be governed, and the plutocrats who humbug them, though they are so far democratic that they must for their own sakes keep their slaves alive and efficient, use their powers to increase their revenues and suppress resistance to their appropriation of all products and services in excess of the minimum. Substitute a plebeian government, and it can only carry on to the same point with the same political machinery, except that the plunder goes to the Trade Unions instead of to the plutocrats. This may be a considerable advance; but when the plebeian government attempts to reorganize production collectively so as to increase the product and bring the highest culture within the reach of all who are capable of it, and make the necessary basic material prosperity general and equal, the dread and hatred of government as such, calling itself Liberty and Democracy, reasserts itself and stops the way. Only when a war makes collective organization compulsory on pain of slaughter, subjugation, and nowadays extinction by bombs, jet propelled or atomic, is any substantial advance made or men of action tolerated as Prime Ministers. The first four years of world war forced us to choose a man of action as leader [David Lloyd George, Prime Minister 1916–22]; but when the armistice came we got rid of him and had a succession of premiers who could be trusted to do nothing revolutionary.... Even Franklin Roosevelt won his first presidential election [1933] more by a photograph of himself in the act of petting a baby than by his political program, which few understood: indeed he only half understood it himself. When Mr Winston Churchill, as a man of action, had to be substituted for the *fainéants* [idlers] when the war was resumed [Churchill was Prime Minister from 1940 to 1945], his big cigars and the genial romantic oratory in which he glorified the war maintained his popularity until the war was over and he opened the General Election campaign by announcing a domestic policy which was a hundred years out of fashion, and promised nothing to a war weary proletariat eager for a Utopia in which there should be no military controls and a New World inaugurated in which everybody was to be both employed and liberated.

Mr Churchill at once shared the fate of Lloyd George [i.e., he was defeated (by the Labour Party), in the 1945 general election]; and the Utopians carried the day triumphantly. But the New World proved the same as the old one, with the same fundamental resistance to change of habits and the same dread of government interference surviving in the adult voter like the child's dread of a policeman....

PART VII: LAST THOUGHTS

3. From "Sixty Years of Fabianism," 1947. [*Fabian Essays in Socialism*, pp. 207–31]

[For a "Jubilee" edition of Fabian Essays, *celebrating sixty years of Fabianism, Shaw wrote a substantial postscript. It is full of disappointments ("the new Labor Party failed") and provocations (the support of eugenics and, once more, Russian-style "liquidation"), but Shaw's conclusion about Fabianism—"the name may perish, but not the species"—shows a (justified) confidence not only in the ideals of Socialism but also in the willingness of future generations to continue the efforts to realize them.]*

Although this volume of essays is sixty years old, and I, its editor, am ninety, it is still alive doing its old work, which was, and is, to rescue Socialism and Communism from the barricades, from the pseudo-democracy of the Party System, from confusion with the traditional heterodoxies of anticlericalism, individualist anti-State republicanism, and middle class Bohemian anarchism: in short, to make it a constitutional movement in which the most respectable citizens and families may enlist, without forfeiting the least scrap of their social or spiritual standing.

This aim is apparently accomplished. The Labor Government now (1947) in office is crammed with ex-Fabians; and they are regarded, not as the extreme Left in politics, but rather as the Old School Ties worn by many of them, including the Prime Minister [Clement Attlee, 1883–1967; Leader of the Labour Party 1935–55, Prime Minister 1945–51]....

[Shaw then gives a summary of Fabian Party involvement in British political affairs over the previous sixty years.]

The Fabians have demonstrated beyond all instructed criticism that the private property system, known compendiously as Capitalism, at last wrecks itself. It has done so again and again, and will repeat the catastrophe if the situation is not saved by a great extension of Socialism. But though Socialist may be substituted for Capitalist Governments in twentyfour hours, it by no means follows that industry and agriculture, religion and art and their professions, land and capital, can be transferred from private to public ownership and management in twentyfour hours or completed even within twentyfour years. Crushing proof of this has come from Russia, where the disciples of Karl Marx, the Arch anti-Capitalist, in 1917 established what Marx called "The Dictatorship of the Proletariat." After a few years of anti-Fabian catastrophic policy which brought their country to the verge of ruin and a bit over, they were forced to announce a New Economic Policy which was in fact Fabian, and which has had a prodigious civilizing success, besides carrying its union of Socialist republics through a frightfully destructive defensive war against all the military might of Germany and her Allies....

The Fabians, preoccupied with industrial problems and their solutions, had said not a word on foreign policy, but assumed throughout that the British Parliamentary Party system, with everybody voting for anybody, however incompetent and illiterate, was democratic, and that the socialization of all the vital industries and the nationalization of the rents of land, capital, and ability: in short, of the "Surplus Value" of Marx, would by themselves attract the electorate and solve all the social problems.

This was pure assumption; and the facts soon contradicted it. The economies and powers of the Socialist plan were available as a policy not only to the "Proletarians of all Lands" but to the Capitalist profiteers. Neither the proletariat nor the capitalists understood the Fabian plan; but the capitalists, following the slot of money, automatically grabbed it, whilst the new Labor Party failed. Its Cabinet ministers, inexperienced in diplomacy and mostly jealous of one another, were not all on speaking terms. The Labor Prime Minister [Ramsay

MacDonald] and the Chancellor of the Exchequer [Philip Snowden, 1864–1937; Chancellor, 1924, 1929–31] were personally irreconcilable. The usual post-war landslide brought the plutocrats back with an overwhelming majority [the Conservative Party under Stanley Baldwin gained a majority of 210 seats in the 1924 General Election]....

[Shaw then returns to the subject he saw as central to Socialist principles: equality of income.]

...The first step towards equality of income is not the division of the existing national income into equal parts [the method, Shaw argues, unsuccessfully applied in Russia]. It is the determination of the basic income needed to abolish poverty and ignorance and make every family a potential breeding place for an aristocracy of talent. Fabianism thus becomes Democratic Aristocracy in strong opposition to Underdog Authority or Government by the Unfittest, which is the bugbear of the cultured classes today.

The late H.G. Wells [novelist, 1866–1946] estimated the basic income at £4,000 a year, representing a house or flat in town, a villa in the country, a motor car, a library, a piano, and/or a sport equipment or both; and I arrived at the same figure with a reminder that under Socialism all these amenities could easily be provided for much less.

Meanwhile the average proletarian laborer must put up with a tenth, a twentieth, even a hundreth of the share of the national income pocketed by the Nuffields and Fords, successors of the Carnegies and the Rockefellers, which the scarcity of their industrial talent enables them now to exact. Only by raising the average proletarian wage to the basic income and thereby increasing the supply of directive capacity until it is as cheap as subordinate labor, can we end its present starvation....

What, then, is the test for the achievement of the basic income for everybody. Is it exactly arithmetic? If great inventors, organizers, pioneers, State figure heads, tragedians, prima donnas, painters and sculptors and authors with lucrative copyrights, are still to make £500 while their valets and maids get five shillings, will that upset the whole scheme of equality of income?

It will not matter at all provided the valets and maids have the basic income and habits and are therefore intermarriageable with their employers. At present the economic and consequent social bars to marriage are so omnipresent that sexual selection, which is still the masterkey to eugenics in a healthy population, is most mischievously restricted. It is not only that a duke cannot marry his washerwoman nor a duchess her [chimney] sweep: there are too few dukes and duchesses to be worth troubling about. But in fact snobbery is as prevalent and bigoted among the poor as among the rich. The marriage of the daughter of a skilled artisan to a laborer is a much more disgraceful misalliance than the marriage [in African legend] of King Cophetua to the beggar girl, which has the charm of romance. I have said again and again to British audiences of all classes that instead of the eugenic ideal that every virgin should have all the bachelors in the country to choose from, and vice versa, their choice is in fact limited to two or three who are by no means always their most desired favorites. And I have never been contradicted.

...Roughly, people with the same education and manners are intermarriageable; and when this is secured by the establishment of the basic income exceptionally big incomes produced by lucrative talents will do no harm, and perhaps provide capital for industrial and cultural experiments which no Government dare undertake.

The Fabians will have to fight the claims always made by the skilled workers and directors to have every rise in the wages of the lowest paid proletarians accompanied by a rise in their own, for no better reason than that they are accustomed to be paid more and are to that extent jealous snobs. Only by sounder economic education can this be cured. There is much more levelling up than levelling down to be done so far.

[*These and other Socialist reforms are prevented, however, Shaw argues, by existing democratic principles and structures, including trade unions, which, he says, tend to become "a dictatorship of skilled labor, opposed to the State direction without which basic Communism is impossible."*]

The assumption still current that all these people and parties can be reconciled in the common democracy by giving everyone a vote is a thoughtless reaction from good Queen Bess's [i.e., Queen Elizabeth I, 1533–1603] view that high politics are not the business of the common people, nor even of the average country gentleman and knights of the shire who resent every interference with their habits, and denounce State action as totalitarian (as if all legislation, beginning with the codification of the ten commandments, were not totalitarian). They make a hopeless mess of their political power, running after any ambitious general or loud-enough windbag who promises to get them out of their difficulties by hook or [by] crook....

This haphazard Mobocracy must be replaced by democratic aristocracy: that is, by the dictatorship, not of the whole proletariat, but of that five per cent of it capable of conceiving the job and pioneering in the drive towards its divine goal, which, however, like the horizon or the place where parallel lines (say railway tracks) visibly meet, can never be reached. Providence forbid it ever should!

This does not mean that the people shall have no choice of their rulers. What it does mean is that their choice shall not be between windbags and blatherskites, but between candidates for the naturally qualified five per cent, guaranteed and empanelled by the best available anthropometric authority.

But democracy should not depend wholly on electioneering vicissitudes: it should be fundamental in the constitution. Take the case of the exclusion of women from any voice or choice in government by Salic law [excluding women from dynastic succession] under feudal militarism, and finally by resultant custom. The nineteenth century agitation for Women's Rights concentrated itself in the twentieth on the Parliamentary franchise. The slogan was Votes for Women. A grotesque campaign of feminine sabotage, and the war of 1914–18, won the vote, with the result that at the ensuing general election all the female candidates, however eminent by their ability and public service, were defeated by male nobodies voted for by women. At the present moment, though the proportion of the sexes in Parliament should be 50–50, it is in round figures 600–40. Feminine Mobocracy will not tolerate women in Parliament: the few who are there owe their election to male votes.

Democracy for women, a vital political necessity (women are much more practical and less Party ridden, being trained managerially by housekeeping and childbearing) must be secured by a Constitutional Amendment making the electoral unit a man and a woman (call it the Coupled Vote); for all authoritative public bodies should consist of men and women in equal numbers if authority is to be democratic. I cannot foresee to what extent this suggestion can be carried; but Fabians can hardly oppose it. The Coupled Vote would at least make a landslide into matriarchy impossible. Matriarchy is at present in such extensive private practice that clever and attractive women do not want votes. They are willing to let men govern as long as they govern men.

Some of the worst political blunders are made with the best intentions, and the successes with the worst intentions. Fabians, though their business is mainly economic reform, will find themselves entangled in humanitarian reforms. Our criminal laws are barbarous, wasteful, and ruinously mischievous. There is agitation against capital punishment; but the words are confusing; for the powers of life and death which all civilizations necessarily wield over their citizens are entirely distinct from the savage and unchristian passions which drive us, when we are injured, to injure the injurer, and the instinctive shame which makes us pretend that the two blacks make a white. They don't: and they never will. But what are we to do with incurable criminals?

What do we do with cobras, mad dogs, and fleas? We do not dream of punishing them. We kill them without malice simply because their activities are not compatible with civilization. They are unbearable nuisances....

Socialism, it is to be hoped, being at root humane, will abolish exemplary cruelty. But it will not abolish what is now called capital punishment. It will strike out the punishment part of it; but it will take more seriously, and extend, the capital part of it....

It seems to me that nothing can make us genuine citizens without a general conscience that unless we are of some use in the world, producing and replacing as much as we consume, and a bit over for capital, we may not wake some morning. If we are starving, and our children cry to us vainly for bread, we must steal or rob as the shelterless squat in defiance of the law. Granted, however, that the Socialist State so arranges matters that none can starve if they choose to serve, crime can be dealt with reasonably without cruelty. The great mass of petty torts can be remedied by imposing extra labor on the wrongdoer until the damage is compensated.

But there are people in the world incapable of fending for themselves. In the army, where they are fed and clothed and housed and told what to do: in short, kept in a state of tutelage, they are good soldiers, good workers, and useful citizens. Throw them out of the army on to the streets and they are presently in the dock, "going to the devil" helplessly in their own feckless way. To lock these people up in cells, denying them newspapers and family life, and making their lives a degrading torment to them as we do at present, is senseless barbarity involving the waste not only of their own lives but of that mass of tormenters called warders, governors, chaplains, and hangmen. The way to make them useful and harmless is to give them the tutelage and discipline and guidance they need.

Then there are the incurably mischievous criminals, ignored by the kindly souls who prate continually about reforming the criminal, and, like [prison reformer John] Howard [1726–90], only succeed in making our prisons more cruel. If criminals can be reformed, reform them. We should continue trying to find out how; but this is the business of scientific psychologists, not of sentimentalists. Meanwhile they should not be punished: they cannot help being what they are. But they should be painlessly liquidated, not caged....

[Shaw concludes his essay by returning—after sixty years of Fabian membership—to one of his fundamental tenets: that Fabians must always be pragmatists, not ideologists, or idealists; they "must be unsentimental scientific pioneers of the next practicable steps, not dreamers of the New Jerusalem and the Second Advent or the Love panacea with justice nowhere."]

[And now] I must retire to make room for the Fabians of 60 years hence, by whatever name they will then be called.

For the name may perish, but not the species.

Sources and Further Reading

For comprehensive and up-to-date bibliographies and other important research aids for work on Bernard Shaw in electronic and print forms see the Research Aids section on the website of the International Shaw Society: www.shawsociety.org. The selection here focuses on Shaw's political interests and activities.

Autobiography

An Autobiography: Selected from His Writings. Ed. Stanley Weintraub. 2 vols. New York: Weybright and Talley, 1970.

The Diaries 1885–1897. Ed. Stanley Weintraub. 2 vols. University Park: Pennsylvania State University Press, 1986.

Sixteen Self Sketches. London: Constable, 1949.

Biography

Gibbs, A.M. *Bernard Shaw: A Life*. Gainesville: University Press of Florida, 2005.

———. *A Bernard Shaw Chronology*. Basingstoke: Palgrave, 2001.

Holroyd, Michael. *Bernard Shaw*. 5 vols. London: Chatto & Windus, 1988–92.

Letters

Agitations. Letters to the Press 1875–1950. Eds. Dan H. Laurence and James Rambeau. New York: Frederick Ungar, 1985.

Bernard Shaw: Collected Letters. Ed. Dan H. Laurence. 4 vols. New York: Viking Penguin, 1965–88.

Selected Correspondence of Bernard Shaw. Series Editors J. Percy Smith and L. W. Conolly. Toronto: University of Toronto Press, 1995– [ongoing]. *Bernard Shaw Theatrics*, ed. Dan H.

Laurence, 1995; *Bernard Shaw and H.G. Wells*, ed. J. Percy Smith, 1995; *Bernard Shaw and Gabriel Pascal*, ed. Bernard F. Dukore, 1996; *Bernard Shaw and Barry Jackson*, ed. L.W. Conolly, 2002; *Bernard Shaw and the Webbs*, eds. Alex C. Michalos and Deborah C. Poff, 2002; *Bernard Shaw and Nancy Astor*, ed. J.P. Wearing, 2005; *Bernard Shaw and His Publishers*, ed. Michel W. Pharand, 2009; *Bernard Shaw and Gilbert Murray*, ed. Charles A. Carpenter, 2014.

Plays And Prefaces

The Bodley Head Bernard Shaw. Collected Plays with their Prefaces. Under the editorial supervision of Dan H. Laurence. 7 vols. London: Max Reinhardt, the Bodley Head, 1970–74.

Political Essays

Bernard Shaw on War. Ed. J.P. Wearing. London: Hesperus Press, 2009.

Essays in Fabian Socialism. London: Constable, 1932.

Everybody's Political What's What? London: Constable, 1944.

Fabian Essays. Jubilee Edition. London: George Allen & Unwin, 1948.

The Intelligent Woman's Guide to Socialism and Capitalism. London: Constable, 1928.

The Intelligent Woman's Guide to Socialism, Capitalism, Sovietism and Fascism. Foreword by Polly Toynbee. Richmond: Alma Classics, 2012.

The Matter with Ireland. Ed. Dan H. Laurence and David H. Greene. Second edition. Gainesville: University Press of Florida, 2001.

Platform and Pulpit. Ed. Dan H. Laurence. New York: Hill and Wang, 1961.

The Political Madhouse in America and Nearer Home. London: Constable, 1933.

Practical Politics. Twentieth-Century Views on Politics and Economics. Ed. Lloyd J. Hubenka. Lincoln: University of Nebraska Press, 1976.

The Rationalization of Russia. Ed. Harry M. Geduld. Bloomington: Indiana University Press, 1964.

The Road to Equality. Ten Unpublished Lectures and Essays, 1884–1918. Ed. Louis Crompton. Boston: Beacon Press, 1971.

Selected Non-Dramatic Writings of Bernard Shaw. Ed. Dan H. Laurence. Boston: Houghton Mifflin Company, 1965.

The Socialism of Shaw. Ed. James Fuchs. New York: Vanguard Press, 1926.

What I Really Wrote About the War. London: Constable, 1931.

What Shaw Really Wrote About the War. Ed. J.L. Wisenthal and Daniel O'Leary. Gainesville: University Press of Florida, 2006.

Criticism

Alexander, James. *Shaw's Controversial Socialism*. Gainesville: University Press of Florida, 2009.

Bentley, Eric. *Bernard Shaw*. New York: Limelight Editions, 1985.

Carpenter, Charles A. *Bernard Shaw as Artist-Fabian*. Gainesville: University Press of Florida, 2009.

Conolly, L.W. *Bernard Shaw and the BBC*. Toronto: University of Toronto Press, 2009.

Davis, Tracy C. *George Bernard Shaw and the Socialist Theatre*. Westport: Praeger, 1994.

Evans, T.F., ed. *Shaw and Politics. SHAW: The Annual of Bernard Shaw Studies*. Volume 11. University Park: The Pennsylvania State University Press, 1991.

Gibbs, A.M., ed. *Shaw: Interviews and Recollections*. Iowa City: University of Iowa Press, 1990.

Griffith, Gareth. *Socialism and Superior Brains. The Political Thought of Bernard Shaw*. London: Routledge, 1993.

Hadfield, D.A. and Reynolds, Jean, eds. *Shaw and Feminisms: On Stage and Off*. Gainesville: University Press of Florida, 2013.

Hummert, Paul A. *Bernard Shaw's Marxian Romance*. Lincoln: University of Nebraska Press, 1973.

Innes, Christopher, ed. *The Cambridge Companion to George Bernard Shaw*. Cambridge: Cambridge University Press, 1998.

Kent, Brad, ed. *George Bernard Shaw in Context*. Cambridge: Cambridge University Press, 2015.

Soboleva, Olga, and Wrenn, Angus. *The Only Hope of the World. George Bernard Shaw and Russia*. Bern: Peter Lang, 2012.

Weintraub, Rodelle, ed. *Fabian Feminist: Bernard Shaw and Woman*. University Park, PA: Pennsylvania State University Press, 1977.

Yde, Matthew. *Bernard Shaw and Totalitarianism: Longing for Utopia*. Basingstoke: Palgrave Macmillan, 2013.

www.ingramcontent.com/pod-product-compliance
Lightning Source LLC
Chambersburg PA
CBHW032052090426
42744CB00005B/180